"May, I must talk to you," Yoko said.

She was barefoot, dressed in a floor-length blue-checked flannel nightgown, her black hair tumbling around her face. She lit a Kool, then sat facing me. She seemed to be having trouble beginning.

"Listen, May," she said finally, "John and I are not getting along. We've been arguing. We're growing apart."

During the previous two weeks I had noted that John and Yoko seemed to be avoiding being in the same room at the same time. There had been some talk that they were thinking of attending Masters and Johnson's sex therapy program. I ignored all the gossip about them; I was sure they would work it out.

Yoko continued. "John will probably start going out with other people. I know he likes you. If he should ask you to go out with him, you should go." Yoko looked directly at me. "I think you should go," she said again.

"I can't," I stammered. "John's married. He's my employer. I don't want to go out with him, and he doesn't want to go out with me!"

"I'd rather see him going out with you than with someone else, someone who might hurt him." Once again she looked searchingly at me. "It will be great. He'll be happy. It's cool. Don't worry about a thing. I'll take care of everything. . . ."

So May began "going out" with John, traveling with him, living with him, learning to understand the man the world loved. Most intimately *Loving John*.

Loving John

by May Pang

and HENRY EDWARDS

WARNER BOOKS

A Warner Communications Company

Loving John is the story of the relationship between three people: John Lennon, Yoko Ono, and May Pang. It is based on the firsthand observations of May Pang as well as interviews with a number of people who knew both May and John when they were together. After sifting through the observations and interviews, it is the opinion of the authors that the relationship between May and John was essentially initiated, controlled, and then terminated by Yoko Ono.

Permission to use all copyrighted material is gratefully acknowledged. Unless otherwise noted, all photographs are copyrighted by May Pang.

Copyright © 1983 by May Pang and Literary Ventures Association, Inc.
All rights reserved.
Warner Books, Inc., 666 Fifth Avenue, New York, NY 10103

A Warner Communications Company

Printed in the United States of America
First printing: August 1983
10 9 8 7 6 5 4 3 2 1

Designed by Giorgetta Bell McRee
Cover design by Gene Light
Front cover photo of May Pang © 1983 by Rose Hartman
Back cover photo by Bill Cadge

LIBRARY OF CONGRESS CATALOGING IN PUBLICATION DATA

Pang, May.
Loving John.
1. Lennon, John, 1940–   . 2. Ono, Yōko.
3. Singers—Biography. I. Edwards, Henry. II. Title.
ML420.L38P3 1983   784.5′4′00924 [B]   83-42689
ISBN 0-446-37916-6 (USA)
ISBN 0-446-37917-4 (Canada)

For Linda Lim Pang,
a woman of courage and determination
and the pillar of her daughter's strength.

———————————

Loving John

Part
One

1

As soon as the alarm went off that Monday morning in August I jumped out of bed and headed for the shower. I couldn't wait for the week to begin, because, more than anything, I loved watching John record, and after more than a year's layoff he was about to begin his second week back in the studio. Just thirteen days earlier he had made the surprise announcement to us. "I need pressure," he had said, and I watched as he barricaded himself into the office next to mine in John and Yoko's apartment at the Dakota and began to write furiously. Two days later he emerged with a complete set of new songs. Coincidentally Yoko had just finished her new album, *Feeling the Space.* She had used a new band. "Don't let them go," John ordered. "I want to work with somebody new this time."

And then Yoko told me that I was to be John's *only* studio assistant on the new album.

I loved John and Yoko. I'd worked hard, sometimes around the clock, as their personal assistant since the end of 1970, doing whatever was needed of me throughout that time. And now I would be next to him every night in the studio.

When we went to the studio for the first time, John was very nervous, but he got right to work anyway. By the end of that week he had laid down the basic tracks of the entire album. Despite his nervousness and his year away, John proved capable of working at his usual astonishing pace.

"So keep on playing those mind games forever," I hummed as I approached the Dakota on that beautiful summer morning. It was a line from "Mind Games," a song John had recorded during the previous week. In the song, John wanted to sustain the word *mind* for five long measures, but he didn't have the breath. "I'll splice two vocals together," he reasoned after a few tries, and he kept on working. During that week we saw the results of that and countless other takes and effects.

Rain or shine, night or day, there was always someone hovering outside the Dakota, waiting for a glimpse of John. That morning it was a blank-faced woman. I stepped quickly, pausing only to look up at the stern Indian face mounted above the main portico. The sunlight was so bright and glorious, the Indian did not look nearly as fierce as usual. "It's a hell of a day," said the security guard posted in front of the building as I walked past him and through the gate.

The Dakota is divided into four sections, and John and Yoko lived in Section A. Each section has a main entrance and a service entrance. I walked through the courtyard to the Section A service entrance and took the elevator to the seventh floor. I scooped up the mail in front of the Lennons' apartment, then I opened the rosewood back doors that led directly into the kitchen. I proceeded to my office and sat down behind my desk just as Yoko appeared at the door.

"May, I must talk to you," she said. Barefoot, dressed in a floor-length blue-checked flannel nightgown, her black hair tumbling around the sides of her face, she looked like a tiny unhappy child that morning. I could tell that something was upsetting her.

She lit a Kool, then sat down facing me. I automatically picked up my steno pad, ready for the day's work. Yoko seemed to be having trouble beginning. "Listen, May," she finally spat out, "John and I are not getting along. We've been arguing. We're growing apart."

I put down my pad and stared at her. Yoko rarely confided in me, and I was surprised. I had heard some talk that John and Yoko might attend Masters and Johnson's sex therapy program in St. Louis, because they were having sexual problems.

During the two weeks prior to that day, I realized they never seemed to be in the same room together, and when they did meet they hardly spoke. I assumed that John and Yoko were going through a phase—they had been married for four years and together for five. After five years, I assumed any couple might have problems, especially a couple as intensely involved with each other as John and Yoko. I was sure they would work it out and I ignored the gossip.

"John will probably start going out with other people," continued Yoko. "Who knows who he'll go out with?" She shrugged her shoulders. Then she smiled at me. "May, I know he likes you a lot."

I couldn't believe what I was hearing. What was Yoko talking about? "Me? No, Yoko, not me," I told her. I did not want Yoko to think I had anything to do with her problems with John.

"May, it's okay. I know he likes you. If he should ask you to go out with him, you should go." Yoko looked directly at me. "I really think you should," she said again.

By then I knew that Yoko's suggestions were in fact orders; this new "suggestion" seemed insane. "I can't go out with John," I stammered.

"Why not?"

"He's married. He's my employer."

"It's okay, May, okay. *I still think you should go.*"

"But I don't want to go out with John, and John doesn't want to go out with me. Where did you get such a crazy idea?"

Yoko paused. Then she decided to try a different tack. "May, how old are you?"

"Twenty-two."

"You work very hard. You don't have time for a social life. You don't have a boyfriend. Isn't that right?"

"Yes."

"Wouldn't you like a boyfriend?"

"Yes."

"But you don't have time to find one. Do you?"

I said nothing.

"Wouldn't this be easier?"

By then my mind was reeling, but Yoko wouldn't let up.

"Don't you see? You would be better off if you went out with John. Don't you like John?"

"Of course I like him."

"Do you want to see him hurt?"

"No."

She could see how nervous I'd become. Still she wouldn't stop.

"I know John will start going out with other people. I'd rather see him go out with someone who will be kind to him, wouldn't you?"

"Yes."

"Wouldn't you rather see him with someone like you than someone who's rotten to him?"

I didn't answer.

The fact that I did not respond irritated her and made her even more determined.

"I'd rather see him going out with you. It will make him happy." Once again she looked searchingly at me. "It will be great. He'll be happy. It's cool."

"I can't do it, Yoko. I can't go out with John," I repeated firmly.

She wasn't listening. "I think tonight when you go to the studio would be a good time for you to begin. Now, don't worry. Don't worry about a thing." Yoko got up and snubbed out her Kool. "I'll take care of everything." She glided out of the room.

I knew she meant business. Yoko always meant business. "Yoko's the type of person that will always try to get you to do things you don't want to do," John liked to tell people. "Suppose she wants you to build a building. It would be ten stories, and she'll want it done overnight. You say you can't do it, but she's so determined that she'll get you to do it anyway. She'll bug the hell out of you until you get it done. And the way she goes about it—she'll call you and say, 'Just start doin' it.' She'll keep callin' you and callin' you, man. Like, 'How much have you gotten done? How much have you gotten done?' She'll keep doin' it, and you'll say, 'Okay,' and she'll keep pushin' you. She'll keep pushin' and pushin' you, and all of a sudden you've just built yourself a building. That's the way she does it. Yoko's fuckin' amazin'!''

I had to face it. From everything I knew of John and her together, Yoko had the uncanny ability to make him do anything she wanted. She was able to convince him that whatever she wanted was always in *his* best interest. Had she already convinced him that it was in his best interest to go out with me? Was I to be that day's version of her asking someone to build her a building? What would she do next?

Yoko's coolness shocked me. I was hurt by the ease with which she was trying to hand over her husband, a man respected and loved by so many people.

I did not want to have any trouble with John and Yoko. I loved my job and did not want to leave it. I just wanted the conversation with Yoko to go away. But it wouldn't. It kept replaying in my head: *I'd rather see him going out with you. . . . I think tonight would be a good time for you to begin.* I couldn't believe what was happening to me.

I felt trapped and sick, and the more I paced, the more distressed I became. I stopped to look out the window at Central Park. Awash in sunlight on that brilliant summer morning, the park had never seemed more beautiful. I stood there looking out, and suddenly I began to cry.

2

I had never dreamed of meeting John Lennon, much less becoming his personal assistant. In the fall of 1969, after a year at New York City Community College, I was so anxious to join the real world that I decided to leave school and interview for the first job that came along. I went to a bicycle company at 1700 Broadway, and the interviewer told me he would let me know. When I went back down to the lobby of the building, I looked at the directory. Apple Records was listed as one of the divisions of ABKCO Industries. Apple—*the Beatles!* I went back upstairs.

To my great surprise I was hired as an office floater: secretary, receptionist, switchboard operator, typist, file clerk, and clerical worker—all at the lowest salary the company paid, ninety dollars a week. I was told to report on the following Monday at ten to start working for the company that managed the Beatles and the Rolling Stones!

I remember so clearly that first Monday. Eager to begin, I arrived half an hour early. The entire office was deserted. At a quarter to ten a secretary arrived, and I introduced myself. She took one look at me and knew how nervous I was.

"Have some coffee," she said. "Relax. Don't worry about anything. When Mr. Horowitz gets here, he'll tell you what to do." Alan Horowitz was the controller of ABKCO Industries.

The secretary, whose name was Marcy, made the coffee. "This is the only quiet part of the day," she said. "You can't believe how busy we are." Fifteen minutes later, at ten sharp, Horowitz arrived. In his business suit, he reminded me of a young bank officer. He led me to a little desk in front of a large office.

"You'll work here. The office behind you belongs to Harold Seider. He's our legal counsel. If he needs you for anything, his secretary will tell you what to do for him. Meanwhile you can spend your time posting checks."

For my first three days on the job I posted those checks; I also roamed around, getting to know the office. By the end of my first week I was also working the switchboard, and whenever I took my place at the receptionist's desk, I stared at the elevators. At any second I wondered if a Beatle or a Rolling Stone would emerge from the doors. Soon I realized my fantasy was in vain. ABKCO was all about *business.*

I had expected ABKCO to be like the record companies I had read about in *Rolling Stone.* I thought the walls would be plastered with gold records and that music would be playing in every office. I also thought there would be lots of rock stars hanging out and that everyone would be talking about rock 'n' roll all day long. I suppose I expected that everyone there would love music as much as I did. I was wrong. Every executive looked like a young banker or an insurance agent. Their secretaries were generally sweet middle-aged women who had been with the company for a number of years—friendly women who never mentioned rock 'n' roll.

There wasn't much organization at ABKCO, but there was always plenty to do. There was also a lot of pressure. The reason for that was Allen Klein, ABKCO's president, who wanted to convince his new clients, the Beatles, that their decision to make him their manager had been the right one and that his method—total financial control resulting in maximum profits—was the way the job should be done. Klein endeavored to create a company that was all efficiency and cost control, a rock 'n' roll management company with the feel of a conservative accounting firm.

The management of both the Rolling Stones and the Beatles made Klein one of the most powerful people in the music business. Some members of the press labeled him the Robin

Hood of Pop. In the late 1950's he began his career as a show business accountant. After discovering that a client—a major recording star—had been underpaid $100,000 in fees and royalties, he went on to track down other large sums of money that had not been paid to the performers whom he represented. When he negotiated a multimillion-dollar advance in royalties for the Rolling Stones in 1965—a staggering sum at the time—his reputation as a man who could make his performers rich as well as protect their money was secure. So was his reputation for always being in lots of trouble.

Klein had owned a record company, Cameo Parkway Records. The stockholders were suing him because they were suspicious about the way he managed the company, the New York Stock Exchange had suspended trading on Cameo Parkway, and at the same time he was being investigated by the Securities and Exchange Commission. There were fifty other lawsuits against Klein, and the IRS was after him for failure to file income tax returns.

Then, on February 3, 1969, at the urging of John and over the objections of Paul, the Beatles appointed Klein their manager.

At the end of my first month with ABKCO I still had not seen the legendary Klein. Then, one morning during my fifth week there, I heard legal counsel Harold Seider yelling, "Get out of my office!"

"Harold, all I'm asking you is to spend five minutes with the guy," I heard a gruff voice reply.

"I told you, Allen, I don't have five fucking minutes. I don't have any time to waste!"

I heard Seider's door slam after a short, squat man stepped out. He reminded me of a young James Cagney, especially in *The Public Enemy,* the movie in which he pushed a grapefruit in Mae Clarke's face. Klein stood there staring at Seider's door, then he opened it. "Didn't I tell you to get out of my fucking office?" yelled Seider, and he slammed the door shut in Klein's face. Klein opened it. "Don't you ever knock?" Seider roared, slamming the door shut again. This time Klein did knock, and Seider opened the door. "I told you," Seider shouted, "I don't have five minutes. Get out of my fucking office!"

I stared at Klein, who was now muttering to himself as he walked away from Seider's door. That was the Robin Hood of Pop?

Two weeks later Klein's secretary was fired, and I was assigned as a temporary replacement. Most of his secretaries were either fired or they quit under pressure. I made up my mind that I would not be let go. Every morning before I went to work I looked at myself in the mirror and said, "May, today you must be perfect." I couldn't help laughing after I said it.

Klein was the first "actor" I had ever met, a man who changed his personality to fit the situation. Sitting behind his huge desk with his back to the New Jersey skyline and an overhead spotlight shining down on him at all times, he could present a fierce image. I often found him sitting there by himself, lost in thought. He was in that brooding mood one afternoon when I answered his phone and a voice said, "This is John. Let me speak to Allen." The voice was unmistakable. I put John Lennon on hold and buzzed Allen. "John wants to speak to you," I said.

Klein replied hesitantly, "Oh, tell him I'm not in. . . . No, tell him I'm in conference." I repeated the information.

"He's duckin' us," I heard John say to someone. "Just tell him we called. Tell him we're lookin' for him," and Lennon hung up.

After working at ABKCO for sixteen months, it was obvious that the only real excitement there stemmed from John and Yoko, no matter what they were up to or how far away they were. They rented large billboards in twelve major international cities and plastered them with the slogan WAR IS OVER! IF YOU WANT IT. They gave a concert in London, then went to Toronto to announce plans for a peace festival that would take place the following summer, as well as to meet with Prime Minister Pierre Trudeau, Canadian Health Minister John Munro, and Marshall McLuhan. John also autographed his erotic lithographs for fans. Every time they made a move our phones rang. Often these calls—requests for interviews, opinions about their politics, suggestions of new stunts they could perform—were as zany as what they themselves were up to.

Then I had to apply for a copyright for Yoko Ono's "Why," a song on her first solo album, scheduled for release simultaneously with John's solo debut, *John Lennon/Plastic Ono Band.* Yoko's lyric consisted of one word, *why,* which she shrieked and gurgled repeatedly. The copyright office refused to copyright a lyric unless it was at least eight lines long. Regardless of the rules, the Lennons demanded that "Why" receive a copyright. In an attempt to dissuade them we made an endless series of phone calls to London, but they held firm: "Why" had to be copyrighted! We called the copyright office, but the government was as adamant as Klein's clients. Lawyers specializing in copyright law were called in, but they said they could do nothing. John and Yoko called ABKCO to complain to Klein; Klein called and complained to his staff; we called the Lennons. For weeks all we did was call each other as we tried to solve the problem. Finally the melody of "Why" was copyrighted; the one-word lyric never was.

I finally did meet some Beatles. Ringo and George each visited the office once, prompting my memory of walking past the Plaza Hotel one day in 1965 when the Beatles were in New York City. Thousands of screaming, crying girls were pressed against police barricades, calling out for their heroes. I stood on the sidelines, watching the display. It seemed inconceivable to me then that any of them—that anyone I knew, that I myself—would ever meet a Beatle.

Although meeting Ringo and George was exciting, it was not enough to make me want to stay at ABKCO. I wanted to do something creative in the music business. Whenever I could I listened to the tapes that were submitted to the company by new artists who wanted to be managed by ABKCO. I believed I had a good ear and that with practice I could pick potential hits, but no one was interested. At ABKCO the creative projects were not generated within the company but by the acts ABKCO managed. ABKCO worked for its acts—acts like the Beatles; it did not have a creative life of its own.

For me the climate there got worse when, at the end of November, copies of John and Yoko's *Plastic Ono Band* solo albums arrived in the office. I played Yoko's "Why." It was as noisy as I had expected it to be. I did not play the rest of her album. On the other hand, John's album was fascinating. It was the album we were told was inspired by John and Yoko's experience with primal therapy, and it became known as the primal album. After John read a book about primal therapy by psychologist Arthur Janov, he located Janov and he and Yoko spent three weeks with the man in England. Later, in June 1970, they went to Los Angeles to spend four months at Janov's Primal Institute.

John's songs were raw and filled with frank observations about his pain—the pain of his childhood, the pain of becoming as real a person as he could be. For me the album cast John in a new light distinct from the phenomenon of the Beatles. He was a man determined to find himself, to be a real person. It was impossible then not to care for him as a human being as well as a rock 'n' roll original.

The album fascinated me, yet everyone at ABKCO seemed to take it for granted. It was "product"; it only existed to be sold. I decided that after the Christmas holiday I would look for a job in the creative department of a major record company.

One morning in early December I arrived at work as usual at nine thirty. As I stepped into the lobby of the building John Lennon and Yoko Ono were waiting for the elevator.

They both looked surprisingly scruffy. Their hair, cropped short as part of their campaign for peace, was growing in again and was uncombed. John had a short, straggly beard. He was wearing overalls. Yoko was dressed in her uniform, black trousers and a black sweater. I had known that some day they would turn up at the office; nonetheless, I was still taken aback when I saw them, and the surprise made me speechless.

Just then ABKCO treasurer Henry Newfeld arrived. He would know what to do. The elevator doors opened. John and Yoko got in. I followed them, and Newfeld followed me; thus he didn't see John and Yoko until he stepped into the elevator and came face to face with them. Even though he was an executive he too was speechless. In 1970 the unexpected sight of John Lennon could make anyone lose his tongue. We all traveled up to ABKCO in an uncomfortable silence.

My phone was ringing when I got to my desk. I picked it up. "They're in Allen's office. Ask them if they want anything," Newfeld said nervously. I quickly did as I was told. When I walked into Klein's office, they were sitting on a couch, looking peaceable and happy. "I'm May," I said as I approached them. "Can I get you some tea or coffee?"

They smiled at me. "No, thank you, May," John said quietly. He spoke in the throaty, wry voice I recognized from *A Hard Day's Night.*

"No, thank you," Yoko murmured, sounding just like a shy little girl.

"If you need anything," I replied, "please call me."

"Don't worry, May," John said slowly, a gentle smile forming on his lips, "if we need you, we'll do just that."

3

The very morning after I first met them I got a call from Alan Horowitz. He explained that John and Yoko had come to New York City to make two feature-length movies that they would film, edit, and show within a record two weeks time. A "John and Yoko Film Festival" had already been scheduled at the Elgin Theater, a movie house specializing in offbeat films. Horowitz told me that almost all of the Lennon staff was in England at Tittenhurst Park, John and Yoko's huge mansion in Ascot. They needed help in New York, and I was assigned to work with them. I was ecstatic; this new assignment had to be more creative than filing copyright forms.

Horowitz told me to meet with Paul Mozian, ABKCO's young director of creative services, who would brief me on my new responsibilities. Paul did his best. "The first film we're doing is entitled *Up Your Legs Forever*. John and Yoko want to photograph three hundred and sixty-five pairs of legs for peace."

"How will photographing those legs help peace?" I asked.

Paul shrugged. "I just work here." He then explained that my job was to help find three hundred and sixty-five people willing to stand still while the camera slowly panned up their legs.

"What is the second film about?" I asked.

"It's called *Fly*. Yoko wants to film a fly crawling over the body of a naked woman. We have to find a woman who can lie still while the fly crawls on her," Paul continued, "and we've got to find a fly that will do what it's told."

"How will you find the girl?"

"They plan to have screen tests." We looked at each other and started to laugh.

"Don't laugh. It's December and it's freezing outside. If you think getting the girl is a problem, think how hard it's going to be to get *any* fly during the winter, no less the *right* one."

We both laughed again. Yoko's ideas were unlike any I'd been exposed to before. They may have sounded crazy but they also sounded like fun and they certainly beat sitting in the office doing clerical work. I couldn't wait to begin.

That afternoon I had my second meeting with John and Yoko. They were wearing exactly the same clothes as the day before and looked just as scruffy. They smiled sweetly when they saw me. John was alternating sips from a can of Dr Pepper with puffs on a cigarette. He was quiet and relaxed.

"May, do you know what your job is?" asked Yoko. I replied that my job was to help get people to appear in *Up Your Legs Forever*. "Here's our address book," she said, handing it over. "Start calling everyone in it. Say: 'John and Yoko want you to come immediately to have your legs photographed for peace.' " She looked at me, making sure I understood. "Use our names," she repeated. "And make sure you tell them it's for peace."

I nodded my head in agreement.

"Don't leave out the peace part," John said. I was still wondering why photographing legs would help peace, but I didn't ask: No one asked.

The Lennons brought one staff member over from England, a boyish, friendly, energetic man named Dan Richter. Dan had choreographed the ape sequences in *2001: A Space Odyssey*. He had also played the lead ape, the one who threw the bone into the air that turned into a spaceship—a fact that intrigued John. Dan had met Yoko in the mid-1960's in Japan. Impressed by the quality of her art as well as her determination to succeed, they became friends. Later, in London, he and his wife were neighbors of Yoko and her second husband, Anthony Cox. Yoko and Tony Cox lived across the road from the Richters in a seven-room apartment that had wall-to-wall carpeting but no furniture. After Yoko married John on March 20, 1969, she asked Dan to work for them, and he had stayed with them since.

Dan explained to me that preparations had already begun on *Up Your Legs Forever.* A cameraman had been hired, a young man named Steve Gebhardt, who had the technical expertise that John and Yoko lacked but who would not try to take over the direction of the films.

Early the next morning I went to a large dance studio near Lincoln Center where the filming would take place. The studio was already set up for the shoot. A podium was erected at one end of the room. White screens shielded the podium from the rest of the room. A dolly was placed in front of the podium with a camera stationed on it. When a button was pressed, the dolly would rise. Whoever was standing on the podium would be slowly photographed, starting at the toes and moving up to the tops of the thighs.

Steve Gebhardt sat in front of the podium. With him was a friend, a young architect named Dick Ward, whom he had drafted to push the button and activate the dolly. Another friend, Bob Fries, Gebhardt's partner in a film production company, was arriving at any moment from Cincinnati to operate a tape recorder stationed near the podium. Yoko wanted a tape made of the names of each of the subjects and their reactions to the shooting. She planned to create a sound collage from those tapes to use as the sound track for the film.

John and Yoko, still in their scruffy gear, were both chain-smoking. It appeared that they planned to sit on director's chairs in front of the platform and "direct" the subjects. Equipped with two new high-speed cameras, John had also decided to photograph the subjects for his own pleasure while Dan Richter got them onto the platform and coaxed them into showing their legs.

The studio was equipped with telephones. I sat down and took out John and Yoko's address book. All day long I called their "friends," including Andy Warhol, Robert Rauschenberg, John Cage, and Jasper Johns. The responses were for the most part friendly, and some people said they would be right over. Not one asked why photographing legs would help peace.

Meanwhile Paul stood at the door with a batch of releases. The lawyers had instructed John and Yoko to have each subject sign a release, agreeing to a fee of one dollar for appearing in the film.

When the subjects arrived, they were ushered into makeshift dressing rooms where they changed into bathrobes. Then they were directed to stand on the platform. Dan would say, "Please take off your bathrobe, or if you feel more comfortable, just lift it." Some people dropped their bathrobes and stood there unashamedly before John, Yoko, and everyone else. I looked at them, astonished by their boldness.

As one woman raised her bathrobe Yoko leaned forward to study her legs. "Move your toes closer together," she said. The woman obeyed. "Hold the robe higher." The woman raised her bathrobe. "Do you think you could lift it a little higher?" The woman followed instructions. "Your thighs are beautiful," announced Yoko, glancing at John, who was clicking away with his camera.

John smiled at the woman. "You've got lovely thighs, my dear," he said, "but we need a little bit more leg on this."

Over and over again in their roles as directors, Yoko especially, then John, taking her lead, coaxed strangers to display their legs. Yoko seemed to enjoy making people do what she wanted them to do.

As people walked by him, John snapped their pictures. Strangers nodded to him, and he nodded back. He seemed to be having a good time. Occasionally someone would venture over and chat with him or ask for an autograph. When people spoke to him, John's responses were clever and quick-witted and often sprinkled with references to song titles, television programs, political figures, and great works of literature. People expected him to be like the John of *A Hard Day's Night,* and he did not let them down. It was hard not to feel good being near someone that funny and bright.

Still, I remember wondering about security. I never believed that famous people, as famous as John, should mix so freely with the public, yet that was the way the Lennons said they wanted it.

As the morning progressed Paul Mozian occasionally went to John to keep him apprised of the costs, as John had asked. John simply acknowledged the information and never objected to the cost of anything.

During the afternoon, while I was making more phone calls, I looked up. Yoko was standing near me, staring into my face. I smiled at her, but even though she knew I was looking at her, she ignored me. She said nothing. Finally she murmured, almost to herself, "You know, I was famous before I met John." Then she walked away.

It seemed as if Yoko had wanted me to eavesdrop on her own thoughts by creating the illusion that I wasn't there to hear. It was a very strange moment.

But then again, the day was filled with strange moments. By the end of the first day I had talked to more famous people and had seen more bare legs than I would ever have thought possible. The things that might make other people crazy—the lack of routine, the confusion—exhilarated me. I couldn't wait to go back to work on Monday.

Over the weekend the *Up Your Legs Forever* footage was processed and then sent out to be edited. Meanwhile we found a location for *Fly*, a top-floor loft in a dilapidated building on The Bowery. Yoko kept telling us she was going to direct *Fly* herself and not with John, and she kept insisting that every detail be "perfect." She had difficulty articulating her definition of perfection. In reality everything became a test: One had to guess what Yoko meant, then do it, then want to find out if one had done the right thing. She had difficulty explaining what she wanted, and it was left to Dan Richter and Steve Gebhardt to create an environment that would satisfy the definition of perfection that existed in her mind. Richter knew Yoko well enough to make his guesses informed ones. He and Steve had a corner of the loft painted white; they shopped for an oriental rug to put on the floor; they found an attractive bed for the actress to lie on while the fly crawled over her. Then the actress had to be found, and screen tests were given to find a woman who could lie perfectly still for an unknown number of hours. Actresses took off their clothes, climbed onto the bed, and were studied to see how long they could remain motionless. I learned later that even my name had come up, but I was quickly passed over. "She's too innocent," Yoko had said. "She needs to be protected." Finally Yoko chose a woman who had long green fingernails and appeared to be in a state of almost total paralysis.

When I arrived on Monday evening, that woman was already in place on the bed. Two cameras were set up, each with a special lens that could fill the screen with an extremely small portion of her body. A facial pore could be magnified to look like a giant crevice, a fly magnified to the size of a prehistoric monster. John, Yoko, Dan, and the crew were clustered around her.

"Put the fly on her nipple," said Yoko. A fly was placed on the woman's nipple. It flew away. John and Yoko looked at each other. Yoko frowned.

"Do it again," she said, and the process was repeated.

It was tried over and over again with the same results. Those flies would not listen to John; they would not listen even to Yoko; they didn't care at all about conceptual art; they didn't care about an ex-Beatle's desire to help his wife. The woman was painted with honey. The honey didn't work. Neither did sugar, nor flour and water. She was sponged down and left lying there while everyone sat down to discuss the fly problem. Dan Richter pointed out that when he had worked on *2001*, a similar problem had occurred. The solution was to gas the flies with carbon dioxide. Then a stoned fly could be placed on the woman's body. We stood around, waiting until the fly recovered enough to start crawling.

"But when it wakes up, then will it do what I want it to do?" Yoko asked.

"The fly will do what *it* wants to do, Yoko," Dan replied. "But at least it will stay on her body long enough for us to get a shot."

Yoko said nothing, but everyone could sense her disappointment. Still, this seemed to be the only practical solution.

The flies were almost gone, and we needed a new batch as well as a tank of carbon dioxide. Paul Mozian found six college students who wanted some extra money. Paid two dollars an hour, they were equipped with fly nets and directed to go into the kitchens of all the restaurants in neighboring Greenwich Village to catch as many live flies as they could. "If anyone asks, say the flies are for John and Yoko," the kids were told. Enthusiastically they set out, much to the chagrin of the neighborhood's restaurant owners.

Another fly squad was dispatched to an uptown cafeteria that we heard was fly-infested. We were also to tell all our friends that John and Yoko would pay twenty-five cents for every live fly brought to the loft. A case of fruit flies used for medical research was ordered, but after unpacking it we discovered that many of the flies were dead.

By noon the loft was overflowing with people: a squadron of ABKCO employees assigned to make sure that John and Yoko had everything they needed, old New York friends of Yoko's who had come to say hello, as well as miscellaneous hangers-on. Throughout the morning the sponged-down star of *Fly* had lain in bed and not stirred at all. She would not move for the day and a half it took to shoot the film.

"Is she all right?" I asked Dan.

"She is feeling no pain, no pain at all," he replied.

I looked down at her and realized my naiveté: The woman probably was so stoned, she could not move a muscle.

By early afternoon enough flies had been gathered to enable us to try again. The loft was cleared. Then a fly was placed in a plastic cup and gassed with carbon dioxide.

"Put the fly on her toe," said Yoko. Gingerly the fly was removed from the cup. In the process its wings were broken. Another fly was gassed. "Put the fly on her toe," Yoko repeated. This fly was successfully transferred from the cup to the toe; it promptly fell off. A third fly was gassed. "Put the fly on her toe," Yoko said again. This time the fly remained in place, and the shooting began.

Working with the flies continued to be a nightmare, and it seemed to take forever to get a good shot. Yoko and John studied the shooting. After a while John became restless and began to strum a guitar. Yoko headed for a corner of the room. She began to stammer, whisper, and moan—her interpretation of the sound of a fly crawling over a woman's naked body. She planned to record the sounds and use them as the sound track for the film. None of us had heard anything like that before. Yoko believed that her vocalizing was "the music of her mind."

Often Yoko interrupted her warbling to give orders. Though she never raised her voice, her tone had a brusqueness to it that caught us all off-balance. Everyone involved in the production wanted to do his best. There was nothing that we wouldn't do for John and Yoko—and do as well as we could—so Yoko's slightly defensive air unnerved people. So did the fact that she constantly changed her mind. Flies would be placed on one breast, then the other, then below each breast, then above them, while she tried to decide what she wanted to film.

John seemed restless—perhaps he was bored—but he was determined to give Yoko support. John and Yoko often whispered together. Yoko listened, thought about what John had to say, then stepped forward to issue another order, but she wouldn't let John give any orders of his own. Once he got up and watched the cameraman focus his lens. He studied the shot, then made a suggestion out loud. "John, that's not your job," Yoko said. When he suggested a camera angle, she said, "You don't know anything about it, John. Let someone who knows do it." So John remained quiet while he watched what was going on. Occasionally he paced back and forth or retired to the back of the loft to talk to whoever approached him.

At two in the morning, after twelve hours of nonstop filming, *Fly* was nowhere near completion. A packet of heroin had been delivered to John, and he became glassy-eyed and began to weave as he walked. I hated seeing him behave so self-destructively. I did not take drugs. I had been brought up to believe in being in control and I hated seeing John out of control. I wanted to rush over to him and say, *"Cut it out!"* but I didn't. No one did. It began to amaze me more and more that no one dared to criticize John Lennon even for his own good.

Two hours later, at four in the morning, I watched Gebhardt dropping behind the camera. "Put a fly on her crotch," Yoko directed. The cameraman stared at her and did nothing. "I can't do it," he finally said.

"I want the fly to go in, and then I want it to come out."

"You do it," said Gebhardt.

Yoko took the fly and bent down over the model's prostrate body. Yoko squinted and got up. She looked down again, clearly displeased. Then she reached out and grabbed a Tampax string protruding from the woman. She yanked out the Tampax and placed the fly in position.

That night, after more than forty hours of filmmaking, the work was almost done. "I want the fly to fly out the window," Yoko said. There was no way to make a fly do that. "The fly has to fly out the window," she insisted. There were not many flies left, and no one wanted to waste them. However, to please Yoko, we tried to make the flies do as she wished. Almost to the end none cooperated. Finally there was one fly left. As it revived it suddenly made a dash for freedom.

"Get it," said Yoko. We all chased after it. John climbed up a chair and made passes at it, trying to capture it between his hands.

"John," said Yoko, "you know you're afraid of flies. What are you doing?"

The fly was impossible to catch. Gebhardt decided to pan to the window so quickly that viewers would get the impression that the fly itself had flown out of it. In the early hours of the morning everyone packed up to go home. I was among the last to leave. I looked around the loft. Fifty people had tramped through it for two days and it was a mess. There was garbage everywhere: piles of cigarette butts, empty beer cans, plates filled with uneaten food. When I looked up, I noticed that the skylight was covered with flies. Captured, brought to the loft, and gassed, they were then awake and buzzing furiously against the glass.

I dashed down the stairs and into the night. After those weird two days, I was glad to go home to the safety of my mother.

*   *   *

While the editors rushed to complete the film in the Regency Hotel suite that had been set up for them, Yoko and Paul Mozian went on a foray to inspect the Elgin Theater. The Elgin was showing *El Topo,* a violent, surrealistic epic directed by Alexandro Jodorowsky, a Chilean filmmaker. Yoko adored the movie. She saw it again with John, and John loved it too.

Jodorowsky met with John and Yoko. He was an attractive man with a great deal of charm. The Lennons complimented him, and he in turn complimented them. He was a superb flatterer, and while everyone was struggling to complete their films, John and Yoko were being flattered into financing *The Magic Mountain,* Jodorowsky's new film.

Meanwhile, not for a second did the pressure of trying to complete the films let up. "Don't worry. Don't worry about a thing," Yoko kept saying, while she repeatedly urged everyone to hurry up. She even sat in an editing room at the Regency and did some editing herself.

An hour before the film festival was to begin, the films were still not completed, and Bob Fries dashed to the Elgin to beg for more time. Finally the festival got under way. The audience sat through a number of short films by John and Yoko, including *Erection,* a short study by John of the construction of the London International Hotel. Then they saw *Up Your Legs Forever,* which lasted an hour and twenty minutes, and *Fly,* which lasted fifty minutes. People became restless as they watched pair after pair of legs appear on the screen. "This is boring," someone called out, which elicited a round of applause. "What the hell is going on?" someone else shouted. People tried to hush the hecklers. The audience grew louder and more hostile and began to boo and hoot. Jonas Mekas, a leader of the New York avant-garde film community and an old friend of Yoko's, suddenly stood up and yelled out, "This is art. The work of two great artists. How can you behave like this?" The audience burst into hysterics and booed and hissed Mekas.

John and Yoko did not attend the screening. They had already left for Japan, dreading the stopover in Los Angeles, because John had been asked to testify at the Charles Manson trial about the meaning of several Beatle lyrics. Manson had said that he believed that the Beatles were the four long-haired angels cited in the Bible's Revelation 9. Using as his guide his interpretation of such songs on the *White Album* as "Helter Skelter" and "Piggies," he had led his Family into slaughter.

John could not imagine how anyone could extract a message of violence from those songs. He knew that Manson was insane and said that it worried him that some other psychopath might use the Beatles' music as a rationale for acts of similar madness. He said that he had sometimes seen the same mania that had motivated Manson in the eyes of some of the people who were his fans and who waited for him. Nonetheless he did not want to testify.

"Why should I?" he asked. "I didn't write 'Helter Skelter'! Paul did."

4

Some things become so easy to see in retrospect. Looking back now at those first encounters, John and Yoko had already become a centerpiece in my life. I stayed on at ABKCO. I waited for them to return. I *wanted* them to return.

The three dull months after they left town were enlivened only by the gossip and information that reached us from England. After their holiday in Japan, they returned to Tittenhurst Park in Ascot, and John immediately went into his home recording studio, even though it was still under construction, to make a new solo album, *Imagine,* which he hoped would show the world where he stood in relation to the solo albums of Paul McCartney. It would make a meaningful statement and not be *wallpaper music*—the term John and Yoko used to describe the music of the Beatles. He was also determined that it be more successful than McCartney's solo albums.

Our office was jumping with talk about what had gone on during the *Imagine* sessions. It seems all of the musicians' parts had been written out, and Yoko kept telling the musicians that they could not deviate from the scores. It was hardly the way pros like keyboardist Nicky Hopkins liked to work. George Harrison, in particular, was dismayed by Yoko's attempt at control. We heard that when he wasn't recording, George would go into the billiards room and mutter about her to whoever was hanging out. At another point, as John was about to record "Imagine," the album's title track, Yoko reportedly demanded that Nicky Hopkins and not John play the keyboards. "Nicky is a better piano player than you are, John," she told him in front of the other musicians. John brushed aside her suggestion and insisted on playing the piano on "Imagine," and he did.

Finally, in early April, I received a call from Alan Horowitz. "They'll be here any minute. As soon as they land I want you to go straight to the Park Lane Hotel."

At that point I realized that one never knew what to expect from John and Yoko, but when I got to the hotel, I discovered that *they* were the surprise. Each appeared to have lost fifteen pounds. They were wearing chic, well-tailored clothes and looked healthy and well groomed. As usual, they both were chain-smoking, and John was guzzling a Dr Pepper. As John talked to me, his eyes never left the television screen except for an occasional glance directed at Yoko.

He was really excited as he explained that he had journeyed to New York to record the backing tracks to *Imagine*. Time had already been booked at the Record Plant, the only studio in New York City with sophisticated quadrophonic recording equipment, quadrophonic—or four-channel—sound being the rage at the time. John told me an arranger, Torrie Zito, had been found to write the string arrangements and that King Curtis would play saxophone on a number of the album's selections. He was bursting to get to the studio the next day.

Yoko was silent. When John looked at her for encouragement, her face remained expressionless but for an occasional wan smile. When John was through, Yoko told me to unpack their suitcases. She wanted their clothes hung up just so. She also told me to pick up after them. I looked around the room. They just seemed to drop their clothes wherever they happened to be standing. When I was finished, I told them that I was going back to the office and would be available whenever they needed me.

The next day John and Yoko went to the Record Plant for the first session, a simple one during which John would overdub some guitar lines and Yoko would so some vocal over-dubbing.

Roy Cicala, who ran the Record Plant and who would en-gineer *Imagine,* asked Yoko to go into a small drum booth to record her background vocals. John remained in the control booth with Roy and Jack Douglas, Roy's assistant. Dennis Fer-rante, a happy-go-lucky twenty-year-old who worked at the Re-cord Plant as a gofer, stood behind Roy. Ferrante looked into the drum booth to see Yoko's face contorted with rage. Her headphones refused to stay planted on her head and kept fall-ing to her neck. She shook them fiercely, then put them back on her head. As soon as she let go they slipped down again. Dennis could feel her anger. He left the booth and headed for her. "Yoko, can I help you?" he asked gently.

She looked at him. "The phones are broken."

Dennis realized that she did not have much recording ex-perience. The first thing a musician does before recording is adjust the metal band that holds the two headphones so that they fit snugly on his head. He took the headphones from her and adjusted the band. Then he put them on his own head and tested each headphone to make sure that it was working. "They're fine now," he said, handing them back to her. She took them and placed them on her head. They fit perfectly.

"Is everything all right now?" he asked. Yoko stared at him. She was still furious but she said nothing. "Is everything all right?" he repeated. Yoko remained still. "If you have a problem, please call me and I'll do everything I can to help." Dennis turned to leave the booth.

Suddenly Yoko flung a torrent of abuse at him. The words came so quickly, he didn't understand any of them—except for the last two: "Fuck you!"

Dennis turned back. "Fuck you, too," he responded auto-matically. There was a minute's pause as he realized what he had just done: He had just told Yoko Ono, John Lennon's wife, to go fuck herself. Nervously he stepped out of the drum booth, convinced that he would be fired on the spot and that his career in the recording industry was over before it had begun.

Roy, Jack, and John were all staring at him. Shaking in his boots, he slowly made his way to them. "Do you know what you just did?" Roy said as soon as Dennis stepped into the control booth.

"I'm sorry," Dennis said sheepishly, "but I was trying to be helpful." On the verge of tears, he looked at John. "I don't know what came over me," he told him. "Please forgive me. I wanted to help her. I didn't want to hurt her."

"You know what this means?" asked Roy.

"Can I have one more chance?" Dennis pleaded. "One more chance?"

Suddenly John jumped up and headed for Dennis. For a moment Dennis was afraid that John was going to hit him. John, however, extended his hand. "Dennis," he said, "I like you. I want you to work with us."

Dennis shook John's hand gratefully. John turned to Roy and Jack. "I love him! He's great!" he said. "I like someone with balls."

Everyone laughed.

Then he turned back to Dennis. "Don't do it again." John's expression said it all: "You can get away with it once but not twice."

Dennis remained at every session of *Imagine*, working side by side with John. As time went on John began to trust him because he always gave John his honest opinion. To John's credit he appreciated someone who could be counted on to tell the truth instead of yessing him because he was John Lennon.

Another colorful presence during the sessions was Phil Spector, who hovered occasionally in the background. Like John, I believed that Spector was the greatest producer in the history of rock 'n' roll. Since 1958 he had created a string of hits that had become legend: "Be My Baby," "Walking in the Rain," "You've Lost That Loving Feeling," "Da Doo Ron Ron," and many more, for dozens of different artists. More than anyone, Spector knew that rock 'n' roll was about rebellion and romance, and to drive it home he utilized an army of musicians as well as his technological wizardry to develop the famous Spector "wall of sound," in which huge rhythm sections, vocal choirs, horns, strings, echo, and electronic effects were melded into a lush, throbbing, orchestral sound.

Spector had coproduced *Imagine*'s basic tracks with John at Tittenhurst. He had known the Beatles since 1963 and had been invited by Allen Klein to pull together their troubled album, *Let It Be,* in 1970. He had then produced John's single "Instant Karma!" and worked with John on the primal album. He had also coproduced George Harrison's *All Things Must Pass* and produced the *Concert for Bangla Desh* album.

A short, wiry, nervous, man, Spector had been painted as an extravagant character by the rock magazines. To be sure, he was the first person I'd known who always traveled with a bodyguard. Still, for all of the buildup, during the *Imagine* sessions in New York he kept himself in the background. He may have been *a* legend, but John was *the* legend.

The three-week recording period went smoothly. John knew exactly what he wanted and wasted no time getting it. Yoko, on the other hand, was quiet. It seemed that they had reversed the roles they had played during the making of Yoko's *Fly.* While recording, John was affectionate toward the "passive" Yoko. He would hug and kiss her, and she would smile adoringly back at him. It was automatically expected that Yoko would be a monster. Instead everyone who was introduced to her during the making of *Imagine* found her to be the most quiet, adoring person they had ever met, except for that one brief outburst with Dennis, which everyone was eager to forget.

One day Yoko approached Arlene Reckson, the Record Plant's affable young receptionist, with whom I became fast friends. "We need people to work for us in the United States," she said softly. "Would you like to help us?" Arlene had studied fashion and film and had spent three years as a shoe designer. Then she decided that she had to work in the music business—at the end of the 1960's nothing seemed as exciting as the music business—and she chucked everything to work at the Record Plant. The Lennons took to her and eventually gave her a number of odd jobs to do. Because of her background in fashion, John even asked Arlene to shop for Yoko, who had absolutely no interest in clothes and would wear the same things day after day. "I want her to look chic," he told Arlene.

Occasionally, on Saturdays, the Lennons' limousine would pick up Arlene. The chauffeur would take her from store to store while she picked up blouses, slacks, shoes, boots, and jackets for Yoko. She had been told to use her own American Express card and that she would be reimbursed by ABKCO. Since she did not have much money and had always used her credit card sparingly, the luxury of the limousine and the uninhibited use of her own credit card made her nervous, especially when she would end up spending hundreds of dollars in an afternoon. Still, she went from Bonwit Teller to Bergdorf Goodman to Bloomingdale's, hunting for pretty, stylish things for Yoko to wear. When she was finished, she would go to the Park Lane and lay out the purchases for Yoko. Then she would leave. What Yoko disliked she simply threw in the garbage.

Usually I wore what is known as the "layered look," a turtleneck sweater, a blouse over it, and a vest over the blouse, all in subtle earth colors. One evening when I walked into the studio during a session I noticed for the first time that John was wearing the layered look. "I liked what you were wearing this morning and I copied it," he said when he saw me staring at him. I looked at Yoko. She too was wearing the layered look. "I liked what John was wearing," she said, "so I copied him."

Despite the ease with which *Imagine* was falling into place, John's insecurity and nervousness did manifest themselves in two areas. He insisted that he was "not a great singer" and that he wanted as many special effects as possible to give his voice the unique quality he thought it lacked. "Fuck up me voice," he demanded, and he was delighted when the engineers applied echo chamber and electronic distortion devices to his vocals. John also thought he was just an average guitar player. Dennis said to him, "An average guitar player only knows three chords. You know more than three, John. You're better than average." John's response was to become even more nervous. In those matters he was so insecure, he would not listen to reason and kept insisting that he was neither a distinguished vocalist nor guitarist, yet he did acknowledge that he was a good songwriter.

His insecurities troubled me, mainly because I hadn't yet been near him long enough to know if they were normal or if they were the signs of a dark turn ahead.

After John finished *Imagine,* he and Yoko remained in New York City. They would get up anywhere between 10:00 A.M. and 4:00 P.M. When they awoke, they called for their "medicine," little white pills that they washed down with orange juice. When I asked him, John told me he was taking methadone.

John was a man of great energy and intensity, but when he didn't have a project to occupy his attention, he became lazy and could spend all day in bed, watching television. Yoko, however, was a nonstop worker. She was always spinning off ideas for new projects of her own. To do her work, Yoko needed John. It was his money that was being spent, so when John refused to work, she could not work. John had an extremely busy mind. When he was idle, his mind could run riot and his nervousness and paranoia would rise to the surface. It was at those moments especially that he turned to Yoko.

Yoko was an extremist and was even more intense than John, taking any idea or comment of his to the limit. If, for example, he complained about any of his fellow Beatles, she would hint that that Beatle had always been an enemy, implying that John should never deal with that person again. Her extreme positions fascinated John and helped him take his mind off himself. But when she became self-involved and paranoid herself—her paranoia usually dealt with her career, her fame, and the fact that even though she had always been famous, everyone conspired to keep her from getting even more famous—he had no place to turn. His insecurity about his solo career, his childhood, his relationships with the other Beatles, the way the public perceived Yoko, overwhelmed him and he became more and more involved with drugs.

Soon they were both locked into escalating paranoia: The world was against them; no one could be trusted. John had taken to his bed to relax, and bed became a cave in which to hide. Only when John was alone in bed with Yoko did he think he might be safe. They both became so fearful that if they left their hotel room and saw someone in the corridor, they would back into the room and hide until the corridor was empty.

I watched from a distance as John and Yoko transformed themselves into paranoid victims. In the short time I had known them I had seen them both play a number of roles: John had been a devoted, loving, supportive husband; a brilliantly capable professional musician; and then a paranoid victim. Yoko had been an aggressive conceptual artist; a meek, shy wife; and then she too had transformed herself into the role of a victim. They both obviously had many gears in their personalities and they could switch back and forth at random. They were like actors who can take on any number of parts and play each one with so much conviction that they become trapped by the roles they choose to play.

Once they took to bed, the only thing that usually got them out of it was a shopping trip. Because John was not recording, they could shop for themselves. Their chauffeur would take them to the boutiques on East Sixtieth Street—Madonna was among their favorites—then on to DeNoyer, which they both loved, then downtown to an herb store that supplied Yoko with her favorite perfume, essence of apple, with which she drenched all of her clothes.

Their shopping technique consisted of Yoko trying on things to see if they pleased John. When she found something that John liked, she bought it in every color. If they did not have a color in her size, she'd buy the item in a size smaller or a size larger. It was as if she needed to demonstrate to herself that she had enough money to buy anything. Because she was always changing her mind but wanted to appear as if she knew what she wanted, she also would make sure that every option was available to her—even if none of the options fit. The hotel moved two large clothing racks into their suite; quickly they were filled with John's and Yoko's new wardrobes.

When John and Yoko didn't want to go shopping, I would call their favorite boutiques to send a salesperson to the hotel to show them the latest styles. I often found them in bed in the afternoons, watching a fashion show put on by someone eager to sell them thousands of dollars worth of clothes. When the salesperson was finished, John and Yoko would choose what they wanted, and the garments would be delivered to the hotel and hung on the racks.

Periodically Yoko became so restless that not even a shopping trip could satisfy her. She was interested in creating a New York image for herself and John. She wanted to meet the right people and be seen in the right places. The right people usually included avant-garde artists and people like Jerry Rubin, who embodied "radical chic."

Yoko would have me call these people and invite them over to the hotel. Many times after an appointment was made, Yoko would cancel it, reschedule it, and then cancel it again. No one ever minded the endless shifts in schedule, because everyone wanted to meet John and Yoko. I had to schedule three different meetings with Andy Warhol. When the right person would arrive, he or she would be ushered into the Lennons' bedroom, and John and Yoko would hold court. When Yoko had had enough, she would tell the visitor apologetically that there was business that John and she *had* to attend to. Responding to her cue, the guest would always leave, never knowing that Yoko had given him the boot.

Mostly John watched television. He was fascinated by television talk shows—especially Johnny Carson's—and he always watched the news. He believed that the media were filled with people selling something: stars selling their latest films or records, politicians selling their latest policies or palatable images of themselves. To him the media were the vehicle for "adverts," for whatever a person wanted to sell. Yoko was a creator of "events." Since every move John made was covered by the media, he and Yoko decided to create a series of events that would be commercials for peace. They staged "bed-ins" for peace; sponsored a Nuts for Peace campaign; plastered billboards all over the world, and took out full-page newspaper ads, with the slogan WAR IS OVER! IF YOU WANT IT; as well as recorded a theme song for peace, "Give Peace a Chance." John believed that if all prominent people created commercials for love and peace, the general tenor of the world would be improved.

In many ways John was an innocent with a utopian vision of the way the world worked. It was this innocence that led him to be impressed by Jerry Rubin's flamboyance. Jerry introduced John to David Peel, a radical street musician who led a group of street musicians who would turn up unexpectedly on street corners to play antiestablishment songs. John liked the fact that Peel belonged to the streets. John felt that he had essentially been a street person himself, one who was losing his common touch because he was rich and lived in expensive hotels. "The world knows you as a working-class hero," Yoko told John, suggesting to him that he really belonged on the streets. She also suggested that John start thinking about writing music that would encourage social change, not merely wallpaper music. Yoko suggested that he turn his music into political street theater and that he give "events" and "happenings" rather than concerts. She suggested that they lend their support to those radicals who used public display and street theater and perhaps start playing basic, primitive music on the streets themselves. John, who loved to throw himself into new things, was hooked.

After two weeks of alternating bursts of activity with entire days in bed, John and Yoko decided to return to England to work on a film version of *Imagine* to accompany the release of the album. Yoko called me and asked me to hurry to the hotel to pack their clothes, since they were planning to leave the following morning. I arrived at 6:00 P.M.

I began to pack at 7:00 P.M. and finished at 2:00 A.M. Two months earlier John and Yoko had arrived in New York City with two suitcases; now they were going home with three suitcases and five large steamer trunks, four of them filled with clothes, and one of them packed to the brim with shoes alone.

I got to the hotel at eight thirty the next morning. Yoko was in her nightgown, studying ten outfits. She would pick one up, then discard it for another one. At nine thirty the limousine arrived to take them to the airport. Yoko still hadn't decided what to wear.

"We have to leave," John snapped. "Get dressed."

Yoko seemed paralyzed by indecision. Finally, moping, she picked an outfit, ran into the bathroom, and changed into it. I scooped up the other nine outfits and threw them into a trunk. Then I called for a bellhop. The phone rang. It was the front desk. They had to leave or they'd miss the plane. John grabbed Yoko's hand and pulled her to the door. They waved good-bye and were gone.

I sat down on top of one of the trunks to catch my breath. It took four bellhops to get their luggage out of the room.

5

A week later, in the middle of June 1971, Alan Horowitz approached my desk. "John and Yoko want the print of *Erection* returned to England, and they want it immediately. We know you've got a passport. We want you to take the print and go tomorrow."

The last thing I expected was a trip to England, and I said so.

"Believe it," Horowitz replied. "We want to fly someone half-fare, and you're the only one on the staff under twenty-one who's available to go. You're going."

Barely a full day later, the print of John Lennon's *Erection* on the seat beside me, I was being driven in a large Land-Rover through a huge wooden gate and up the snaking drive of the Lennons' home, Tittenhurst Park. Even in the dark the stately old mansion looked enormous. Inside, John and Yoko had knocked down a number of walls and combined little rooms into large modern spaces. Somehow it seemed as if the inside of the house were at war with the outside. I wondered why anyone would buy a beautiful old house only to dispense with so much of its charm by making the inside sleek and ultra-modern.

A few minutes after my arrival, John and Yoko trailed into the room. They looked very tired.

"Hi, May," Yoko said. "How was your trip?"

"Fine," I told her.

"It's good that you're here," John said.

"Thank you," I replied.

"See you tomorrow," Yoko said. They turned and left. The interview was over.

Eventually, I wound up in the kitchen, where I ran into Dan Richter. I made coffee as Dan started to talk about life at Tittenhurst, in particular something that had happened the week before I arrived.

There were certain of John's fans whom John referred to as "the weird ones," fans who *insisted* on seeing him face-to-face. There had been one in particular, whom I'll call Steven, who had sent a number of telegrams from a mental hospital somewhere in the Southwest, insisting that he could be "cured" only by looking into John's eyes. Dan had predicted that one day Steven would turn up at the gate. Sure enough, as soon as he had been discharged from the hospital, Steven found his way to Tittenhurst Park and camped out to wait for John. John did not want to see him. "I don't want anyone to believe I can cure him. I'm John. That's all I am, John," he said, and he took refuge in the house. The police kept removing Steven from the road, but no matter where they dropped him, he found his way back to the house and would not leave. He had been there for days.

"I don't know what to do about him," John told Dan. "I don't want him hurt, but I do want him to go away."

Dan tried to convince John that the only way to get rid of Steven was indeed to look into his eyes. John became more upset. Dan kept after him, and finally, after much discussion, John acquiesced. Then Dan got the idea of filming the meeting for the *Imagine* film. John balked again. He did not want Steven exploited. Dan persuaded John that since the film was to be a photographic document of his life—and that this was a rather strange moment in his life—it would be permissible to film the meeting. They could decide later whether to use the footage in the finished film.

On the appointed afternoon, with the film crew poised, John went to the gate. Steven walked toward John and slowly stared into his eyes, and John looked back. Steven was speechless. He had trouble believing that his dream had come true.

He searched for something to say but he was too overwhelmed to speak. He continued to stare at John for a long, long time. Then, with tears in his eyes, he turned and walked slowly down the road. He was never seen again. Dan, the crew, and John all realized that John had "cured" Steven. John turned and walked back to the house. He was shaken by this incident, and the startling image of the "cure" continued to haunt everybody else.

Early on the morning after my arrival I was in the kitchen again when a group of children suddenly burst through the door. Among them was Julian Lennon, John's son by his first wife, Cynthia. Julian was eight years old and small for his age. He bore an uncanny resemblance to his father and had the same impish, intelligent eyes.

"Good morning, Julian," I said, extending my hand. He shook it politely.

"Come and play with me," he said.

"Go ahead," someone said. "John and Yoko don't get up until noon anyway. You've got plenty of time."

I followed after Julian, who was heading straight for a golf cart parked outside the house. "I'll give you a ride," he said.

He climbed onto the driver's seat, and I sat beside him.

"Do you get scared easily?" Julian asked me.

"No."

Julian drove the golf cart fast. His one intention was to frighten me. He headed for rocks and swerved around them at the last minute. He pretended to crash into trees. He had used his little-boy charm to get me into the cart, and once he had me where he wanted me, he gave me a real run for my money. I was really very frightened but I managed to laugh instead of scream. When Julian saw that he could not scare me, he calmed down.

By the time I got back to the house the day had officially begun. The house was filled with people, and none of them seemed to know what to do. The gardener, the grounds keepers, the housecleaners, the chauffeur, the Lennons' secretary—everybody just wandered about. They were waiting for instructions from their master and mistress, who had still not made their first appearance of the day. The film crew also paced back and forth. They too were paralyzed until John and Yoko got up.

"Believe it or not," said Dan, "this *is* the easiest part of the day, the time before they get up." Then he added, "Have you seen the burglar alarm system?"

I followed him to a panel near the stairway. Dan explained that the system, unlike other alarm systems, was wired to lock people in. "At night, after John and Yoko go to bed, it is the job of the last person to go to bed to set this switch. After it is set, no one can come into their bedroom, and they can't leave it, without triggering the alarm. If it goes off, it rings in the police station, and the police are here in a matter of minutes."

A little while later John and Yoko burst into the room. John had never seemed speedier. Yoko looked extremely tense.

"Have you seen the house?" she asked me.

"I certainly have. It's beautiful."

"Did they show you the burglar alarm system?"

"Yes."

"Isn't it wonderful?"

I did not know what to say to people who enjoyed being prisoners in their own home.

After they spoke hurriedly to their film crew, Yoko asked me to go upstairs with her. A number of small rooms had been combined to create a large space for them, empty except for a mattress against one wall. From the mattress you could see the beautiful lake. I walked to the window and looked out at it.

"John wanted to see water when he got up . . ." said Yoko.

". . . so I had them build me a lake. It's almost real, except for the rubber bottom," John finished, laughing.

"Look at our bathroom," they said.

I followed them into the bathroom. It was bigger than the bedroom I shared with my mother. Four people could fit comfortably in the tub, the kind you expected to see in Hollywood musicals.

"What a big bathroom," I said.

"Very big," John said happily.

"It *is* a big bathroom," echoed Yoko.

"Has anyone explained the film to you?" John asked.

"No."

"Well, in the movie I'm Errol Flynn and Yoko's Rita Hayworth. And now we're gonna get dressed. Go downstairs and wait for us."

"Do you need me to help?" I asked.

"No," Yoko told me, "not now. Later!"

I joined the film crew, who were still waiting to begin. Twenty minutes later John marched down the stairs. He was dressed as a gaucho. Yoko, wearing a beaded evening gown, followed him. When they got to the bottom of the stairs, they stood there waiting to be admired. Yoko studied John. Even though he was in good spirits, I sensed that she thought that he was not enthusiastic enough about her outfit. "I've got to change," she said and ran upstairs. Ten minutes later she reappeared, bearing a cigarette holder and wearing a long scarf. "Do you like the holder?" she asked. We all said that we did. Then *we* did not seem enthusiastic enough. "I'll change again," she said. "I'll change, too," said John, and they both ran upstairs. Fifteen minutes later they returned, wearing completely different outfits. They conferred with the film crew, then Yoko decided to change again. Dan told me that on the previous day Yoko had changed her clothes approximately forty times before she was ready to begin work. After she went upstairs, Dan said, "Shooting the film is easy. The hard part is getting them ready to do anything."

That day it took three hours before Yoko was ready to start filming. Eventually they went outside.

The *Imagine* film was to be an odyssey of the life of John and Yoko. In the early 1970's many rock stars made their own movies based on their lives. Often the films were elaborate home movies, designed to show just how wonderful the private life of a rock star really was. *Imagine* seemed to be a shining example of that genre.

First they were photographed running through the woods. Afterward they changed their clothes and were photographed near the greenhouse. After that shot, they changed again. The filming occurred in starts and stops, with most of the time devoted to waiting for the stars to appear in their new costumes. When it grew too dark to film, everyone trooped inside.

Yoko and John cooked themselves frozen peas and French fries in their microwave oven. For the ten days I was in England, that was the only food I saw them eat.

After dinner, they had themselves locked in their bedroom. Watching Yoko change her clothes all day had exhausted me, and I went to bed, too.

On the following day Yoko and John appeared at noon, dressed in black robes. When the cameras began to roll, they planned to leave the house and get into the black hearse they used as their personal car. Then Dan would drive them down the road to the man-made lake. John and Yoko would leave the hearse and enter a rowboat that John would row to the island built in the middle of the lake. A small table had been set up in the gazebo on the island; on it rested a chess set. John and Yoko planned to walk slowly to the gazebo, seat themselves at the chessboard, and begin to play. In order to film the shot the camera had been attached to a rig extending from a helicopter. As soon as John and Yoko left the house and headed for the hearse, the plan was to have the helicopter rise into the air. It would rise higher and higher until, by the time they were at the chessboard, they would be mere specks in the center of the screen.

Dan Richter gave the cue, and John, Yoko, and he headed for the hearse as the helicopter began its ascent. The hearse sped down the road as the helicopter rose higher. When the helicopter reached the top of the trees, the rig suddenly caught on a treetop. The pilot tried to free the camera by lowering and raising the helicopter, but the more he tried, the more entangled it became. We were all hypnotized by the weird surrealistic scene of the tree fighting the helicopter. From the ground it appeared that the tree might even pull the helicopter down. Meanwhile the hearse had reached the lake. In the distance I could see John and Yoko rowing across to the island, unaware that they were not being filmed. Suddenly the helicopter broke loose, and we all burst into applause. When John and Yoko received the news, they took it with relative calm. Later the scene was repeated with no hitches.

At the end of the day a farmer delivered a huge hog to the mansion. It was John's notion to parody the album jacket photograph on Paul McCartney's *Ram,* which showed Paul wrestling with a ram; John would wrestle with a pig. We all went outside and stared at the large surly animal. It was much bigger than any of us had expected. John circled the animal warily. He liked the idea, but he didn't like the hog.

Dan stood poised to snap the picture. "Climb on its back, John, and grab its ears," he said.

John looked doubtful. He stepped closer to the animal. It let out a shrill, strange sound. John stepped back, but we all urged him on. "You can do it, John," I said. John approached the animal once again. "I can't hold the friggin' pig for too long. You get one shot and one shot alone," he told Dan.

John climbed onto the animal's back and grabbed its ears. The animal shrieked. Dan snapped the camera. John jumped off the pig and headed for the house, Yoko behind him. Inside they ate their microwave oven dinner and had themselves locked in their bedroom.

The following morning John and Yoko filmed the scene that accompanied *Imagine*'s title track. John sat the piano and played the song while Yoko opened the shutters one by one. As John played the room grew brighter and brighter. By the time he was finished the room was filled with bright morning sunlight. It was simple and quite touching. Because they were beginning filmmakers, John and Yoko worked by trial and error. When their instincts were right, their work could be very beautiful.

Some ten days later, at noon, John and Yoko walked into the kitchen, and Yoko said, "May, it's time for you to go home. We're going to follow after you in a few days. You must pack all our clothes."

After packing the five steamer trunks two weeks before, I suddenly found myself packing them again. Early in the evening, just as I was finishing up, John and Yoko entered the bedroom.

"May, you'll leave in the morning," Yoko told me. "You'll take the trunks with you."

"Wouldn't it be easier if you shipped them?"

"No, May," Yoko replied. "We must have our clothes waiting for us when we get there, and we trust only you. We don't trust anyone else."

She looked nervously at John. "We trust you, May," John echoed.

"You could send them with a courier," I told them.

"We don't trust a courier," Yoko replied. "We trust only you. I think you'll have to take our clothes."

I tried another ploy. "When I get to the airport, I'm sure there'll be a huge duty on these clothes. I suppose you'll want me to pay it at the airport."

"I don't think there will be any duty on them," Yoko said.

John shrugged his shoulders; he didn't care.

Yoko looked directly at me. "Don't worry. There will be no duty." She said it with so much conviction, I had to believe her.

"Why don't you take this back with you also," John said, handing me an old Rickenbacker. "It's the guitar I used when I was with the Beatles."

I took it gently. I wanted to tell him how thrilled I was. Before I had a chance, they left the room.

The next morning I went to the airport with the five steamer trunks and the guitar. When it came time to inspect the trunks, I opened them. The customs inspector stared at me.

"These are my clothes," I said impulsively. "I brought them with me from America." The inspector looked at the labels, all of which were American. He must have assumed I was a wealthy young woman who always went to London with many steamer trunks filled with the most expensive clothes.

"Close them up."

I was on my way.

More important, Yoko had been right. There was no duty. I sat on the plane, thinking about what had just occurred. What had prompted me to say what I had to the customs inspector? What was there about Yoko that made people believe her? What was there about her that made people do things that would make her assumptions come true?

If Tittenhurst was frantic, strange, *unpredictable,* it was only the beginning. The months that followed would be even more bizarre.

When I returned to New York I found the ABKCO offices in an uproar. During my absence George Harrison had gone to New York to see Allen Klein. George's friend, the Indian sitar player Ravi Shankar, had told him about the plight of Bangladesh, the eastern sector of Pakistan, and George had decided to give a benefit concert for the victims. Allen Klein approved the event, and "The Festival for Bangla Desh," a benefit concert starring George, had been scheduled for August 1, 1971, at Madison Square Garden.

From the moment the concert was announced pandemonium reigned supreme. It sold out in three hours, and tickets were being scalped for a thousand dollars a pair. The public also believed that at the concert the Beatles would reunite for the first time in five years. The word was that George himself desperately hoped the Beatles would reunite for this event, which meant so much to him.

A number of superstars volunteered to appear on the bill. George, however, knew exactly whom he wanted, and he turned down, among others, Mick Jagger; Crosby, Stills and Nash; and Joan Baez, choosing instead friends like Billy Preston, Leon Russell, Eric Clapton, and, of course, Ringo.

I plunged in as, all day long, flights, hotels, and limos were booked and confirmed for the musicians, many of whom were traveling from Los Angeles or London. Rehearsal space had to be found and electronic equipment rented. In addition, the concert was going to be filmed and recorded by none other than Phil Spector.

While Ringo agreed instantly to appear at the concert, neither John nor Paul seemed capable of making up his mind. Paul called, then John called, each deliberating whether he would appear with George. It appeared that Paul would go on if John did; John said he would do so if Paul did. Then their business problems began to surface, and old angers reemerged once again. Finally Paul refused, while John remained a maybe.

A few weeks went by before John and Yoko arrived. John continued to waffle about performing with George. He did want to do it; however, his restless, intense mind kept telling him why he shouldn't. To do it, after all, meant that he would have to be a Beatle again—which would stand in direct opposition to everything he had stood for publicly since the group had split up. Yoko, however, had no difficulty making up her mind. She wanted to do it, and she wanted to appear as a solo artist—an idea that appalled George. He wanted John and John alone and refused to allow Yoko to appear. Yoko told John that he should use his powers of persuasion over George so that she could appear as a solo artist. George, however, was adamant.

A day or two before the concert I was at the ABKCO offices when I received an emergency call from Dan Richter. He urged me to go immediately to the hotel. When I got there, Dan was sitting in the living room of the suite alone. "What should I do?" I asked.

"Just clean up. We're probably going to have visitors."

The Lennons' suite was its usual mess, and I began to tidy up. On the floor in the corner I found John's wire-rimmed glasses. They had been crumbled and lay in a knot.

"Where's John?" I asked.

"He's gone. Yoko's still here. She's in the bedroom."

I spent the afternoon in the suite, waiting for instructions. Occasionally Dan would appear to tell me to hang on. By the end of the day I had had nothing to eat, so I picked up the phone and called room service. The food arrived, and I sat down to eat. While I was eating the doorbell rang. I answered the door. George was standing there, accompanied by bass player Klaus Voormann and Mal Evans, who had been the Beatles' road manager.

"I want to see John," said George.

"He's gone."

George looked puzzled. "Where did he go?"

"I don't know."

George grew even more puzzled. He seemed stuck. Then he decided to try again. "Isn't John here?"

"John isn't here," I replied. "But Yoko is."

"And John isn't?"

"No, he isn't. Why don't you call Allen?" I suggested.

"Do you think he's coming back?"

"I think you should call Allen."

"Let's go." George marched off.

I learned later that only that morning John and Yoko had had a violent argument during which John told Yoko that he was considering appearing in the festival and, further, that it made no sense to do so except in the guise of a friendly Beatle; the festival could not be a showcase for either Yoko's avant-garde shenanigans or John and Yoko's peace propaganda. If he did it, Yoko would have to stand in the wings. As they argued John became so angry, he crushed his glasses in his fist. Finally he decided that the only way to deal with the problem was to leave. He ordered Dan to take him to the airport. They dashed from the hotel, jumped into a cab, and went to Kennedy Airport. When they got there, John took the next plane out to Europe and wound up in Paris.

Later Yoko went to see Allen Klein. When she returned, she said, "Allen told me to go after him. Pack my bags."

I packed her things, and as soon as I was done she too was gone.

Two weeks later, on August 12, 1971, I found myself unpacking those trunks that I had either packed or unpacked four times in less than two months. John and Yoko arrived in New York to stay.

John, as usual, was staring at the television set, Yoko lying by his side.

"England is a dead country," said Yoko.

"I can't live in a place that doesn't have all the action," John added. "And New York has television twenty-four hours a day."

They were really in New York to stay.

The very next day the Lennons took over a large portion of the seventeenth floor of the St. Regis Hotel. They lived in Suites 1701, 1702, and 1703; I was given room 1707 to use when there was too much work and John and Yoko kept me too busy to go home. A group of musicians, including such distinguished Los Angeles players as drummer Jim Keltner, was flown in from Los Angeles to record *Fly,* the sound track to Yoko's movie. John's plan was to accompany every one of his albums with one of Yoko's. *Fly,* a two-record set, would be released at the same time John released his solo LP *Imagine.*

On a typical day I would arrive at ten in the morning, knock on their bedroom door, and call room service to order them their breakfast: cinnamon toast, tea, and coffee. After they had eaten, gotten up, showered, and dressed, Yoko would give me the errands to do as well as the list of people to call. I also had to answer the phone and screen their calls. The errands might include a quick trip to Chinatown to buy Yoko's favorite herbs or a trip to the Godiva boutique to buy John his favorite chocolates. John, like me, was a chocolate freak. Or I might search for an outfit for Yoko to wear. I also did the correspondence, held the petty cash, and kept the records of expenditures up to date. In addition to all that, I booked the studio time at the Record Plant and made sure that the right equipment was ordered so that the musicians could perform properly each night.

I did my job in the midst of nonstop pandemonium. Besides the film crew roaming through the suite were Tom Bassaleri, their driver; Dan Richter and Peter Bendry, who had been in England with the Lennons; a number of other assistants sent over by ABKCO; a few musicians who were moved into the hotel along with their wives, mates, and children; a number of visiting avant-garde artists and culture heroes of the moment: lawyers; accountants; as well as a number of models ready and eager to show the Lennons new clothes, since they were still up for shopping. Iain Macmillan, the English photographer who had shot the *Abbey Road* cover, also showed up, eventually to be assigned by John and Yoko to photograph them in such a way that their pictures, when put on a record label, would merge into one face as the record spun on the turntable.

Soon after they moved into the St. Regis, John and Yoko had a meeting with me. John explained that he wanted Yoko to get as much favorable press as possible. He felt that too many people hated her and blamed her for the breakup of the Beatles. John's position was that people had to learn that artists like Yoko, not the Beatles, were the true visionaries; they were the ones who would really change the world.

Yoko shook her head in agreement. "It's good for the world," she said.

A plan was established in the setting up of interviews. The writers would meet John and Yoko together. John would discuss how badly Yoko was being perceived, then he would get up after a while and leave the interviewer alone with Yoko. Before any interview I was to chat with the reporter and then brief Yoko about the reporter's prejudices, and the topics to talk about or stay away from. Yoko had watched John, whom reporters always found funny and likeable, and during her own interviews, she played the role of a charming, likable, subdued woman. All the journalists who met her told me afterward how, despite their preconceptions about her, they found her to be a lovely human being. For the press and for anyone who would listen, John and Yoko spoke with total conviction about how they loved each other, how much support they gave each other, and how wondrous their devotion to each other was. They said it; they meant it; they believed it—they were *on*.

I believe they did love each other, but their love was unlike any concept of love that I have known or read about. They spent enormous amounts of time in bed together, but they rarely kissed or touched. As far as I could see there was nothing sensual about their relationship. I had met other couples involved in rock 'n' roll, and it was natural for them to caress each other. Not John and Yoko: They behaved more like children snuggling against each other to ward off any demons that might be loose in the night.

The *Imagine* film was not yet completed, and Yoko kept driving the film crew mercilessly. In response, some of them would roll huge joints and smoke them on the roof of the St. Regis.

Then, one day in late September, inspiration struck. John learned that Fred Astaire was staying in the hotel. He was then my favorite movie star; John loved him, too. Yoko was less impressed. "He is not avant-garde," she told John. Nevertheless John sent me to Astaire's room to invite him to meet them.

I knocked on Astaire's door, and he opened it. Astaire was wearing a blue bathrobe over blue trousers and a pale blue shirt, and he looked just like *Fred Astaire!*

I explained to him that I worked for John and Yoko. "They would very much like to meet you. They're in Suite Seventeen-Oh-One," I told him.

Astaire replied that he had to catch a plane and was running late. He told me to thank them for their interest and conveyed his apologies. He was extremely gracious. Entranced, I went back to 1701 and explained the situation to John. I was going over the meeting when the phone rang. I answered it. It was Astaire, and I gave the phone to John, who spoke to him for a few minutes. Then he hung up the phone. "Let's clean up the fuckin' place," he bellowed. "Fred is coming over."

"Let's change for Fred," said Yoko, and she and John then fled into the bathroom.

I was embarrassed by the mess and ran around, trying to clean up as quickly as I could. In a few minutes John reappeared, dressed rather conservatively in an elegant dark suit with a necktie. Yoko followed a few minutes later; she had not opted for a conservative look. She was wearing a leotard without tights, a huge picture hat, and extremely high-heeled patent-leather shoes. It was a most unusual costume.

When Astaire arrived, I took him into the bedroom to meet John and Yoko. They talked for a while, then John explained about the *Imagine* film. He asked Astaire if he would participate. The movie star replied that he'd love to, and the camera crew was called in.

Astaire's shot involved his walking through the bedroom door with Yoko. After he rehearsed it, he did a take. He stood there thinking, then shrugged his shoulders. "I think I can do it better," he said. "May I please do it again?"

John and I watched him respectfully. Fred Astaire was the consummate professional and he always wanted to be perfect—no matter what he was doing. John and I were thrilled to have met him.

A less attractive experience was the making of "Happy Xmas (War Is Over)," which also occurred at the end of September. The Harlem Baptist Choir, a choir of black children, had been recruited to sing on the recording. The kids and their parents gazed respectfully at John and Yoko.

"Give me a fucking cigarette," said Yoko. Everyone shuddered. Yoko then and there decided that *fucking* was the only word to describe everything. She talked about the "fucking kids, the fucking weather, the fucking musicians, the fucking song."

John became more and more agitated. He knew it was wrong to use foul language in front of the children—even for Yoko—and he didn't like it. Finally he couldn't stand it anymore. "Yoko, cool it," he shouted. "Just cool it."

Yoko clammed up. Muttering, she walked into a corner, resentful that she had not been allowed to do precisely what she wanted to do. She could scarcely believe that John had reprimanded her in public.

"I've invented a new clothes line," Yoko told me one day. "These are the clothes of the future, and I want you to model them." She then showed me her sketches, which included a T-shirt with the breasts cut away and a pair of slacks with the crotch missing.

"Which would you like to model first?" she asked.

"No, thank you," I replied.

"You're so prudish. Are you ashamed of your body? You must liberate it."

"Not today," I said firmly.

"You could be my kid sister," Yoko said patronizingly. "It's my responsibility to help you free yourself."

A few days later I was raving to John about the Chuck Berry show I'd seen the previous night. I noticed Yoko glaring at me and I wound up my description quickly.

"I would have liked to have gone," said John.

"There'll be other concerts," Yoko said icily.

Later, as she was prowling around the living room, she

realized that we were playing a Chuck Berry album. He was John's favorite rock 'n' roll artist. She said, "Get that off. I don't want that played around here." Rock 'n' roll was banished from the suite.

Most of September had been spent in a frenzy of activity to prepare for "This is Not Here," a museum show of Yoko's at the Everson Museum of Art in Syracuse, New York. The show was scheduled for October 9, the day of John's thirty-first birthday. All of us worked on compiling and then addressing and mailing one thousand invitations for Yoko's list of important people. Each invitation was submerged in a small plastic bag filled with water. Since the show was a water event, the invitations were designed to arrive wet. Five hundred artists and celebrities had been asked to contribute a water piece to the show, and Yoko told me to nag them until their contributions were delivered to Syracuse. I had to call John Cage, Dick Cavett, Ornette Coleman, Willem de Kooning, Bob Dylan, Henry Geldzahler, Dennis Hopper, Jasper Johns, Paul Krassner, Spike Milligan, Jack Nicholson, Isamu Noguchi, Andy Warhol, and Frank Zappa to ask them where their water pieces were.

After much persuasion, compasses, steam engines, poems about water, test tubes filled with colored water, india ink bottles, microphones immersed in tanks of water, Mason jars, ice cubes, fish tanks, a refrigerator, and stacks of blotting paper began to pour into the museum in Syracuse.

I compiled a press list. I chartered planes. I rented hotel rooms. Suddenly Yoko appointed me hostess for chartered flights to Syracuse.

There was an awful moment at the airport. I was standing there trying to herd record producer Phil Spector, Ringo, Apple executive Neil Aspinall, bass player Klaus Voormann, drummer Jim Keltner, and keyboardist Nicky Hopkins onto a plane. Then the plane we were to take was delayed. A second plane was also delayed, and we were told that we would have to wait for a plane that was returning from Syracuse.

Spector became frantic. I did my best to calm him down,

but all he wanted to do was yell. He turned to Voormann and shouted, "Have you ever heard of this airline?"

"Sure," replied the musician.

"Yeah. Only after a crash!" He pointed at the musicians. "You . . . you . . . you . . . come with me." He was so dramatic and so emphatic, everyone did as he was told.

"Phil, Phil! Listen to me!" I screamed.

Spector would not listen. He took the musicians to another airline and insisted on flying on his choice of plane, not ours. That night, at John's birthday party, he had a vicious argument with Paul Krassner about, of all things, the death of Lenny Bruce, and John had to intervene to calm them down. It seemed as if there were an inevitable commotion whenever Phil Spector was around.

When we all got to the museum, it was already packed with thousands of Beatles fans trying to get a glimpse of John. All of the plumbing had been hooked up, and the fans flushed the toilets, overflowed the bathtubs, and broke the water-filled balloons. Within an hour there were inches of water on the floor.

I sat with a grim Yoko and John in the museum library. They had been up for days and were both very cranky.

The staff would appear with reports of the latest damage. "They just broke the glass hammers," someone reported.

"Do you know what those fuckin' hammers cost?" John scowled. "Thousands apiece."

"If they were broken, that was the way it was meant to be," Yoko replied sullenly but with a kind of Zen calm.

"I told you to put 'em under glass. I told you to put the whole fuckin' show under glass. I told you not to let 'em touch everything. I told you they'd break whatever they get their fuckin' hands on!" he shouted.

Yoko was impervious. "What was meant to be, was meant to be," she said again.

A museum aide suddenly appeared. "Another toilet is overflowing."

"I suppose that was fuckin' meant to be, too," said John.

"Yes," said Yoko. "Yes."

That night we stayed up until dawn celebrating John's thirty-first birthday. The next day, exhausted, we climbed into a limousine. "New York City, please." The car drove us all the way home.

During the month following the museum show a decision was made to move from the St. Regis Hotel to an apartment. Yoko got on the phone and put out the word to everyone she knew. Joe Butler of the Lovin' Spoonful wanted to sublet his apartment on Bank Street in Greenwich Village. The apartment consisted of two rooms: a small living room and a large bedroom. There was also a minuscule kitchen.

I told Yoko I thought the apartment was much too small for their needs.

"Listen, May, artists have always lived in Greenwich Village," she replied. "This is the kind of apartment people like us should have."

During their sixteen months on Bank Street, John and Yoko made appearances at such radical events as the Attica benefit at the Apollo Theatre in Harlem (November 1971) and a benefit for Detroit radical John Sinclair in Ann Arbor, Michigan (December 1971). They also fought the immigration authorities. John's visitor's visa expired, then his visa extension was revoked, the authorities citing his 1968 marijuana bust as their reason for the action. It seemed certain that he was going to be deported. Meetings with lawyers to try to figure out a way to stay in the United States went on continually.

Also during those sixteen months John and Yoko created their first joint album, *Some Time in New York City,* and Yoko made another two-record solo album, *Approximately Infinite Universe.* Geraldo Rivera asked them to give a concert for the Willowbrook handicapped children's institution, and they gave two benefit concerts on August 30, 1972, at Madison Square Garden. "This will be our Bangla Desh," Yoko kept telling everyone.

To make the records and give the concert, they needed a backup band, and Jerry Rubin set up a meeting for John to meet Elephant's Memory, a six-man New York–based band that had a reputation for being radical. Elephant's Memory was the regular attraction as Max's Kansas City, the in rock club at the time. Elephant's Memory were all in their late teens and early twenties. They loved to party and they hung out in the East Village, their loud, fierce playing earning them a reputation among the radical chic community John and Yoko were courting.

Over the following weeks John and Yoko and Elephant's Memory played together, ate together, and hung out together. John was friendly, unpretentious, and occasionally sharp-tongued, but the band appreciated his outspokenness. The group found him nervous about his work, but they viewed his nerves as normal for a creative artist who had set himself the task of writing a series of political songs—songs dealing with Attica, John Sinclair, Angela Davis, the oppression of women, and the situation in Northern Ireland—songs that sounded more like slogans than music.

In April 1972 a single from John and Yoko's album *Woman Is the Nigger of the World* was released. It failed. The album followed in June. The reviews were pretty bad, and the sales were disappointing—164,000 copies, compared to *Imagine*'s 1.5 million. Radio would not play the single because of the word *nigger,* and John was furious. "All they want is *Imagine,*" he grumbled, but he was honestly upset. "It's like a mantra. You set up a pattern. 'She loves me, yeah, yeah, yeah . . . she loves me, yeah, yeah, yeah.' Once you've set it up you can say whatever. Like 'Give peace a chance . . . give peace a chance.' "

That time, however, John's mantras had not worked. He was so taken aback, he refused to record again for over a year.

By then everyone was in the midst of an eight-week rehearsal period for "One-to-One," the Lennons' benefit concerts for Willowbrook. John was so petrified of performing live that he began to gag and throw up. He was also concerned about Yoko. He did not want her booed; he did not want things thrown at her. So everyone rehearsed diligently at the Butterfly Studio in the East Village. For the final two weeks they moved into the Fillmore East and practiced nightly, setting up the equipment on stage as if they were playing Madison Square Garden.

Still, when they moved into the Garden, the amps

wouldn't work, the sound was filled with echo, and the equipment malfunctioned. There were also security problems. At Madison Square Garden there were fans in the dressing rooms as well as in the wings. The guest list had been hastily prepared, so strangers had no trouble talking their way backstage. The whole experience unnerved me terribly.

A few months after the concert, Harold Seider got the Lennons Robert Ryan's apartment at the Dakota, a stately old apartment house at the corner of Central Park West and West Seventy-second Street. Seider had been Allen Klein's legal counsel. After John fired Klein, he had hired Seider to represent him, figuring that since Seider knew Klein inside and out, he'd be the best man to represent John in Klein's breach-of-contract suit against him.

After they moved in February 1973, I was assigned to work in the Dakota full-time. On the first day I went to work Yoko showed me the apartment. Double doors opened into a sitting area that led to a large living room. Yoko decided that one of the many bedrooms would be converted into a huge closet for her clothes. There were three more bedrooms, a small room that would serve as an office, a main dining room, a butler's pantry, and a large kitchen, as well as numerous bathrooms.

"Isn't this a great place?" she asked. "I found it myself."

"It's a beautiful apartment," I said. "I know you'll be happy here."

Yoko stared out the window. When she spoke, she seemed to be addressing Central Park.

"Our life here is doomed," she said quietly. She lit a Kool. "A few nights ago John and I went to a party. John got drunk. Very drunk." Yoko shook her head to emphasize the point. "He went into a bedroom and fucked a girl while I was in the other room. Everyone knew."

I said nothing. I was very uncomfortable. Neither of us said anything. Yoko got up and stared down at Central Park. She mumbled, "I did primal therapy with him. I watched him go back to his childhood. I know his deepest fears."

It was a dark, horrible moment, and I wanted to forget it as quickly as I could.

Every day at the Dakota was filled with crises, and Yoko's response was always the same: "Ask May." But the confusion didn't bother me. I reveled in the lack of routine and the fact that there was always something new for me to deal with.

During that time John was exceptionally quiet. Sometimes, however, he would lose his temper and shout out in anger if he was displeased with something. Or he would rivet you with a fierce, frightening stare. He seemed fully aware that he need only raise his voice or change the expression on his face and people would become hurt and frightened. That's how much we loved and wanted to please him. It really upset us to see him unhappy—and he knew it.

A month or two after the move to the Dakota, John informed us that he wanted to practice typing! He took the office next to mine, and a couple of times a day he'd pop in and show me how his typing was progressing. Those visits were all quick, funny, friendly, and, so I thought, harmless.

Then that spring Yoko decided to record a new album, *Feeling the Space*. She did not want to work with Elephant's Memory anymore, and she asked drummer Jim Keltner to put together a new band for her. The band was to include a handsome, talented, spunky young guitarist named David Spinozza. I went to the studio every night with Yoko and I could see that Spinozza fascinated her. Later I was to learn that she had found out he was getting divorced from his childhood sweetheart and that she had written him a number of sympathetic letters. During the sessions, however, she remained aloof, except for a moment or two when she and Spinozza would wind up speaking to each other or laughing together. Spinozza was fascinated by Yoko's interest in him. After all, she was John Lennon's wife, Yoko Ono—literally one half of the John and Yoko team—and he was merely a young, relatively unknown guitarist.

One night during those sessions Yoko sent me back to the Dakota to fetch her a tom-tom.

John was watching television. He got up and found the drum, which was on a closet shelf.

Back at the studio, Yoko asked me, "Was John there?"

"Yes," I replied.

"Was he nude?"

"No."

Yoko giggled. "Sometimes John walks around nude."

"I did not see John in the nude."

"Oh," she said, "are you sure?"

"I'm very sure."

Yoko looked disappointed. It seemed as if she had wanted me to see John naked, which really confused me.

At that point I had no idea what was on her mind.

I had been with them more than three years that August when John suddenly began to write again. By then I knew full well just how central John and Yoko were in my life. Then that Monday arrived, and with it Yoko's terrifying "suggestion." I suddenly realized that, like it or not, I was about to become a central part of theirs as well.

Part
Two

6

*H*er words continued to ring in my ears. *It will be great. He'll be happy. It's cool. . . . It's cool. . . .*

It was *wrong*. That was my only reaction to Yoko's plan for John and me, and I wanted no part of it. My one hope was that if I just worked hard enough for the rest of that day, this new project of Yoko's would just go away.

Then at noon she appeared in the doorway. "I'm still trying to get John to go to the studio tonight. That really would be a good time for you two to begin." At two she appeared again. "I don't think John wants to go to the studio tonight. He's probably going to cancel." At four she returned to announce, "John probably will cancel, but don't go home until he makes up his mind."

A little after six I got up and wandered into the kitchen to get a drink of water and came face to face with her. Just then John buzzed from the bedroom. I stared at the phone. For the first time since I'd gotten to know John, I was afraid to talk to him.

"May, answer the phone. It's John." Automatically I picked it up. "Yes, John." John's silence told me everything— he too had been informed of Yoko's plan. "John?" I said.

"Is Yoko there?"

I handed her the phone, then got up and walked out of the kitchen. I did not want to hear her pressuring him to go to the studio. A few minutes later she walked into my office. "The studio has been canceled today. You can go home now, May."

As I walked slowly along Central Park West I tried to sort out the day's events. I felt numb. I was terrific at handling complications—that was my job—but Yoko's proposition had pulled me way beyond my limit.

As I waited for the bus I thought about quitting. I didn't want to quit. I really loved John and Yoko. I also knew I wouldn't be able to get a job that exciting anywhere else. And—if I was to quit—would Yoko find it necessary to destroy my credibility in order to make sure no one would believe me if I ever discussed her "suggestion" with anyone else? What would she tell prospective employers who called for recommendations? I knew Yoko, always an extremist, had the power and the will to make it difficult for me to get a job in another part of the music business if she felt I had betrayed her by leaving. I decided to stick it out as long as possible.

The next morning Yoko's aims were undiminished. Exactly at nine forty-five she marched into my office. "I think today will be the day. You'll go to the studio with John tonight." She smiled sweetly. "Don't worry about a thing."

Once again I kept myself busy, wondering all the while what she would tell me next, but Yoko left me alone for the rest of the day. I assumed that her absence meant that John had balked, and as the day went on I began to feel relieved.

At the end of the day John came into my office. "We will be going to the studio tonight," he said matter-of-factly. It seemed to be business as usual: There was not a clue from him that there was anything else on his mind but going to work, his professional manner indicating that the drama was over. I thought John and Yoko must somehow have worked it out and I felt grateful and relieved as I packed John's lyric sheets and cigarettes and took some money from the petty cash drawer in case I had to buy him anything during the session. Then I called the front gate to make sure the limousine was waiting for us.

John was at the front door when I walked out of my office.

We left the apartment and went to the elevator and rang for it. Neither of us said anything. When the elevator arrived, we both stepped into it. As soon as the elevator doors closed, John turned to me, grabbed me, and pulled me to him. He took my face between his hands, put his mouth to mine, and began to kiss me. "I've been wantin' to do this all fuckin' day," he said.

I pushed John away. He could see that I was really upset and he was puzzled. Yoko gave him a center. It was necessary for him to believe that no matter how outrageous the things she told him were, she was always right. We said nothing as we left the elevator and headed through the Dakota courtyard to the limousine parked on West Seventy-second Street. There was an embarrassed and heavy silence as we traveled to the studio, in contrast to the small talk that usually went on.

The session was the first devoted to vocal and guitar over-dubs. John planned to add two or three vocal harmonies to most of the basic vocal tracks he had recorded the week before. This takes a lot of time; therefore only two or three songs could be completely worked out during each of the sessions. As usual, he was also concerned about his vocal ability. He wanted to hear how he sounded when layers of echo were applied to the vocal tracks.

John was in wonderful voice that night, and the session, though arduous, was as smooth as any I had seen. Periodically during the session John walked over to me and asked, "What do you think? What do you think?" Sometimes when he talked to me he became so excited, he would jump up and down. "May, are you hungry? Do you need anything?" I realized that John had two ways of courting a woman: by relying on her judgment and by trying to please her.

While John was at his best, I was the uncomfortable one, especially when John began to sing "Mind Games." I realized that somehow I had been caught up in the mind games that went on between John and Yoko. It seemed to me that Yoko had instigated the elevator incident and I was equally certain that when John got home he would report to her. She would then invent some excuse that would turn her mistake into a plausible piece of strategy that was part of her grand plan. The next day the sun would rise and Yoko would come up with another scheme—hopefully one that didn't involve me.

Then, at the end of the session, after John packed away his guitar, he came over and sat down beside me. "I'm gonna come home with you tonight."

"I'm dropping you off." I got up and headed for the door. He took my arms and pulled me to him.

"Come on, May," he said. "I want to go home with you."

I pulled away. "No!"

"Come on. Come on." I stared at him. He sounded just like a pleading teenager.

"John, I am dropping you off and that's that!"

He didn't answer. Once again there was an awkward silence as the limousine headed up Eighth Avenue. The car finally pulled up to the Dakota, and John opened the door to get out. With the door open, he leaned back. "Beware of the little green men," he said enigmatically. "They may come through your window tonight." Then he closed the door.

The following morning Yoko walked into my office. "Did you two get together last night?"

I did not look at her. I kept my head down and kept on working, but I could feel her staring at me. She then said with surprising gentleness, "If anything happens, don't be afraid." After a while, I heard her leave the office. She did not appear for the rest of the day, nor did I see John until it was time for us to leave for the studio at six. That night John was his old self. He didn't try to make a pass at me, we bantered in the elevator and in the limousine, and we kidded in the studio. The session, another night of vocal overdubbing, went smoothly. I allowed myself to relax.

As soon as the session was over, however, John once again announced that he wanted to go home with me. I said nothing, but as soon as I got into the limousine I directed the driver first to take John home to the Dakota.

"The little green men may get you tonight," he said when the car pulled up to the building.

As I lay in bed that night I thought about John. There was a part of me that did find him attractive. I liked his wit, his sweetness, his intelligence, his talent. I also liked his soft hazel eyes and his regal nose. Why, then, was I so unresponsive? Was I a coward? Had I been so brainwashed by my strict Catholic upbringing and my equally strict father that I would not even allow myself to consider the adventure of an affair with John? What would I do, I wondered, if it had been John's idea and not Yoko's? Would I be behaving differently? It would never be John's idea, I thought. I realized that even though I was bright and hardworking, I had been trained to believe that men like John—men who were talented and famous—never picked women like me. We *worked* for men like John, we did not have affairs with them. Finally I pushed all of those questions out of my mind. After all, I believed it was Yoko's idea and not John's, and I was determined not to be taken advantage of by either one of them.

On Wednesday the same pattern was repeated: Yoko did not appear all day, and John appeared only when it was time to go to the studio. Again it was like old times, but mindful of the previous night's events, I was still ill at ease. That session was devoted to recording John's solo guitar parts and it was a fascinating one. Whenever John had a guitar solo he would play it a number of times, inventing a different phrasing each time he did so. He'd do a clean version, then a spacey version, then a raunchy version of the same solo. Each of these was recorded on a different track, and later John would select the performance he liked best to include on the album. Even though he did not feel confident about his guitar playing, the grittiness of his work that night made it apparent that he was a consummate rock 'n' roller.

Often during that session, after John laid down a guitar track, he asked me excitedly, "Do you like it? Do you like it?"

I loved his playing and I told him so. As soon as he heard my praise, beaming, he picked up his guitar and started playing again.

At the end of the session John announced for the third time that week that he wanted to go home with me.

"No, John," I said.

"We're gonna take a cab to your house."

"We are taking you home in the limousine."

"There's no limousine. . . . It's been sent away." John glared fiercely at me.

"I'll call another one."

"You know how long it will take to get a limousine. We're gonna take a cab."

John took me by the arm and led me out of the studio and onto the street. It was a hot, sticky August night. Eighth Avenue was almost deserted, and there were only a few cars traveling uptown. Finally a cab appeared, and we flagged it down.

"We need two," I said.

"You can't go home alone, and I don't want to stand on the fuckin' street by meself. I don't want you standin' on the street by yourself either. Get in." John hustled me into the taxi. As soon as he closed the cab door he said, "Tell the driver your address."

"We're going to the Dakota."

John's temper suddenly flared. He shouted, "No fuckin' way. I'm goin' home with you."

The driver looked into the rearview mirror and began to study John's face. Suddenly he spun around, astonished to be looking directly at John Lennon. "Tell the man where you live," John ordered. I always hated to be involved in a public scene with anyone; with John it was especially intolerable. I could see the cabdriver grinning in the rearview mirror, as if delighted to see that even John Lennon could have difficulty getting a girl to give him her addresss.

"Eighty-ninth and Third," I blurted out. I did not give my exact address, believing that when I got to my corner, somehow I could convince John to go on to the Dakota. When we got to the corner of my block, I told the driver to continue on to the Dakota, but John would have none of it. "I'm takin' you to your door." He paid the fare, and we both got out of the cab.

"Where do you live?" he asked again as we stood on the street corner.

"We've got to get you a cab," I replied.

"I've got to see you to your door."

"That's all right, John. Let's call a cab and send you home."

Once again John began to shout. "May, I've got to see you to your door." I was afraid that if I continued to resist, John would become more noisy. So I began to walk to my house, not saying anything, hoping that the silent walk would calm him down enough so that I could convince him to take a cab home. When we got to my building, I looked at him to say good night. John opened the outer door for me. "May," he said very quietly, "I'm comin' upstairs with you."

"Yoko has put some ideas in your head that are just not true," I replied evenly.

"I'm comin' upstairs with you because I want to. It has nothing to do with Yoko. Nothing at all. All Yoko did was tell you the truth. Understand? Yoko is very smart and she knows how much I like you. And that's it."

John glared at me. It was obvious he wasn't going to leave.

"All right, John," I said quietly. "But only for a few minutes."

Slowly we began to walk up the stairs to my apartment. When we got to my door, John said, "Open it," and I did. I stepped inside, and John followed me in. I turned on the light and stood there. It was two in the morning, and John and I were standing in the center of my small studio apartment, looking at each other, saying nothing. I didn't know what he was doing there; I didn't know what would happen next. It was too much for me and suddenly I began to cry. "John," I sobbed, "I've had a terrible week. All of this is very frightening. I'm very frightened. I don't know what to do."

John sat down cross-legged on the floor and pulled me down to sit opposite him. He took my hands. "May, I'm just as scared as you. What do you think?"

I looked at him skeptically.

"Look at this." He pointed to his neck. There was a gash on his throat that I hadn't noticed. "I was in the bathroom shavin' when Yoko came in and told me that she fixed it. I didn't understand what the fuck she meant. She told me, 'I fixed it so that you can go out with May.' I just freaked. That's why I couldn't come out of the bedroom the whole day. I couldn't fuckin' face it."

"Where did Yoko get such a crazy idea?"

"Yoko insisted that she sensed the vibes between us. But there's also the possibility that I talked in me sleep, because I know that I do. May, I've just been thinkin' about you for a long time. You just don't know. And Yoko's smart enough to have picked it up."

"You haven't been thinking about me that way. How can you say that?"

John looked quizzically at me. "Why do you think I took the office next to yours? That's as close as I could get to you during the day. You were just on the other side. Don't you understand? I wanted to get close to you, but that's as close as I could get without *bein'* in the office with you. You think I sit in there just to be a fuckin' secretary?"

I shook my head in disbelief.

John stared at me. Neither of us spoke. Then John said softly, "I want to be that close to you. But you get scared off. Look, May, I don't know any more than you do. So let's take it for what it is."

It was so hard for me to believe. "John, you can have anybody," I murmured.

"I fancied you for a long time. You got beautiful, beautiful skin. You got these almond eyes."

I sat there stunned. I'd been to bed with men before, but no man had ever talked that way to me.

"The musicians all talk about how sweet and pretty you are and how they want you, but you're always so busy, they don't know how to get close to you, do they?" John riveted me with his eyes. Then he moved closer, reached out, and gently brushed away my tears.

"You know how I am, John. I'm too busy. I don't want anyone close to me."

"Do you know anything about men?"

"I've been out with a few guys."

"Don't you want me?"

"I don't know. I'm too confused."

"This is just as confusin' to me as it is to you."

John slowly drew me to him and cradled me in his arms. He began to kiss me gently. I felt inexperienced, awkward, an unlikely choice for a man like John. I was sure that he was going to be disappointed. Sensing my discomfort, he whispered, "Just do it."

I realized that I wanted him to make love to me. The feeling of passion and desire that I felt for him overcame the guilt and awkwardness that I was also feeling.

John enveloped me in his arms and stood up to lead me to my bed. He turned off all the lights and opened the blinds slightly so that the light shone in. Then he began to undress me. His eagerness to have me made him rush, and I tensed. I knew he sensed my tension and I could feel him trying to restrain himself, but he couldn't. I did my best to give myself up to the experience, but we were both very nervous.

When it was over, we lay there quietly for a few minutes, and John lit a cigarette.

Then reality hit me. I was lying next to a man. The man was John Lennon and he was married to Yoko Ono, and I was their assistant. Suddenly I burst into tears. "Please go home," I sobbed. "I want you to go home."

"If that's what you want." Then he tried to comfort me, but I pushed him away. "Please go home," I said again. "This whole scene has made me very nervous."

John got up, turned on the lights, and began to get dressed. He stood at the door. Automatically I remembered my job. "I'll get you a cab," I said.

John laughed. "No. I can do it, May. I'll just see you in the morning." He winked at me. Then he left.

I turned out the light and I tried to sleep but I couldn't. I thought about Yoko. I did not want her to know what had transpired between us. John and I had made love, and it was over, I told myself. I was sure that it would not happen again. It was best, I believed, that it not happen again. But I couldn't deny the truth either. I knew that I wanted to make love to John again.

The next day, while I was getting dressed, I had a nervous flutter. How would I feel when I saw John? Would he ignore me? Would it be awkward and terrible? I didn't know what to do or say.

The day proved to be exceptionally quiet. John popped in and out of the office but did not mention the night before, and neither did I, except when he told me that he'd started to write a song about me, a song that was to become "Surprise, Surprise" on *Walls and Bridges*.

We went to the studio together that night to begin the difficult job of mixing down the album. The mix is in some ways the most creative part of the recording process. During the mixdown each of the album's sixteen tracks is balanced against the others to ensure that the sound works as a whole. It requires "ears"—an intuitive feeling for the sound of the finished record—and it may have been one of John's greatest talents; he could "hear" the finished recording in his head and knew exactly what to do technically during the mixdown to achieve that precise result.

Mixing down takes a lot of time and patience and has always made me restless, even without the kind of emotions that were at play that night. The session dragged on and on while I sat there wondering about what was going to happen when it was over. Finally it came to an end. John said, "Let's go."

As soon as we stepped inside my apartment we began to make love. That night, unlike the previous night, neither of us hesitated.

"Close your eyes and just feel," John said. "Think about yourself and what feels good to you." John liked caressing and kissing my fingers. He took my foot in his hand and began to blow on my toes, then nuzzled them with his lips. He was intent on driving me wild with excitement and giving me the best sexual experience I could possibly have. No man had ever cared about me in that way before—getting his pleasure from pleasuring me. On that second night I allowed myself to discover how much I really did excite him. When I stroked his bare leg, he sighed. Every time I touched another part of his body, he moaned pleasurably, and his sounds excited me and encouraged me to be more daring. I loved pleasing him as much as he loved pleasing me.

After we made love, John said, "We fit like a glove. We're perfect together."

There was an enormous physical chemistry between us; it made me very happy.

Then John suddenly sat up. "I've got to take a shower. Last night Yoko said to me, 'You've been with May, haven't you?' She told me she can smell your perfume all over me. Not that she doesn't know we're together. I just don't want her to get upset every time she smells your perfume."

It seemed so contradictory. After all, Yoko had encouraged John. Noticing my puzzled expression, John took my hand. "Let's take a shower together," he said.

After he was dressed, he put an arm around me, drew me close, and attempted to explain about his concern for Yoko. "Yoko told me that she wanted me to have fun. And you know what fun means to her: gettin' fucked and that's it. If she knew that I felt something for you, I know she'd be hurt. I don't want to hurt her."

He looked at me, hoping I'd understand. The last thing I wanted to do was to be openly affectionate to John in front of Yoko. "John," I said, "you don't have to be afraid of me. I'm certainly too embarrassed to do anything in front of Yoko."

So I continued to go to work every morning at the same time, maintaining the same pace I always had. At work John continued to treat me as an assistant and nothing else, and Yoko, who never again brought up the subject of John to me, continued to give me long lists of things to do.

Keeping our secret proved easier for me than for John. During the day John liked to bolt into my office to give me a kiss or a caress. As soon as he touched me John became sexually aroused, but there was nothing we could do but wait until after the evening sessions were over. In the studio at night he would get up from the console, walk over to me, put his arms around me, and kiss me. That would also provoke a sexual response. His behavior was noticed by the studio crew, who would pretend to look the other way but would watch his every move with fascination, grinning at each other when they saw that John wasn't looking to let each other know that something was going on. At those moments I would pull away, doing my best to discourage John. "John," I'd whisper, "not now."

Always a creature of impulse, John could not be stopped. "I want a kiss," he would reply, "and I want it right now."

At the end of each mixing session for the following two weeks, we rushed to my apartment to make love. We were like teenagers discovering passion for the first time and our passion overwhelmed us. John knew how sexually inexperienced I was, and it brought out everything that was protective and tender in him, and he became my teacher. Again and again he made me concentrate on obtaining as much pleasure as I could for myself. He kept saying, "I want to see what makes you tick," as he led me more and more into intense sexual activity. During lovemaking it seemed as if our bodies were able to talk to each other: There was amazing give-and-take as each of us responded to the other's caresses and sexual sounds. I could not believe how responsive we were to each other.

"We make love with our hearts and souls as well as our bodies," John explained.

He told me that when he was a Beatle, hundreds of groupies had been available to him. He described those experiences as "macho quickies"—encounters that had had no real emotional feeling attached to them. John believed that sex should be charged with emotion as well as desire. "There's gotta be passion there," he told me. "You know you gotta feel."

During these two weeks we spent a lot of time together and we talked. In his role as teacher, John did most of the questioning, and I did most of the answering. He was fascinated by China and when he learned that my Chinese name was Fung Yee, which means phoenix bird, he started to call me Fung Yee when we were alone. John told me that he had always wanted to go to China. He was the first man I had ever known who was really curious about my background.

"Tell me about you, Fung Yee," he said to me again and again.

I told him that my parents were both born and raised in the province of Taison, a rocky farmland in the southern part of China. As was the custom in Old China, their marriage had been arranged by their parents.

"My mother was a docile woman, but it did not stop my

father from beating her," I explained. "In our culture women have never been treated with respect." John listened as I told him some of my family's history.

"In 1935, three years after he was married, my father set out for America. And it wasn't until 1947, two years after the war had ended, that he finally sent for his wife. By then my parents had been married for fifteen years and had spent only four of those years together."

It was hard to read John's reactions to my story. His own past had left him extremely conflicted about parents, especially fathers: John's had abandoned him when he was a little boy.

"Listen to this," I said. "My father made one stipulation when he sent for my mother: He did not want his child, a daughter, to come to America. He wanted a son so badly he sent her money and told her to adopt one. He told her to bring the baby boy with her and leave her daughter behind."

"Fuckin' amazin'!"

"In China couples who did not have sons could *buy* them. My mother bought a ten-year-old boy for five hundred dollars. She left the girl behind and set out for the United States."

I was born three years after my mother's arrival, on October 24, 1950. "My father flew into a rage when he heard that I was a girl and not a boy and refused to come to the hospital to see me.

"My arrival at home did not please my father, who was a very violent man; it also upset Peter, his thirteen-year-old adopted son. When I was two months old, Peter took me from my carriage, placed me on the ironing board, and tried to scald me."

I showed John the scars on my wrists and arms.

"He was a fuckin' bastard to hurt you, Fung Yee."

To change the subject, I showed John the jade necklace my mother had given me. "It's a good luck charm. I've promised never to take it off."

We talked about my Catholic schooling. "Giggling was sinful, talking was sinful, even going to the bathroom was made to seem sinful. I really did believe in Hell."

And we talked about rock 'n' roll, about how when I was seven years old I discovered Dick Clark's *American Bandstand,*

and how day in and day out I stopped whatever I was doing to watch the show. "I was hypnotized by the good *feelings* I got when I listened to the music."

"At seven!" John said. "Way earlier than me!"

Listening to rock 'n' roll was a passion that we shared. John rarely listened to rock at home, because Yoko did not like it or understand it. But to us the music symbolized escape from childhoods that were confining and limited—it meant freedom. We would turn on the radio and switch from station to station, searching for singles we both liked. We loved to hear new groups, the new songs, the new sounds. We also wanted to hear the hits. John listened for unusual hooks—in the arrangements, in the instrumentation, in the production of the record. As he listened he'd get very excited. "Listen, May," he'd say, "listen to the way they've double-tracked the guitars on this record." John and I knew the words to almost every rock 'n' roll and rhythm and blues standard. He also knew the "B" side of every record and often favored the songs that had not become hits like Carla Thomas's "I Can't Take It." When a song that he loved was played on the radio, John would start singing along with it, then he'd say, "May, you sing, too," and we'd sing together. That was what I had dreamed about as a teenager—having a loving, kind boyfriend who would listen to music with me. I guess we were teenagers together.

During my workdays, from the time John and I became involved, I tried to avoid being in the same room with both John and Yoko. I was successful for nearly two weeks, until, for the first time since my affair with John had begun, the three of us wound up together in the living room. I felt very uncomfortable. I sneaked a look at John, but his head was averted. Yoko, however, seemed quite at ease. She looked at me with a rather merry smile and began to giggle. John looked at Yoko and also began to laugh. I didn't feel like laughing at all.

"I hated it when the three of us were together today," I told John that night. "I think I'm going to quit."

"It was awful," John said. "I had this awful feeling."

The next night John said to me, "Yoko thinks that if it

weren't for her, we wouldn't be together. She thinks it is very unfair for you to leave just because you're embarrassed. So just think about that before you do anything." John studied my face for my reaction. "Okay?"

"I still don't like it."

"I don't want to make Yoko unhappy."

The thought that Yoko might become upset seemed to agitate John. I could not stand seeing his distress. Finally I told him that at least for the time being I would stay.

John was in the middle of a strange situation: His wife and mistress were coexisting, for the most part, under the same roof. The way he chose to deal with the strangeness was to ignore it. Yoko, on the other hand, seemed to enjoy watching and attempting to supervise the situation. I knew that it was a tradition in Japan for wives of the upper class to understand the need of their husbands to have a mistress. In Japan often the wife and mistress were friends. I was not a Japanese mistress, however, and the arrangement did make me uncomfortable and embarrassed.

The morning after we had that discussion Yoko entered my office. She asked how I was. Then she said, "I know you get very embarrassed when I talk about it, but John and you have the right to have some time together. So I've decided to attend a feminist conference in Chicago. I will be gone for a week. I think that's fair." She added, "I've told John that I think the two of you should carry on your normal business while I'm gone, so no one will gossip about what's going on. You should continue to do your work while John finishes his album. Why don't you pretend that nothing's going on? I think that's fair also."

"Did she tell you she's goin' away?" John asked me later. He grinned at me. "We'll have a whole week together. That will be wonderful. We just have to pretend nothing's goin' on." John was very amused by the idea of pretending.

On the night that Yoko left, John insisted that I stay over at the Dakota. I felt uncomfortable with the idea at first, but he told me that I would really enjoy myself, adding that a twelve-room apartment at the Dakota would be far more comfortable for us than my little studio apartment. Any discomfort about staying at the Dakota was soon submerged in the greater pleasure of finally being able to spend an entire night with John. I did not want to sleep in their bedroom, so John pulled a mattress into the living room. Even then I was too excited and I couldn't sleep. John, who slept calmly, held me in his arms throughout the night. Toward daybreak I finally dozed off.

In the morning, while we were having coffee, I told him that I couldn't spend a night at the Dakota again. I just felt too uncomfortable.

John agreed. "As soon as I finish the album we'll get the hell out of here," he announced.

Until that moment I had never thought about going anyplace with John, and his idea took me by surprise.

During the week that Yoko was away John and I complied with her wishes. I did my work during the day, and John spent his time watching television, composing, or playing the guitar. In the evening we became a young dating couple. Yoko loved limousines, and to please her, John was used to taking limousines everywhere. "You'll like walking," I coaxed. "You'll see, it's painless. You can't window-shop if you're sitting in a limousine." He also hated any kind of exercise. Finally, after much prodding, he and I walked a block or two. "I like it," he said. Soon we were walking to the movies or to dinner, or we spent the early evening strolling through Central Park. Then John would go to my apartment as we had agreed after my first—and only—night at the Dakota; he would leave before sunrise so that no one would think that he hadn't slept at home.

As strange or incredible as it may sound, Yoko had arranged a relationship for me, a relationship that was making me happier than I ever would have believed.

One day John walked into my office, holding the *Mind Games* jacket artwork in his hand. On the album cover a small figure of John stood in the foreground in front of a huge mountainlike photograph of Yoko tilted on its side. On the back side of the jacket John was much closer to the camera and loomed larger.

"The idea came to me in me sleep," he told me, "and I just figured it out. Look at these pictures."

I studied them, then looked back at John.

"What I'm doin' is walkin' away from Yoko! Can't you see?"

I looked again. John was right. He was walking away.

During that week Yoko called once or twice a day. Our conversations were always the same.

"Are you getting along?"

"Yes," I would reply.

"Are there any problems?"

"No."

"Good." Then she would ask to speak to John. Their conversations were cordial and brief. Yoko kept her word. She seemed to be doing everything she could to allow John and me to grow closer. Toward the end of the week John wound up his work on *Mind Games*. Then he learned that Yoko was thinking of flying home over the weekend. "I think we should go somewhere for a while," he told me. "Let's go to Los Angeles. Harold will be there, and we'll have someone to hang out with. Elliot's also there. We can hang out with him." Elliot was Elliot Mintz, a local L.A. radio and television personality who had become Yoko's friend after he had interviewed her. He had paid Yoko a number of compliments after their interview, and, pleased, Yoko had begun to call him, and Elliot flattered her again. After a number of these conversations Yoko told John that Elliot was "all right" and she had encouraged John to become his friend.

That night, then again in the morning, John mentioned the idea of leaving for Los Angeles. I felt ready. Although the idea of going away with John was very frightening, I selfishly wanted him all to myself. But because Yoko was keeping her word to us, I told John that he had to call and tell her that we were going on holiday. We just couldn't sneak away. John agreed. Later he told me that he had spoken to her. "She's very happy for us," he reported. "She's glad we're really gettin' along." He looked relieved.

I knew that Tony King, a very special friend I'd made at Apple during one of my whirlwind ABKCO trips to London, was in Los Angeles, and I wanted to see him again. Tony had always said he wanted to get to know John better. I was sure they would enjoy each other's company and I called Tony to tell him we were coming to L.A. He told me that he had just finished working on Ringo Starr's new album, *Ringo,* and was planning to go home to London. "Please stay," I urged him. Tony agreed to stay a few more days.

"We won't disappoint him," John told me when I gave him the news.

On the following Saturday afternoon Harold Seider met with John to bring him up to date with respect to the negotiations to dissolve the Apple partnership. I was at home when John called and asked me to go over. "I'll leave the front door open," he said. "Come to the Dakota. Come directly into the bedroom. I don't want Harold to know that you're here." I went to the Dakota and found John in the bedroom, watching television and waiting for me. He closed the door, and we made love. Then I left the apartment, stood outside the door, and rang the doorbell. John went to get me. "May's here to do some work," he told Harold.

At the end of that meeting Harold announced that he had to go to the airport; he had decided to go to Los Angeles that night. John got up and dashed into my office. "May, we're goin' to L.A.!"

"When?"

"On the seven o'clock flight."

It happened so quickly, I didn't have time to think. I went downstairs, took a taxi home, and threw some things together. Then I called my mother and told her I had to go to Los Angeles on business. "Who are you going with?" she asked.

"With John."

"Is Yoko going?"

"She's in Chicago."

"I see." I did not think she suspected anything. I had never lied to my mother before and I knew that if she questioned me then, I would tell her the truth—a truth that would challenge everything she believed was right. Going away with John stood in direct opposition to everything I too had believed in, yet I couldn't wait to go.

During the ride to the airport Harold once again laid down the law to John about money. "John, you're a very rich man," he told him, "but at the moment you have to realize that you have almost no cash flow. All your money pours into Apple and it stays there. At this rate God only knows when the corporation will be dissolved. It looks like it could take forever. The only money you have to spend comes from your receivership. Yoko spends all of that. The money you've been living on has been money advanced to you by Allen Klein. That's over now, too. At the moment you really don't have a cent. There are legitimate business expenses that you can put on a credit card and write off, but any money that you spend now is not Allen Klein's money, it's money to which you don't have access or money that you haven't earned yet. The only cash that is readily available to you is cash we can borrow. To keep you going we've got to get you a loan."

"Ah, fuck! What a fuckin' pain in the ass!" John turned to me. "I hate to borrow," he said firmly.

John's attitude about money had been formed early in his life, just as mine had. I had been taught never to borrow; so had he. John, who had been taught to be frugal when he was a little boy, was by nature a cheap man.

"We'll do as little borrowing as possible," said Seider. "In the meantime the only sensible thing for you to do is exercise some real control. Do you understand me?"

"My parents have never earned more than four thousand dollars a year," I told John. "I know how to stretch a buck."

It was agreed to borrow $10,000 from Capitol Records. While we promised Harold we would make the money last, John felt enormously frustrated by the fact that he was both so very rich and so very poor at the same time.

Harold knew exactly what was going on between us. He understood that we had chosen to act as if nothing were going on and said nothing. I knew that other people would also catch on—it was impossible not to—yet, John knew how obsessed Yoko was with her image and he felt it was imperative that we continue to pretend. "We must keep this real quiet," he said during the flight. "It would drive Yoko mad."

"It would drive me mad," I replied. "What would happen if it got into the Chinese papers? My parents would be too ashamed to go to work."

"What about the nuns? What would they say if they learned that their innocent little May had run off with me?"

The image made me shudder and laugh at the same time. "They'd say temptation finally had gotten its way."

Just before the plane landed Harold asked, "Where are you two going to stay?" Before John had a chance to answer, Harold said, "Stay in my apartment. I can stay with friends." Harold kept apartments both in New York and L.A.

"Harold, are you sure it's goin' to be okay?" John asked.

"I'd rather see you save a buck. Remember, you're very rich and you're also very broke. Next year you can afford to go to a hotel."

Harold lived on West Harper Avenue, a pretty block in West Hollywood, lined with mansions and small apartment complexes, all of which looked like old Spanish castles. His apartment was in one of the complexes just below Sunset Boulevard. Tiled steps led from the street into a beautifully landscaped courtyard. The complex consisted of twelve duplex apartments, each with its own separate entrance opening onto the courtyard. There were palm trees and lush foliage in front of each entrance. The atmosphere was pretty and soothing.

Harold gave us a set of keys. "When you're inside, keep the key in the inside lock. If you lose it, you won't be able to get out."

Harold's apartment was a duplex. The first floor consisted of a living room and a small kitchen. A staircase led to the bedroom and the bathroom. "This is a furnished apartment, in case you haven't guessed," he said. "That's why everything looks like it came from a fire sale at a Holiday Inn."

We stared at Harold's bed. It was a large canopied four-poster bed, totally out of style with the rest of the furnishings.

"Don't ask me how this thing got here," said Harold. "This is L.A. Nothing makes too much sense."

He told us that in case we needed anything, there was an all-night grocery store a block away. He also gave us walking directions to the nearest restaurants.

"Are you two kids going to be all right?"

We assured him that we would be.

"I'll give you a call tomorrow and I'll arrange something, because I know you both don't drive." Harold headed for the door. "Okay, have a good night and don't spend any money."

After Harold left, John turned on the television, and we curled up on the bed.

"This bed is fuckin' awful."

"Let's save up for a new box spring," I replied.

John looked at me and laughed. He kissed me, and then we made love. Later that night we got hungry and went out for a walk. It was a mild summer night, and we felt wonderful. John and I were both fascinated by the huge lit-up billboards hovering over Sunset Boulevard. "Well, here we are," he suddenly exclaimed.

He remembered an all-night coffee shop on Sunset Boulevard and we walked to it. The place was filled with oddball characters: hookers, pimps, some hippy weirdos, a transvestite or two. He told me that a lot of music people had breakfast there at four in the morning after their session work was finished. "It's very L.A.," John said as we looked over the menu. "In this city everybody's up all night with no place to go. This is the City of a Million Nuts."

We ate our dinner, delighted to find that our check came to less than ten dollars. John laughed when he saw it. "So this is what it's like to have a Saturday night date with a Beatle," he said. "I think I can afford to pick this one up."

After dinner we went back to the apartment. We undressed, and I climbed into bed beside John. He cuddled me in his arms. "What are you thinkin'?" he asked.

"We don't have any money," I said. "We don't have an apartment, we don't have a car. And I've never been happier in my life."

"It's fuckin' great!" replied John. Then, wrapped in each other's arms, we drifted off to sleep.

7

The following morning we got up early. "What are we going to do today?" I asked John.

"Let's make a few discreet calls. Who should we be discreet to?"

"I'll call Tony King and tell him we're here."

"Then I'll call Mal Evans." John had known Evans from the early 1960's, when Evans had been the Beatles' assistant road manager.

"We ought to call Harold and tell him we're all right."

"Then we'll call Elliot Mintz."

"Elliot?" I asked.

"Yoko is going to tell him anyway. You know they talk every day. As soon as he finds out we're here, he'll be here in a flash, so we might as well call him."

"Is there anyone else?" I asked.

"I'd like to see Jim Keltner." Keltner, by this time, had played with John on *Imagine, Some Time in New York City,* and *Mind Games,* and had worked with Yoko on *Fly* and *Feeling the Space.* John found him a superb drummer and liked Jim's loving, positive nature.

I shared John's feelings. "That's a wonderful idea."

We called Harold, who said he'd drop by later. Then we spent the rest of the morning lying in bed, talking on the phone. Tony King was especially delighted to hear from us. "I'll come over after work tomorrow and take you to dinner," he said happily. "You talked me into staying, and now that we're all here together, I think we should celebrate."

Then John spoke to Elliot Mintz. "He made me an offer," John said after he got off the phone. "If we rent him a car, he'd like to be our chauffeur."

"It will do for a day or two," I replied. "I can drive, and I'm going to get my license. Then we can rent a car for *us*."

John also spoke to Mal Evans and Jim Keltner and made dates to see them as well. I called my mother to tell her I was all right. John listened intently while I spoke to her, doing his best to break me up while I was on the phone.

Then he said, "I think we should call Yoko and tell her we're all right."

He found her Chicago number and dialed it. As soon as Yoko heard John's voice she asked for his Los Angeles number, and he gave it to her. He answered her questions about the plane ride, the trip in from the airport, and the apartment. "I like it here, Yoko," he said. "I like it much better than I thought I would. I may even want to record here." He stared at me. He wanted affirmation, and I smiled back. Until then I had had no idea that John was even considering recording in Los Angeles. I had assumed we were staying only two weeks. I wondered if he was planning to stay longer. John handed me the phone. "Yoko wants to say hello."

"May, how are you?" she asked.

"Fine."

"How's the weather?"

"It's beautiful, Yoko. How's the weather in Chicago?"

"It's very humid. But fall will be here soon anyway. When I get back to New York, I'm going to have to go over my fall clothes." She paused. "Are you happy, May?" she asked suddenly.

"I'm very happy."

"Good. John sounds wonderful, too. Listen, May, this is just the beginning. It's a wonderful beginning. I'm so pleased for the two of you. I want you to have a wonderful time."

I thanked her and gave the phone back to John, and they exchanged good-byes.

"I'm glad," John said after he got off the phone. "I'd hate

to see her upset." He poured himself a cup of coffee. "I wonder if Yoko will find somebody to hang out with."

"I really don't know," I said quietly.

"I hope she does." He smiled at me.

"John, are you really thinking of recording in Los Angeles? I thought we were only staying for two weeks."

"Let's play it by ear," he replied.

That night the phone rang. John was used to having all of the calls screened by Yoko and insisted that I pick it up first. It was Yoko, and she wanted to report the events of her day and wanted to hear how we had spent our time. She quizzed me, then she quizzed John.

Early the next morning she called again. It was clear that she planned to call at the beginning and end of each day. Yoko, indeed, had no intention of leaving us alone. She had once told me about the Japanese puppet theater. Unlike an American puppet show, the Japanese puppet masters were in full view of the audience, and the puppets didn't have strings. Even though I was three thousand miles away from Yoko, suddenly I felt part of one of those shows.

After Yoko's morning call, we decided to go out for breakfast. That time we walked in the other direction, to Santa Monica Boulevard, and discovered an International House of Pancakes.

"All right! Fuckin' blueberry pancakes, I love 'em!" said John.

Our breakfast was a happy one. The truth is, we liked doing simple, sappy things together and felt no need to dress up, to go to fancy places, or to eat fancy food. John knew he was a star, but at that moment he did not feel the need to prove it by flashing his wealth and fame and by living extravagantly.

He told me during breakfast that he was looking forward to seeing Tony King, and I was thrilled. While at the Dakota John never wanted to meet new people or see old friends and felt relieved when Yoko screened his calls, read all his mail, and scrutinized his visitors before she allowed them to meet with him. John believed that people had an expectation of him because he was John Lennon. The thought that he might not fulfill that expectation made him nervous, and he preferred to meet as few people as possible. At the Dakota, Yoko scheduled John's social life, and he spent his time with her friends or the people she thought he should meet. When he met strangers, John would always cascade them with dazzling displays of wit. Invariably most people found him brilliant and extremely funny. That was the John of *A Hard Day's Night*—the John they expected to meet. It was a role he could play to the hilt. People often mistook his public performances for self-assurance, never realizing that John's wit masked deep-seated discomfort and was his way of keeping most people at a distance.

John mistrusted most people. Did they want to know him because he had been a Beatle? Were they only after his money? It took him a long time to trust someone enough to let down his guard and show his gentler, more sensitive side. I thought that he might remain true to form and insist on keeping his distance from everyone, even Tony, someone he had known casually from his Beatle days. Instead all day long he looked forward to the dinner.

When Tony arrived, John was perfectly at ease. Tony, however, was quite nervous about seeing John. "I know a wonderful restaurant," he blurted out. "It's called Lost on Larrabee. Everyone hangs out there."

When we arrived, Tony couldn't manipulate his huge car into the parking space. No matter what he did the car refused to fit. "Tony, what's the matter?" John finally said.

"It's you," a flustered Tony replied. "Being in the car with John Lennon is making me nervous."

John took my hand, and we both got out. Tony still couldn't park the car. "I'm not in the car now," John told Tony. It was a tease—a gentle tease. John smiled at Tony, and Tony began to laugh.

John led me toward the restaurant. "Tony will never park the car until I'm out of view. He really is anxious, and now that he's had a laugh, maybe he'll calm down."

When Tony walked into the restaurant, we all laughed again. "Thank you for understanding," Tony told John.

John and Tony talked about the times they had met in England when they were hanging out at such English clubs as the Scotch, St. James's, and the Ad Lib. They recalled the evening at the Scotch when the Beatles' table was given to Princess Margaret and they were forced to get another table. They laughed merrily as they remembered how annoyed they had become because Princess Margaret had been shown precedence over the Beatles.

Tony and John talked about their fatherless childhoods. The fact that Tony also had not had a father made a deep impression; it helped John decide to make Tony a real friend. Then they talked exuberantly about one of Tony's oldest and dearest friends, Elton John, who, at that moment, was the most popular rock star in the world. "Elton has always desperately wanted to meet you," Tony said.

"Really?" replied John, laughing. "Then I'd like to meet him."

Only once did they both get deadly serious.

"America," said John. "I always felt I was an American. Tony, even though you're English, I can tell you're really an American, too. *You've got to move here.*" John nailed Tony with his fierce stare, and Tony knew John meant every word.

Recently Tony said to me, "I'll never forget that moment. John changed my life that night. He knew how to care."

It seemed to me that our first days in Los Angeles were enchanted. Indeed, it had been only a few days when suddenly we found a beautiful house to live in—a magic castle that was ours.

We were at the Rainbow, a popular Los Angeles rock club, when we ran into an old friend of John's, Andrew Oldham, who had been a press agent for NEMS Enterprises in the early 1960's and had discovered the Rolling Stones and had been their original manager and producer.

"Where are you living?" Oldham asked John.

"In Harold's apartment," John replied. Oldham knew Harold. "Harold's representing me in the Klein case."

"How would you like a house? A friend of mine has lent me a great house that I've been living in. I'm going back to England the day after tomorrow, and the house will be empty. I suggest you move in and keep the bed warm."

Andrew Oldham's friend was Lou Adler, the music business giant who had produced the Mamas and the Papas and who eventually produced Carole King's enormously successful albums. Lou Adler was living in his beach house, and his city house was unoccupied.

"I don't know Lou Adler," John told Andrew.

"I'll speak to him for you."

The next day Oldham called to tell us that Lou Adler had said he'd be delighted to have us stay in the house. "It's yours," he said. "I'll be gone tomorrow. I'll leave the keys in the mailbox. Come up anytime tomorrow and move in."

"It's like magic," said John. It was. Then John added, his eyes twinkling as he said it, "And it's rent-free!"

That night we ate with Tony again. During dessert John suddenly handed him a cassette of *Mind Games*. "Here's my new album," he said. "What do I do with it?"

Tony took the cassette and stared at John. Was it possible that John Lennon did not know how to promote an album?

"Yoko and I were very pleased with the way you handled our albums in England. I need your help now. I want to know what to do."

Tony remained silent.

"Come on. You can always tell me the truth. I'm famous for it."

"To be honest, John," Tony finally replied, "you have to do interviews, lots of interviews. You should start doing them now. Between your *Rolling Stone* interview and your *Some Time in New York City* album, everybody thinks you're a very angry man. That's all you've put out about yourself during the last three years.

"The public deserves to know that you're okay. You should talk to the press and tell them that you're okay. Let them see you as you really are. You're not angry, you're not a radical. You're an intelligent, sensitive, gentle, caring man— and you're also a musician, not a crusader. That's the message the press should give to the public. When people *like* you, John, they *want* to buy your albums. When they don't like you or they're afraid of you or they don't understand where you're coming from, they don't want your records in their homes. It's as simple as that."

By the time we got home John was wildly enthusiastic about Tony's advice. "Tony's right," he said. "Being liked is important. Everybody liked the Beatles, and look what happened. I've never been able to get the press to like Yoko. If the press liked her, the public might begin to like her. Then some of them might buy her records. I've tried to push Yoko and radical causes for the past few years and it doesn't seem to work. I'm a little tired of it now.

"I just want to make albums. That's it. The best person for Yoko now is Tony," meaning Tony Cox, Yoko's second husband. "He knows her better than me and he knows how to get the things done.

"Our friend from Apple is right," John repeated. "The time has come for me to help me."

An hour later Yoko called. "Yoko," John said excitedly, "we had dinner with Tony King tonight. You remember him?" Yoko didn't, and John explained to Yoko who he was. Then John said, "He's going to do the press campaign for *Mind Games.* Do you remember all the good things he did for our albums in England?"

When I looked at John, I could see his changes of expression as he talked.

"Yes . . . have it your way. . . . Yes, Yoko . . . yes . . . yes . . ."

By the time the conversation was over, there was a haunted look on John's face.

"What's the matter?" I asked.

John told me that Yoko had made no response to his news about *Mind Games.* Instead she told him that she had something she wanted to talk to him about. In her concern about her image, Yoko was afraid that the press was going to find out that they had separated. If asked, she wanted to tell the press that she had thrown John out and that John had not left of his own accord; she wanted him to promise that he would not contradict her, and John told me he had agreed to her version of the story. Then he told me Yoko wasn't content with that.

Of course John and I should be together when we went home at night, John told me she had told him, but to avoid any problems with the press we had to continue to pretend that nothing was going on between us. In that way the press would never know a thing about us and there probably wouldn't be any questions at all. John told me that she had cited a number of instances when she had learned from "friends" that we had been seen holding hands and kissing in public. We were never to touch in public. She suggested that we ride in separate cars, and she said that even in front of friends who knew, like Tony King and Harold Seider, we should keep up the pretense. She suggested that we have no visitors when we moved into the house.

"If it's going to help Yoko's ego to make the public think that she threw you out, it's fine with me," I said evenly. "I'm happier, much happier, in the background. But you've got to realize that none of this makes any sense. Whether we do or don't ride in separate cars, people are going to find out the truth, aren't they?"

John stared at me. "No one's controllin' me mind," he said. "I wouldn't be with you if that was the case."

"John, I'll do whatever you want, but we've got to be able to tell each other the truth. You can't fool yourself into believing that pretending really works. Yoko wants us to spend our time doing these things because she wants us to spend all our time thinking about her. This is her way of making sure that we don't get too close."

"Yoko is very smart. She's taught me a lot. I don't want to hurt her."

"Yoko is a wonderful woman and she's taught me plenty also. But that's no reason for us to be isolated and alone. Haven't you enjoyed going out? Aren't you happier making new friends? Do you really want to spend your time hiding out with me, being paranoid, spending our time worrying about whether or not we're pleasing Yoko?"

I knew John was very upset. When he spoke to Yoko again, he told her that I had disagreed with her. When John got off the phone he told me that Yoko was hurt. " 'I was so nice to her,' " he quoted Yoko. " 'I helped put you together. I've always been nice to her. Is this the way it's going to work out?' " John looked disapprovingly at me. He sympathized with Yoko—somehow Yoko's pain was *my* fault. I knew John was in a bad position. He cared about me and he also cared about Yoko. It appeared that Yoko had the power to speak directly to the deepest, most insecure part of John, and it was essential to him to do what she said, to defend her against criticism, and to believe her if she criticized me. That connection defied all logic and it was a truth that I had to accept, even though it saddened and threatened me. I wanted to do everything I could to help John trust himself, then he would not have to turn to *anyone* to be told what to do. I also hoped that I would never have to call Yoko and ask for her help because I did not have the ability to speak to John the way she did.

John sat beside me. "Well, here we are in Los Angeles, together on our own. I love you, Fung Yee. But I'm going to tell Yoko that we're doin' what *she* wants. Then we'll do what *we* want. It's the only way to keep the peace."

Yoko called early the next morning, and I wished I had the courage to unplug the phone. John repeatedly reassured her that he would comply with her wishes. He also gave her the number of Lou Adler's house so she could reach us after we moved in. Then he hung up and looked at me. "Yoko's cool," he said and winked at me.

Later, when Tony called, John said, "I really want people to hear *Mind Games*. So I'm goin' to do whatever I have to do, and I'll talk to anyone who wants to talk to me. Don't turn anyone down—come one and come all. I'm not angry anymore and I'm ready."

Not more than a few hours later we were settled into Lou Adler's house. True to Oldham's word, it was a small, elegant mansion on Stone Canyon Road in Bel-Air, one of the most luxurious neighborhoods in Los Angeles. Just as Andrew had promised, the keys were in the mailbox. John and I strolled through the house. It was comfortable and spacious. Behind it there was a small pool in which we could swim and an area for sunbathing. It was perfect, and we knew it.

"I call our first week in Los Angeles a success. Don't you, Fung Yee?" John said happily. "We have a lovely home. . . ."

"And Tony's a terrific new friend," I added.

John looked at me and smiled. Suddenly he scooped me up, carried me into the bedroom, and threw me onto the bed.

He reached down, grabbed my T-shirt between his hands, and ripped it in half. No man had torn my clothes from my body before. It was a little frightening but very exciting. We made love for what must have been hours. There was only one on-going interruption: The phone kept ringing. It rang and rang. Finally John got up and answered it. I could hear him from the other room. "Yes, Yoko . . . right . . . right . . . anything you say, Yoko. . . . Yes . . . yes . . . yes, Yoko . . ." I wanted to rip the phone from the wall.

8

That damned phone! John believed that because Yoko had given him his freedom, he owed it to her to take every one of her calls instead of telling her to call only when she had something important to say. Soon Yoko was calling all day long. "Why did she call this time?" I'd ask. "She just went to the store," he'd reply. There were times when she called to tell John that she was hurt or suicidal or that she thought I didn't care about her. At these times John would do his best to pacify her. It seemed to me that by telling him these things Yoko was giving John the illusion that *he* was controlling *her.* Whether John did or did not really believe her, he insisted that he had to be nice to her; otherwise, if she ever did kill herself, her death would be our fault.

I hated the phone game but didn't know what to do about it, as I knew anything I might do could be construed by John as proof that what Yoko said about me was true, and I was not being nice to her when she was being nice to me.

Deep down I also knew I had my own reasons for not trying to stop John from taking those calls. John had spent his life surrounded by people who wanted to manipulate him and his feelings. I could not have lived with myself if I became one of them. I did not want to be John's new mother. He had already begun to ask my opinion about his every move. He wanted me to be Mother, but I would not do it. I wanted John to stand on his own and I wanted to play straight with him. Rather than betray him by attempting to control him, I let myself hope that I could help John feel secure enough to limit the endless calls himself.

A day after we moved into the house, the *Mind Games* interviews began. Tony told me that invariably when he picked up journalists to bring them to our house, they were excited to the point of hysteria. "John doesn't realize how beloved he is," he said. "Everyone—absolutely everyone—is a devoted fan."

The interviews went splendidly. John knew that his job then was to be himself. He was so charming and terrific that reporters, following his lead, did not challenge him and insist on straight answers to difficult questions about the breakup of the Beatles, a possible Beatles reunion, or any of his controversial activities since he had met Yoko. When asked why he had gone to Los Angeles, he explained his visit by saying, "That's where Phil Spector lives, isn't it? Phil is my favorite producer. Maybe I'll record with him."

Among the interviews that Tony had set up was one with *Record World,* the music business trade magazine. That interview became a two-part series. Tony told John that it was essential to tell the industry (which Tony believed then viewed John as some flaky radical) that he was back on the track, not making music that would hector people but music they could enjoy.

As I listened to those interviews I realized that there were some more basic truths that I did not want to face. At his core John was a very frightened man. He dealt with his fear of women by allowing himself to be manipulated; he dealt with his fear of men by manipulating *them.* He could do it by fixing them with his piercing stare, by speaking to them firmly in an unmistakably authoritative voice. He could also do it by being the public John—a man of startling honesty and common sense. In reality John allowed almost no one to become his close friend; even though his truthful, direct style enabled him to create an illusion of startling intimacy, he used his bluntness as a way of keeping people at a distance.

When we spoke alone, John was always simple, direct, and brief. But during those interviews he was on. Stunningly articulate, he had a public voice and he knew how to use it. Suddenly I was afraid. I did not want to think about the fact that John could turn on a public voice whenever he wanted to. It would make me question his truthfulness and wonder if he was ever using his public voice with me. I decided always to believe him, no matter what he said. I had to believe him or I couldn't have stayed with him.

In the midst of the burst of publicity generated by Tony King, *Mind Games* was released. The album reached the ninth position on the popularity charts, and the single went to number eighteen. People seemed to feel that *Mind Games* was a bland album but a welcome relief after *Some Time in New York City*. John was discouraged by the mild success of the album, but he also found a way to rationalize it. "Now they know I don't automatically make number ones all the time," he told me. "If I did, they'd expect every album to be number one. Now the pressure's off me to keep producing."

At the beginning of our third week in Los Angeles, while we were having our morning coffee, John said, "You know what kind of album I'd like to make next? I'd like to make an album of all the songs that made me fall in love with rock 'n' roll in the first place. All the songs I loved when I was in me teens. It's something I wanted to do even before I became a Beatle."

It sounded like a wonderful idea, but what he said next did not sit as well with me.

"Phil should do it. He's the greatest rock 'n' roll producer. I'm goin' to let him produce and I'm just goin' to be the singer in the band."

"But the people have already seen what Phil has done," I managed, wanting to be careful in the face of John's enthusiasm. I couldn't understand why John, a wonderful producer in his own right, wanted to make a *Spector* album, when in the past he had hired Spector to make *Lennon* albums.

"I love him and his music," John said. "Him and his wall of fuckin' sound."

"Can you at least coproduce it with him?"

John didn't listen. He was intrigued by the idea that Spector could do for him in 1973 what the producer had done in the early 1960's for groups like the Ronettes and the Crystals. I thought that even if Spector was the sole producer, the album inevitably would wind up a collaborative effort. So I decided not to worry and to trust John. The recording studio was the *one* place where John *always* knew what he was doing.

After a number of calls had gone back and forth—Spector was never easy to reach—the producer invited us to go to his house the next evening to have a meeting. John told him that we didn't drive, but Spector insisted we go to *him* anyway. He did not know that we weren't taking taxis or renting limousines, but were depending instead on Elliot Mintz to be our chauffeur.

Yoko, as usual, called many times that day, and during one of her phone calls John told her about his idea for a new album. Toward the end of the afternoon I heard John say to her, "Yoko, these songs are what I grew up with, and I *want* to do it."

When she called the following morning, she brought up the subject of the album again. "These songs are *classics,* Yoko. They fuckin' never die. I don't always have to do an album of new songs all the time. I'm *not* the avant-garde one, Yoko. I'm a rock 'n' roller."

Lodged in between her endless description of her day and her questions about ours, Yoko made one critical suggestion after another about John's new project. They were small criticisms, criticisms that could easily be dismissed, yet John responded sharply to each of them. Nonetheless he remained in good spirits and looked forward to his meeting with Spector and to hearing Spector's reaction to the project. Right before we left for Spector's house Yoko called again. "Yoko, I'm goin' now," John said with ultra-sweetness. "I'll be sure to send Phil your love."

Spector lived in Beverly Hills, right near Sunset Boulevard. As Elliot drove us up the hill to Spector's house John gleefully pointed out the devices the producer had acquired to protect himself from the outside world. Spector's house was surrounded by a small brick wall. "A brick wall," observed

John. The wall was surrounded by barbed wire strung from tree to tree. The barbed wire could easily be stepped over or cut through, but it was there anyway. "Look, barbed wire," said John. There was a heavy metal gate in front of the mansion. "A metal gate," said John. Six No Trespassing signs hung on the gate. "No Trespassing signs," said John. When you got to the gate, you reached out and pushed a button in a box. A signal rang in the house, then the gate might or might not swing open, depending on Spector's mood. I pressed the button, and the gate flew open.

"Into the jaws of the dragon," John said merrily as we drove into the courtyard.

The house, like many Los Angeles mansions, had no main floor. Spector's front door was opened by his butler, who led us down a long hallway to Spector's dimly lit sunken living room, where he formally announced our arrival to an empty room.

We sat and waited—and waited. I smelled trouble. John saw I was getting restless. "Maybe Phil's in the bathroom," said John.

We waited some more.

"Phil likes the upper hand," explained John. "He likes to keep people waitin'. It's his style."

After fifteen minutes, even John had become restless. Just as we were about to leave, Spector suddenly dashed down the stairs and John jumped up to shake his hand. "You remember May," he told Spector. I extended my hand to shake Spector's. Spector, however, did not extend his hand to me in return. Instead he stepped back, ignoring me, and said angrily to John, "She's one of Klein's. I recognize her from Klein's. How can we trust her?"

"She's all right, Phil," John replied.

Spector stared at me. "I'm all right, Phil," I said quietly.

Spector glared at me. "How do *I* know we can trust you?" he asked.

"You can trust me. You can trust me," I said.

"I don't know that. How can I believe you?"

"I'm tellin' you," said John, "that you can trust her."

"But she worked for Klein. Don't you realize I saw her—I saw her working for Klein."

"She works with me now. And I trust her."

"But she could be in touch with Klein, couldn't she? Are you in touch with Klein?" he asked.

"No."

"Phil, I have something to talk to you about," John said briskly.

"You want to talk in front of someone who may not be trustworthy? What's wrong with you?"

"Phil, sit down," John snapped.

Phil glanced at me. There was an enigmatic expression on his face. He struck me as very strange. He had to know that even though I had worked for Allen Klein, I could not have been privy to any secret information. It was as if he moved in clouds of anger, fear, and drama. Spector made me really nervous, and I did my best to ignore him.

John, on the other hand, had enormous patience with him. He accepted the fact that Spector's genius went hand in hand with his unpredictability, and so he looked the other way, brushing off Spector's shenanigans. Paradoxically he was also very relaxed with Spector. When he was with Spector, he did not have to worry about anyone's expectations of *him*, because with Phil in the room it was impossible to pay attention to anyone else.

John explained that he wanted to record a group of his favorite golden oldies and that he wanted Spector to produce the album.

"Who is in control of this album?" Spector asked.

"You are."

"Do I have *total* control?"

"Yes."

"Total—total control?"

"Yes. Yes, you do. I only want to be the singer in the band."

Spector was quiet. "In other words," he finally said, "I have total control."

"You have total control."

Spector stared at me, trying to gauge my reaction. "We should think about some songs," he said. "And then start thinking about the musicians. I'll get back to you."

"So you're going to do it," John said with delight.

"Only if I have total control."

On the way home John was really happy. "You heard him," he told me. "Phil's goin' to do the album."

I was concerned about Spector's "total control." Nonetheless I had seen John record *Imagine, Some Time in New York City,* and, most closely, *Mind Games.* While he had had his moments of nervousness, he had always known what he was doing. Once again I tried not to worry.

That night John told Yoko that Spector had agreed to do the album and that he had given Spector control. The next morning, during one of her calls, I heard John say sharply, "When you want to do a rock 'n' roll album, you go after the best! And Phil is the best!"

That afternoon, after many tries, John got Spector on the phone. Spector could be wildly enthusiastic, and John loved being swept away on the tidal wave of Spector's enthusiasm. "It's going to be the album to end all albums," Spector told him. "It's going to be the greatest. Baby, it's going to be a classic. That's what it's going to be, a classic. Now, don't worry about a thing."

Acting on John's behalf, I called Capitol Records and informed the director of finance of John's plans. The standard procedure in situations like that is to budget an album, then studio time is booked and musicians are contracted and the bills are forwarded to the label. Of course, everyone was always interested in cost control, but in the early 1970's the music industry was going through an extraordinary boom. Hit albums could generate fortunes, and money flowed when superstars like John were involved. No record company would ever attempt to restrain an artist like John unless he went berserk and began throwing away hundreds of thousands of dollars with no end in sight. I knew Capitol would pay the bills on John's new album without questioning them. Still, I thought it important that, just as we were living on a budget at home, we not spend unreasonably in the studio.

I called Spector's office and spoke to his secretary. Finally, after many tries, I got Spector on the phone. "I've contracted John's albums before," I told him, "and I'm prepared to do it again. I can sit with you, and we can budget the album together."

"My office will do everything," Spector replied.

In those days musicians were booked for three-hour sessions at a cost of ninety dollars. Payroll records had to be kept so that the musicians would be paid and the proper information forwarded to both the IRS and the musicians' union.

"If you tell me who you want to hire, I can contract the musicians and take care of the paperwork," I told him.

"My office will take care of the musicians."

At that time the studio costs were one hundred and fifty dollars an hour. When people worked inefficiently, those costs could mount astronomically.

"I can book the studio time," I volunteered.

"We'll take care of that, too."

"When the bills come in, I can go over them and then send them on to Capitol."

"We'll mail the bills directly. Don't worry about a thing. All you have to do is turn up."

There was nothing for me to do but call Capitol Records and tell them that our bills would be sent directly from Spector's office.

John heard me making those calls and he laughed. "You're not used to total control," he said. "You're one of those people who likes doing all of the work. You've got to sit back and relax."

Meanwhile word was getting around that Spector and John were planning to create an album of rock 'n' roll classics, and that Spector had decided to have every top sessions player in Los Angeles make a guest appearance on the album. As the word spread everyone who was anyone in Los Angeles decided that he had to play on the album. We began to get calls from friends who wanted to play with John and wanted to recommend their friends to play as well. John directed those calls to Spector. Then John would ask Spector to tell him what was going on, and Spector would tell him nothing.

Spector's game fascinated John. His silence made John even more curious and enthusiastic.

John did insist, however, that Jim Keltner, his favorite drummer, be hired to play on the album. He also told Spector that he wanted to use his own engineer, Roy Cicala. Despite Spector's total control, the producer readily agreed to John's choices. I realized then that Spector wanted the album as badly as John did. Relieved, I immediately made arrangements to get Cicala from New York. Then I really could relax. No matter what Spector did, John had chosen to surround himself with his musical "family," extremely capable men who loved and trusted John and were loved and trusted by him.

Then John decided to hire guitarist Jesse Ed Davis, and one afternoon Davis came to the house to discuss the album.

"He gives me a bad feeling," I told John after he left.

"Fung Yee," John replied, like a schoolteacher lecturing a narrow-minded student, "he knows every guitar lick imaginable. He's a fuckin' amazin' guitarist. How could you get a bad feelin' from someone like that?"

Meanwhile Yoko continued to pepper her fifteen or so daily calls with negative observations about Spector. Nothing she said, however, could still John's enthusiasm. Yoko reminded John that Spector had sent them a bill after they spent two days as guests in his house.

"Phil has a sense of humor," John replied.

She told him that he shouldn't trust Spector, because his house was haunted.

"Whether it's haunted or not, he's goddamn brilliant," John told her.

Late one night she woke us up to ask John how he could trust anyone who liked to carry a gun, as Spector did.

"He never fired it at anyone," John snapped. "Besides, I'm sure it's filled with blanks." Then John hung up.

Most of the problems I perceived—Spector's secrecy, Yoko's suggestions about Spector, my displeasure about Jesse Ed Davis—rolled off John's back. He was cheerful and eager to begin, and I was delighted.

John and Spector talked on the phone to establish a time to begin a series of planning sessions about the album. It was hard to get Spector; then it was hard to get him to make up his mind after you got him. It would take four or five phone calls to set up the first time. Then Spector would call to change the time, and there would be three or four more phone calls. Spector refused to go anywhere until the sun went down; he insisted upon being home before the sun rose. John and I nicknamed him the Vampire.

One day during this period, when John saw Harold Seider, the lawyer told us that John's problems with music publisher Morris Levy were kicking up again. Levy had filed suit against John, charging that when John had written "Come Together," he had lifted a single line from Chuck Berry's "You Can't Catch Me," a song published by Levy's music publishing company.

"Just settle it," John instructed Harold. "Find out what he wants from me."

The settlement included a provision that John would record three songs published by Levy on his next album. "That's easy," John said. "He's published some great old tunes." John began to go over Levy's catalog to find numbers that he wanted to do on the Spector album.

He would discuss his choices with Spector during their evening meetings. When Spector arrived for these meetings, he generated a great deal of excitement. Once he walked through the door, his enthusiasm was so infectious that you automatically forgot the fact that he was late. "Oh, man," Spector would say over and over again, "it's going to be the greatest. It's going to be fucking great. I can't believe it. I can't believe how great it's going to be." John and Spector were like kids revving each other up, and John would sit and listen attentively while Spector rambled on, talking about the history of rock 'n' roll, life in Hollywood, and the latest gossip about L.A.'s most prominent studio musicians.

Finally they would turn to the subject of material. After they agreed upon a song, they would run through the tune on their guitars and work out a basic approach and arrangement.

They agreed to devote the first session to recording the basic tracks of "Bony Moronie," a novelty hit for Larry Williams in 1957, and the second session to "Angel Baby," the Rosie and the Originals hit.

A day or two later, after another of Yoko's calls, John hung up and turned to me with a bemused expression on his face. He was about to say something when the phone rang again. "I don't know who it is," I heard John telling Yoko. As soon as they hung up she called back immediately. "I don't know who it is," I heard John say again. The calls kept up, and I could see him growing more irritated by Yoko's game of "Guess Who?"

"What does she want?" I finally asked him.

"Yoko says she's goin' out with someone. Someone who really fancies her. She won't tell me who it is. Do you have any idea?"

We started to throw names back and forth. "I bet you it's David Spinozza," John finally said, referring to the young guitarist in Yoko's band whom she had appointed to produce her new solo album.

John picked up the phone and called her back with his suspicions. It appeared that Yoko did not contradict John.

"Aren't you upset?" I asked him when he got off the phone.

"I want Yoko happy," he replied. "I don't want her alone. One of me biggest fears was that she wouldn't find anyone." He paused. "I just want her to be happy."

A few minutes later Yoko called back, and I answered the phone.

"May, go into another room. I must talk to you."

I did as I was told. John did not mind. He was glad to have Yoko off his back for a while.

"Yes, Yoko," I said when I picked up the extension.

"What's wrong with you?" she hissed.

"Nothing."

"I'm disappointed in you. I'm shocked."

"Why?"

"I thought you understood. You just don't understand."

"I don't know what you're talking about."

"*You* told John about David. This makes me very angry. I'm very upset."

I knew Yoko well enough to know that no matter what I said, she was in the mood for giving me the business. To defend myself would only encourage her.

"Don't you realize how upset I am? You've upset me. You just don't understand."

I said nothing.

"You just don't understand."

"I guess I *don't* understand."

"Don't you know it's not your job to give John any information? The information is supposed to come from me. You're not doing your job."

She kept me on the phone, chastising me for not cooperating, not doing my job, not keeping her trust.

After I hung up, she kept calling back and kept insisting on speaking to me in secret. During those conversations she continued to browbeat me relentlessly until she was convinced I would never again give John information until I cleared what I would tell him with her. John ignored the whole thing. "That's fuckin' Yoko," he said. "She's overreactin'." He got a kick out of the whole thing.

Later he said to me, "Suppose she started with David Spinozza while she was in the studio with him." He paused. "Maybe she thought that she could have David and I could have you and we could all live at the Dakota and no one would know a fuckin' thing."

I wondered if John might have stumbled on the truth, then I realized that I might never really know the truth myself.

So it was that our "quiet" L.A. vacation began to heat up. That weekend we went to Las Vegas on impulse with Elliot Mintz to see Fats Domino, who was playing at the Flamingo Hotel. We drove back with Tony King and his friend the composer Michael Hazelwood, stopping along the way at a deserted ghost town in the desert. We roamed around, snapping pictures of each other in the eerie setting. Las Vegas and the ghost town seemed like two different kinds of burial grounds, and we were unnerved by each.

The next night Elliot took us out with a friend of his, Sal Mineo, and we all went to a gay cabaret/discotheque. John was oblivious to the gay ambience. He was curious about everyone's sexuality and liked to gossip about who was sleeping with whom, whether they were gay or straight. John made no judgments about homosexuality but was really curious about who was and who wasn't gay.

He knew that his appearance at a gay club might start rumors about his own sexuality, and it made him laugh. He told me that there had been rumors about him and his first manager, Brian Epstein, and that he usually didn't deny them. He liked the fact that people could be titillated by having suspicions about his masculinity. Then I was the one who was laughing. "How could anyone believe a man who likes women as much as you do is gay?" I told him.

After the show we went back to Mineo's apartment. I was thirsty, and Mineo told me to look in the refrigerator. There was nothing in it but one big bottle of amyl nitrite.

Mineo told John that he knew Ava Gardner. "I'm a real fan of hers. I love Ava," John replied excitedly.

Mineo went to the phone, called London, woke Gardner up, and told her that John wanted to speak to her. John took the phone. "Ava, is that you? Ava, I think you're beautiful. I've seen all your movies. Christ, is it really you?" They spoke for five minutes, then a thrilled John handed the phone back to Mineo.

When I spoke to my mother the next day, she told me that Arlene Reckson had been trying to reach me for days and had finally called her to find out where I was. She had left a number in Woodstock. I realized that it did look as if I had disappeared. I called Arlene.

"May, where are you? What's going on?" she asked.

I explained that John had suddenly decided to go to Los Angeles to record and had asked me to go with him. I did not tell her that we were having an affair.

"What are you doing?" she asked.

I explained that John's budget was limited and that John—as Arlene knew—would do nothing for himself. I listed my activities: I shopped for groceries, prepared meals, cleaned the house, answered the phone, scheduled meetings, coordinated transportation, did the correspondence, and planned John's social activities. I also told her that in two days time we were going to go into the studio to begin recording John's new album.

"You're doing all of this by yourself?" Arlene asked.

"You got it."

"I'd love a change of scenery and I'd love to see you. Why don't I come out? I'll pay my own airfare and I'll help you in return for room and board."

I loved Arlene; I also missed having a friend and I did need help. "Let me talk it over with John," I replied.

John was agreeable to the plan, and I called Arlene and told her she was welcome.

When Arlene arrived the next day, we hugged each other as if we were long-lost friends. "I'm so glad to see you," I exclaimed. "I really missed you." I led Arlene into the living room to say hello to John. Just then the phone rang.

"It's Yoko," John said nervously. "Don't say anything. I don't want her to know you're here."

Arlene looked puzzled. She did not know that John had promised Yoko that we wouldn't have any visitors in our home.

That night Spector arrived at the house to meet with John one last time before the first recording session. When John introduced Arlene to Spector, the producer insisted that Arlene sit through the meeting. Arlene did her best to concentrate, but Spector's incessant rambling made her nervous. She sat there, staring at John, begging him with her eyes to be excused. John noticed her discomfort. "If you're so uncomfortable," he said, "why don't you get up and go?"

"Thank you, John." Arlene fled from the room, and I followed after her. We sat in the kitchen, far enough away from Spector so that his voice was reduced to a dull roar.

Finally I took Arlene to her room, then I went to bed. Always a light sleeper, I awoke as soon as John climbed in beside me.

"Has the Vampire gone home yet?" I murmured.

"Yes." John laughed. He gently began to kiss me.

"How did you do?"

"Phil says it's all goin' to be great."

"It will be."

"Fung Yee, it's goin' to be the greatest," John said enthusiastically. "This album is goin' to be great!"

9

"*I* know Phil's tough," John told Yoko, "but it's worth it. I'm tellin' you, I know anything can happen. That's part of the fun. . . . I like mystery, Yoko, I like it!"

On the first day of recording John was usually agitated and tense. That day Yoko had already called three times, once again mentioning her concern about Spector in the middle of the third call. I wondered why then, of all days, Yoko had chosen to suggest once more to John that he could be making a mistake.

John hung up and turned to me. "Fung Yee, do you think I'm doing the right thing?" He looked intently at me, wanting to be reassured.

"This record can't miss," I said calmly. "Now, come on. It's a beautiful day. Let's sit by the pool." I was making lunch when Yoko called again. During that morning she decided that it was time for *her* to record again, and she wanted to discuss her new album with John. "Yoko's upset," John told me when he got off the phone. "She wanted to make a two-record set, and I told her that I couldn't afford it. Harold warned both of us about money. This is not the time to spend one hundred fifty thousand dollars makin' an album no one will buy."

"Would you like to go for a drive?" I asked.

"No. I want to watch television."

Yoko called again. "You won't believe this," John said

when he got off the phone. "She's got herself booked into Kenny's Castaways. She's goin' to open at the end of the month. I hope she doesn't run the bill up too high." Then he shrugged his shoulders. "I don't want to see Yoko hurt, and you can guess the kind of reviews she'll get." Then he laughed. "At least she can spend the rest of the month drivin' her 'musical director' crazy while I'm makin' me album." Yoko's musical director was going to be David Spinozza.

During the afternoon John's engineer, Roy Cicala, called to tell John that he was raring to go. His drummer, Jim Keltner, called to say he was looking forward to playing on the session that night. Tony King called to wish John the best of luck. John laughed and joked with each of them. Spector had refused to give John any details about that night's session, and John's curiosity was at a fever pitch. He asked each of the callers what he thought Spector would do that night and how many musicians Spector would bring to the session. Everyone gave him more or less the same answer: Be prepared for anything.

In the late afternoon we watched television together. "I don't have anythin' to worry about," John said during a commercial. Then he said, "Jim will be there, and I have me own engineer. So all I have to do is sing me songs and relax." He looked at me for reassurance, and I nodded my head in agreement. John laughed. "I've got a girl named Bony Moronie . . ." he sang lustily to me.

Later Yoko called again. She wanted to tell John about an astrologer she had decided to consult, and he listened with interest. Suddenly he snapped, *"Phil is goin' to be all right."* No matter what Yoko told him, John's good mood remained intact.

At the end of the day we got up to get ready. John went to the bar and siphoned off a flask of vodka from the big bottle on the counter and packed the flask in his shoulder bag. He noticed me staring at him. "I need a little security, Fung Yee," he said a little sheepishly, then, trying to reassure me, "I'll probably only have one drink to relax me." I put my arms around him, and we just stood there hugging each other tightly.

Arlene, who had been doing errands all day, joined us, and we all sat down to wait for Elliot to arrive to drive us to the session. John was very fond of Arlene, and from the moment she arrived we invited her to join us whenever we went out. The three of us were pals who enjoyed hanging out together.

At six thirty Elliot honked his horn, and John bounded out the door. The phone rang. I felt sure it was Yoko. John didn't hear it, as he was getting into the car. I let it ring.

"There will be no more than eight musicians," John said with certainty as we drove down Sunset Boulevard. "Whenever Phil and I worked together before there were never more than eight."

The car was caught up in rush hour traffic, giving us time to study the billboards perched above Sunset. We joked about each of them. "I'm imagining John Lennon's new album up there," I told John, and we all laughed together.

"Yoko thinks it'll be Phil Spector's and his alone by the time it's done," John replied.

Finally we arrived at A & M Records, where we were to record. There were one or two fans outside the gate, and they waved to John as we drove by. He shifted uneasily. John hated unexpected invasions of his privacy. "How do they know I'm here?" he asked. "It's just so fuckin' amazin'. I don't understand it."

"I'll check on security." We were both used to working at the Record Plant in New York City, where everyone was devoted to protecting John so that the recording could go as smoothly as possible.

At the gate Elliot announced to the guard, "This is John Lennon."

"Where are you going?" the guard asked.

"It's *John Lennon*," Elliot repeated.

"Tell him it's the *Spector* session," John said, realizing that Spector had probably instructed the guard not to let anyone onto the lot unless they used the name Spector to get through the gate.

"Why isn't there a list?" I asked, thinking about the Record Plant in New York and its simple and efficient procedures.

"Why *isn't* there?" John replied, shrugging his shoulders.

"Studio A," announced the guard. "To your right." He lifted the gate, and we drove into the lot. Originally the Charlie Chaplin Studio, the record company had retained the original 1920's two-storied clapboard buildings but had painted them a rather dark, shiny gray. The unrelieved monochromatic surface had a strange effect: It made the buildings look as if A & M Records were not real at all but merely the facade of a movie set.

"Very Hollywood," said John as he stepped out of the car and looked around at the old but recently gussied-up buildings. "Very Hollywood indeed."

As soon as we stepped into Studio A we spotted Roy Cicala and Jimmy Iovine, Cicala's assistant, whom Roy had brought from New York. They waved to us. We also noticed Jim Keltner sitting at the drums. The studio, a very large one, was set up for eight musicians. John stepped into the control booth to greet Roy and Jimmy. "Is this the studio we're usin'?" he asked. "Is anybody here yet?"

Cicala shrugged. He was as uninformed as we were. John's eyes took in the complicated equipment: the stereo tape recorders, the multitrack recorder, the mixing console; then he stepped out of the control booth. In rapid succession a sax player and then a trumpet player entered the studio.

"I see we're goin' to have a real horn section tonight," said John.

A couple of assistants walked over and introduced themselves. They shook hands and then stood staring at John while they tried to make small talk. In New York there were almost no hangers-on. If the beloved child of a producer *had* to watch John record, the person was sneaked into the studio and instructed to make himself as inconspicuous as possible in the corner and never to speak unless spoken to. In L.A. every kid acted like your long-lost friend. Meanwhile more visitors continued to arrive and mingle and leave. I approached the studio assistants. "What's going on?" I asked, but they could only tell me that Spector and only Spector had the authority to close the session.

"There's Steve Cropper!" John whispered. He smiled at the legendary Memphis guitarist, and I could see he was delighted to have Cropper on the session. Musician after musician filtered into the studio, and John spotted Leon Russell, Barry Mann, Jeff Barry, Pete Candoli, and Larry Carlton among them. John leaned against the wall, amazed at the group that Spector was assembling. He was excited and nervous. Then Jesse Ed Davis arrived. He looked around and said to John, "This looks like it's going to be a good party." Jesse smiled mischievously.

Within half an hour twenty-seven musicians were crammed into the studio, which had been set up for eight. There were hippies, middle-aged men, rock 'n' roll legends, and laid-back L.A. session types, all with one thing in common: None of them knew a thing.

"Where's Phil?" John kept asking. "Where's Phil?" everyone else kept asking. Everyone knew, though, that Phil, addicted to making entrances, would wait until everyone else had gathered before he entered the studio.

Sure enough, as soon as the last musician had arrived, Spector suddenly appeared, a pistol strapped around his shoulder. His bodyguard, George, walked behind him. Spector greeted everyone and then said, "Let's set up."

It is normal procedure to set up *before* a session begins. Studio time is never wasted on setting up. Where had Spector's assistants been? I wondered. Why didn't Spector have them on the case? If that was only the beginning, I thought, the album would wind up costing a fortune to produce.

"He doesn't have a May to worry about details," John said to me as we watched studio assistants scurrying around, looking for twenty-seven chairs and twenty-seven music stands.

"He doesn't deserve one," I replied.

As the assistants pushed the instruments and music stands into place, Spector walked around, kibitzing with the musicians. It took some time to set up because no one but Spector had known that twenty-seven musicians were going to play on the session. Finally the orchestra was in its place, each musician equipped with a lead sheet with his part written on it. John, just the vocalist, sat on the side.

"Let's run it down," said Phil. He took a guitar and played "Bony Moronie" in the simplest way possible. There were absolutely no frills. When he was done, he paused for a moment, then he said, "All right. Let's all do it." Everyone played the song in exactly the same, very simple way. Some of the musicians looked knowingly at each other. They had played with Spector before and knew that he performed his magic in the control room, taking a simple performance of a tune and using studio equipment to transform it into something that sounded infinitely more exciting and complex than it had when the musicians had actually played it. The musicians who had never worked with Spector seemed confused and looked at him, waiting for instructions.

"Okay, that's it," he said and got up and marched into the control booth and left everyone sitting in the studio while he engaged in intense discussion with the two engineers. After twenty minutes, he got onto a speaker box and asked the rhythm section to play "Bony Moronie." Seven musicians were occupied—three guitarists, two drummers, and the two keyboard players—while twenty musicians, including John, found themselves with absolutely nothing to do. The rhythm section played the basic chart over and over. They played it for three hours. A horn player stopped counting after ten or fifteen performances. Nothing was played back; no one was given any instructions. By never explaining any of his moves, by trying to keep everyone confused and on edge, and by treating everyone as if he were a machine and not a human being, Spector created an atmosphere of suspense and confusion that he alone thoroughly enjoyed. No one complained, however. The mythic nature of the collaboration between John and Spector, as well as the talent and fame of the musicians who had been assembled, was so impressive that it made everybody in the studio want to do his best.

Meanwhile, in the control booth, Spector was busy creating his legendary Spector "wall of sound." By the time he was finished, the rhythm section, the strings, the horns, any number of special effects, and John's vocal would be blended together into what Spector himself called "a tidal wave of sound powerful enough to sweep the listener up with its velocity."

Those musicians and members of the studio staff whom

he especially liked were allowed into the booth to watch the master at work. Anyone who was not part of Spector's "in" crowd was shouted out of the booth. John watched quietly.

"So this is how he makes his wall of sound," he said to me. "Slowly. Very slowly." But he was fascinated as he watched Phil. Slowly, meticulously, Spector kept adjusting the sound of each of the instruments in the rhythm section. He experimented with the tones, making each instrument sound extremely full, then thinning out the sound—to see if he preferred that new effect. When he finally settled on a sound, he added a layer of echo to it; sometimes he doubled or tripled the echo effect, blending together the sound of all the instruments, adding a layer of echo to the new concoction. All the while he slugged down gulps of brandy.

John also had a drink or two, but the alcohol appeared to have no effect on him. He was too intent on doing well. The vocal track would be the last thing to be recorded that night, and John wanted to be in perfect voice for it.

I began to wonder why Spector had hired the best musicians to play a simple chart over and over again. But soon I realized that each time they played their charts, inevitably there were subtle variations. Those were among the nuances Spector would use as he built his wall of sound. I wondered aloud why Spector needed to have the basic track repeated endlessly. An engineer pointed out that almost the same effects could have been achieved electronically, but the result would have lacked the ultimate Spector touch.

John laughed when he caught me frowning because so many musicians were hanging around, doing nothing. We both knew that in more conventional situations these players could work for three hours and record *all* of their parts on an album.

"Turn off the calculator in your head," John said with a laugh. "It's the final result that counts."

Finally Spector was satisfied with the rhythm section. He gathered the horn players together. The saxophone, then the trumpet, and then the trombone players rehearsed their simply arranged parts. Afterward he went back into the booth and ordered the saxophones to begin again. The saxophones played their part five times. "Again," he ordered. It dawned on the saxophonists that they would probably have to play "Bony Moronie" over and over again. They did not complain, however, while Phil put them through their paces.

Spector was still working with the saxophonists when Joni Mitchell sauntered into the studio. She was recording in the next studio and decided to pay Spector a visit. She sat down next to the producer and watched while he worked. Occasionally she looked out at John and smiled languidly. It was clear that she was flirting with him, and he was embarrassed by it. Between glances at John she turned to Spector and asked him questions about what he was doing. The producer spat rapid-fire answers at her, and she responded by telling him that he was wrong. Her corrections only made him angrier. The session ground to a halt while Spector argued with Joni Mitchell. Finally she left, and work resumed.

At last, at three in the morning, six hours after we had begun, all the musicians were gathered to play "Bony Moronie" together as they had at the beginning of the session, while John sang the vocal part.

John went to the microphone. "I'm singin' this for May," he announced. "Come here, May, I want to sing to you." I walked into the booth and sat down beside John. I didn't even think of Yoko's injunction. I was delighted to have John singing just for me. "I love you, May," John said. Then he put on the earphones.

"Roll tape," said Spector. Expertly John laid down the vocal track in less than half an hour.

"Playback," said Spector.

Everyone listened intently. By then we were all so exhausted that anything would have sounded marvelous.

"That's a session," he said, and the first night of recording was over.

John was exultant. I was happy, too—and relieved.

"Listen, May," Yoko began when she called early the next morning, "I heard you were holding hands in the studio last night." She must have had spies everywhere; I felt like I was in a samurai movie. "You know you are not supposed to do that."

I didn't want her to get John upset, so I said, "I'll take care of it." John was still asleep, and Yoko said that she would call back. John and she spoke periodically during the day, but no matter what she said to John, he remained jubilant.

That night Spector came over to the house to work on "Angel Baby," which John and he planned to record the following night. The fact that they refused to plan the entire album in advance and were working track by track seemed inefficient to me, but John pooh-poohed me. He and Spector enjoyed those nights together, nights that gave John yet another opportunity to sit back and be amused by Spector's antics.

Before the second session John once again poured himself a flask of vodka. He looked at me. "We both know you don't need a security blanket," I said jokingly.

"I don't . . . but I'm takin' one anyway."

When John, Arlene, and I got to the studio, the atmosphere was subtly different than it had been on the first night. The mystery and suspense of the first night had evaporated; everybody knew what was in store—a long, grinding evening. The musicians who had been cool and professional with each other on the first evening greeted each other like long-lost army buddies who had suddenly been recalled to fight one more war. Everyone seemed almost too relaxed, too jolly.

After the musicians had gathered, Spector, followed by George, marched into the studio. He was wearing a costume, a white surgical gown with a stethoscope around his neck. Spector was in a wild mood. He took out his bottle of Courvoisier and took a swig. Then he flashed his gun. Everyone cheered. Once again chairs had to be pushed into place to accommodate the orchestra. Chattering wildly, Spector ran from musician to musician, revving each up for the evening's work.

He ran down "Angel Baby," then the orchestra played it together. Then he went into the booth to work with the rhythm section. On the first night the musicians had stayed in their seats, waiting for instructions. On the second night, knowing that the rhythm section was in for a long haul, they got up and went into the hall. John followed after them. John and Jesse Ed Davis had begun to pass the flask of vodka back and forth.

"Come on, have another drink," said Jesse, and John obliged. "Have another one," Jesse said a few minutes later. Once again John did as he was told. Jesse was fascinated by his ability to manipulate John, and John was delighted to have found a playmate eager to encourage the bad boy in him.

Then they circulated the flask. Unexpectedly musicians pulled out their own bottles. Arlene and I looked at each other—we sensed trouble.

As the night wore on, Spector continued to work with the rhythm section. They looked tired and thirsty and cranky and bored. "Again," ordered Spector. "Again."

One of the musicians said to John, "Hey, man, why did he call us for seven? It's already eleven, and we haven't played a thing. We've been here four fucking hours!"

A saxophonist said to me,"You don't know what hell is until you've heard 'Angel Baby' forty times!"

Meanwhile John and Jesse continued to hang out in the hall and swig away at the vodka. John's drinking made me nervous. He marched over, grinned, and kissed me. Then he kissed me harder and slipped his hand into my blouse.

"Please don't drink any more," I said as I pulled away, embarrassed.

"Why not? I'm just hanging out with the boys. Don't you like me to hang out with the boys?"

"I think we should go home."

"I haven't done my vocal yet."

"Please, let's get out of here."

"Don't worry about a thing. You just stay straight so that there will be *someone* who knows what's going on."

John laughed and kissed me on the chin, then sauntered back to Jesse.

When I saw Joni Mitchell arrive, I got up and went back into the studio. John followed after me. Neither of us was in the mood for her. In the studio, Spector was working with the horn section.

Suddenly a clarinetist stood up and put down his instrument. Spector rushed from the booth. "What the fuck is your problem?" he bellowed at the musician.

"I've spent five hours, man, doing twenty minutes of work," the musician replied.

"What records have you done, man?" barked Spector. "Minor-selling jazz artists like Gil Evans? Do you know the records I've made, man? The Ronettes, The Crystals, Ike and Tina? What have you done, man?"

The horn player yelled back. For twenty minutes Spector and the musician harangued each other.

John grew tense. He hated seeing people abuse each other. "Let's go," I kept urging him, but he insisted on staying. While we waited Joni Mitchell waited, too. She did not take her eyes off John.

Finally John marched into the booth. "When are you goin' to get to me?" he asked Spector.

"I'll get to you, I'll get to you," Spector replied, paying him almost no attention.

"You'll get to me!" John picked up a headset and smashed it angrily against the console. It shattered, and the pieces fell onto the floor. There was a moment of dead silence while everyone stared at John and Spector. Then John laughed, and his laughter dissipated the tension.

"Now, what did you do that for? You're slowing things down," Spector growled.

When the strings and horns were done, Spector gathered the orchestra together, and John and I went into the booth. I held John's hand while he sang "Angel Baby." Again it took only a few takes.

When the session was over, I took John by the arm. He was weaving slightly as we walked out of the studio. Outside he suddenly turned, stared wildly at Jesse, rushed over to him, and kissed him. Jesse laughed. He thought it was very funny. He leaned over and kissed John back. John reached out and sent Jesse sprawling across the parking lot. "Faggot!" he screamed.

I had never seen John like that. I approached him and stared at him. His eyes were so glassy, he couldn't see me. Suddenly I realized that liquor was the one thing that enabled him to overcome his desire to be controlled by a strong woman. It was obvious no woman—not even Yoko—could handle him when he was drunk. I was very nervous. Still, I did not want to leave his side.

I looked around. Elliot wasn't waiting for us. Spector and George suddenly pulled up in one car; Roy Cicala pulled up behind them. "In here," said Spector, pushing me into Cicala's car while he hustled John and Arlene into the other.

"I want to ride with John," I said.

"In here," he ordered.

"Do what Phil says," John said drunkenly.

"No, I want to ride with John."

"It's a short drive." Spector grabbed me by the arm and pushed me into the other car.

It was early morning, and the roads were deserted. As we drove I could hear John in the car behind me. He was screaming at the top of his lungs. First he screamed "May." Then he screamed "Yoko." Over and over again I heard him scream "May . . . Yoko . . . May . . . Yoko . . ."

When we got to the house, I dashed out of the car. Arlene got out of the other one and ran to me. She looked very frightened. "John's gone mad," she said. "He tried to kick out the windows of the car. He's been hitting everyone and pulling their hair. Jim Keltner tried to sit on him and hold him down, but it was impossible."

I saw John stagger out of the car and I went to him and put my arms around him. "Let's go inside," I said.

"He's a very skinny man, and it's hard to believe how strong he is," Keltner told me. "I'm much bigger than he is and I couldn't hold him down. I can't believe it. He's stronger than I am. I think he's uncontrollable."

"We should put him to bed," I said.

"He's too drunk to sleep," said Spector. "We should sober him up. Otherwise the alcohol in him is going to make him crazier and crazier. In this condition he's capable of anything. You're in great danger. Don't you understand that? We should sober him up. Do as I say. Make some coffee. Otherwise you'll be sorry. You could be hurt."

"We should put him to bed," I shouted.

"Make some coffee!" Spector bellowed. "Do as I say."

I made the coffee, and Spector tried to get John to drink it.

"What are you bastards doin' here?" John suddenly screamed. "None of you is any fuckin' good."

"Easy does it," said Spector. "Easy does it. Drink some more coffee."

Although Spector had said that he was just trying to calm John down before letting him go to sleep, everything he actually did was having exactly the opposite effect. The more coffee John drank, the more argumentative and violent he became. Suddenly it struck me that Spector had taken total control of that episode just as he had at the recording studio. The same climate of hostility, mistrust, and general pandemonium was beginning to reign at the house.

"Get the fuck out of me house." John started to weave toward Spector. He was too drunk and uncoordinated to do any harm, but Spector jumped as if he were under attack.

"We've got to get him upstairs," Spector said. "Now—we have to put him to bed before he hurts someone. Grab him!" Phil shouted.

George grabbed John by one arm, and Spector grabbed him by the other. Together they began to walk John up the stairs. I followed after them. "Don't come with us," Spector said dramatically. "This man is capable of great danger. Keep your distance."

No matter what Spector said I kept following behind them. They got to the head of the stairs, then took John into the bedroom. I followed after them, but Spector slammed the door in my face.

Suddenly I heard John scream. "I can't see. You Jew bastard, give me me glasses. I can't see!"

I banged frantically at the door, then I tried to force it open, but someone was standing against it.

"What are you doin' to me?" screamed John. "Get away!"

I heard the sounds of a fight and I knew I needed help. I ran to the phone.

"Who are you calling?" Arlene shouted from the bottom of the stairs. "You're not calling the police?"

"Are you crazy? I'm calling Tony King. I need a man here—a man John will listen to." While I dialed Tony's number John's screams grew even louder.

I told Tony that Spector and his bodyguard were in the room with John, that John was screaming, and that I needed help quickly.

After I got off the phone, Arlene and I stood there, listening to the screams. We were both terrified. Finally Spector and George walked down the stairs.

"What did you do to him?" I called out.

"He kicked me," said George.

"We tied him up." Spector glared at me. "He was too dangerous. We tied him up tight so he won't be able to harm anyone and he'll be able to sleep it off. Untie him in the morning. Let's go, George." They headed for the door. "Good night," said Spector. "By the way, wasn't it a terrific session?"

After Spector left, it was quiet for a few minutes. Arlene and I said nothing. We were both too afraid to go up the stairs. Then we heard John scream. "Untie me, May, damn it. You had better untie me or else!"

The screaming continued for another five minutes. I didn't know what to do. I wanted to help him, but at that moment I was just too panicked. Then I heard John thrashing around, as well as the sound of glass shattering. I knew that John had ripped himself loose and had just thrown something through the plate glass window in the bedroom.

"Fung Yee," he screamed, "where are you?" John staggered out of the bedroom and stood at the top of the stairs. He wasn't wearing his glasses. His feet and wrists had been tied with neckties. He had pulled his wrists apart, snapping the ties in the process. Two ties dangled from his feet.

Squinting, John stood at the top of the stairs. "Yoko! Yoko!" he screamed. *Yoko, you slant-eyed bitch, you wanted to get rid of me. All this has happened because you wanted to get rid of me.* He stumbled down the stairs. "Yoko, I'm goin' to get you."

John was lost in a nightmare. His brow was bathed in

At the American Film Institute dinner in honor of James Cagney,
March 13, 1974, the night after the incident at the Troubadour.
PHOTO: RON GALELLA

John and Elephant's Memory, 1972.

OPPOSITE:

Top: John with session guitarist Jesse Ed Davis, Disneyland, 1973.

Bottom: Julian Lennon and Mal Evans the same afternoon.

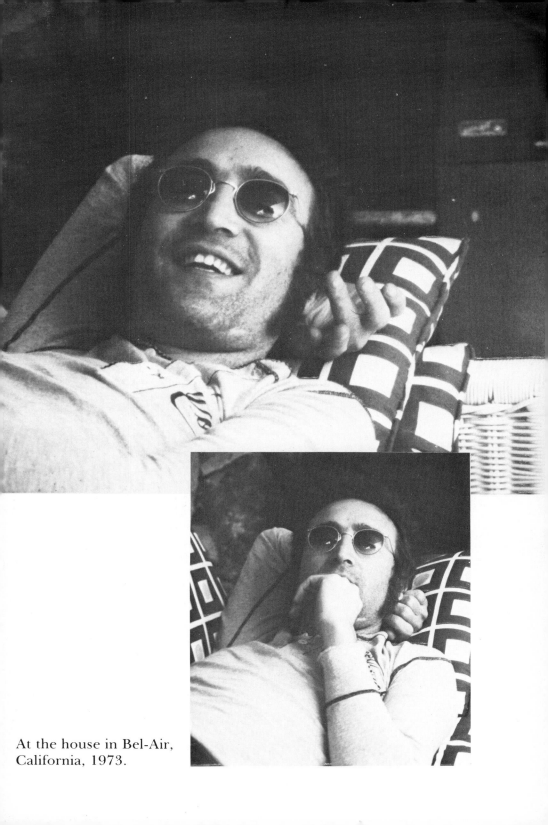

At the house in Bel-Air,
California, 1973.

In the Nevada desert, 1973.

John and May, Palm Springs, 1974.

With Harry Nilsson the same afternoon.

With Al Coury, New York, 1974.

OPPOSITE:

Top: Baron von Moon and Jesse Ed (*behind*) at the Santa Monica beach house, 1974.

Bottom: John, Mal Evans, and Ringo.

A *Walls and Bridges* session with (*left to right*) John, bassist Klaus Voormann, Kenny Ascher at keyboards, and drummer Jim Keltner. The Record Plant, New York, 1974.

John x 3 at the
Record Plant, 1974.

Upstate New York, 1974.

Pete Bennett, Ronnie Spector, John, Bianca Jagger, and May at Hippopotamus.
PHOTO: DAGMAR

sweat and he was literally foaming at the mouth. He began to shake as if he were going to have a convulsion. "Yoko, look what you've done to me," he roared. He tried to focus. Humiliated and tortured, he seemed overwhelmed by confusion. He stood there not knowing what he wanted to do. Then he began to moan. It was the sound of a wounded wild animal. He looked at me, but he did not recognize me. He did not know where he was. "Yoko, I'm goin' to get you," he screamed. He looked at me blindly. Then he charged wildly at me. I had never been more terrified in my entire life.

"John," I screamed. I turned and dashed out the door, Arlene following after me. As I ran down Stone Canyon Road, a Jeep drove down the road, and the driver jammed on his brakes when he saw me, almost hitting me, but I kept going.

Finally I reached the Bel-Air Hotel. As I headed for the entrance I heard John's voice cut through the night. "Nobody loves me," he roared. "Nobody gives a shit about me! . . . Everybody just uses me! . . . No one cares about me!" I hoped no one in that exclusive neighborhood would call the police.

I ran into the hotel lobby, told the desk clerk that I had been locked out of my house, and asked to use the desk telephone. Then I called our engineers, Roy and Jimmy. "Come over now," I screamed. "John's gone crazy, and I'm afraid."

I left the hotel, and then Arlene and I paced back and forth on the road. I could hear John screaming in the distance. He hurled abuse at Yoko and at Spector. He called out for me. He kept screaming, "Why doesn't anyone love me?" I stood in the middle of the road, waiting for Tony. John's voice resounded, and the noise was horrible enough to give me goose bumps. I looked at Arlene and shook my head in amazement. Everything was so peaceful and beautiful on that lovely summer night, and there was John screaming his heart out—and there was nothing I could do.

Finally I spotted Tony. "I'm sorry I'm late," he said. "There was an enormous car crash on Sunset Boulevard."

At that moment I realized how much I really hated Los Angeles. So many people in that city were crazy. After listening to John, Tony told me he wanted to deal with him alone.

He thought it would be too dangerous for me to approach John in his condition. I told him that I had called Roy and Jimmy.

"Stay here," he said. "I'll calm him down. You wait for Roy and Jimmy."

Tony drove up the road and spotted John near the house. John had ripped a large frond from a palm tree and was brandishing it in his right hand, using it as a shield to protect himself. Caught in Tony's headlights, he threw his free hand up to cover his eyes. Even from a distance I could see that John looked like a trapped insane child. There was something so sad about seeing him that way, I couldn't bear to look at him.

Tony got out of the car and slowly walked toward John. Although Tony was visibly shaken by the tortured look in John's eyes, he walked straight up to him and said simply, "What's the matter, John?"

John looked at Tony for a long moment, then collapsed into Tony's arms and began to weep. Tony cradled John in his arms and rocked him back and forth. He stroked him and spoke soothingly to him. "Nobody loves me . . . nobody cares about me," John cried out in despair.

"We love you; we care about you," Tony kept repeating. John thrashed around in Tony's arms, but Tony was strong enough to hold him still. No matter how violently John tossed and turned, Tony held on to him. Eventually John became calm enough to be led inside. I was so upset, I couldn't face going back in. Finally Arlene came out and said, "John's asking for you."

I walked back into the house. John had smashed all of the platinum albums hanging on Lou Adler's walls. Carole King's *Tapestry* lay dented on the floor. An antique chair had been thrown through the window. The chandelier had been pulled from the ceiling. The brass bed had been dented.

John was lying in his bed with his eyes open.

"John, are you all right?" I asked softly.

"I want to get that Jew bastard." He began to rave about Spector, insisting that I get Spector on the phone. He became so agitated, I called Spector's number and woke up his secretary.

"John wants to speak to Phil," I said. Spector would not go to the phone. "John, you'll fire him in the morning," I told him.

"We're goin' home in the morning. It's over. You and I are over." Then he started to rant about Spector again.

Finally John fell asleep. I had to admit that I still felt afraid of him, but I went to sleep next to him anyway because I loved him. Throughout the night John slept peacefully. I couldn't sleep at all.

In the morning I felt John stir. My first impulse was to run. John opened his eyes and blinked at me. "Hello," he said softly.

"Are you all right?" I said.

"Yeah. Why?" John gave me a kiss and put his arm around me. He did not remember a thing.

I got up and made coffee. When he was totally awake, I gently described the evening.

"Did I frighten you?" he asked. "I never want to frighten you." He reached over and gave me a big hug. I could see that he was genuinely embarrassed that I had seen him like that, and he was genuinely contrite.

We got up, and I showed him the damage to the house. He said that it would be repaired immediately. We went back to the bedroom and stretched out beside each other. "I don't think you should drink at the sessions anymore," I told him.

"A little bit of pot always relaxes me. I know that if I drink, I might get rowdy." John sat up and stared at me. "Fung Yee, I'm just so tired of havin' everyone expect so much from me. I'm just fuckin' human like everyone else."

"John, I really love you. I can't tell you not to drink. I'd like you not to, but I can't tell you what to do. I love keeping you organized. I love taking care of you. But I can't control you. You've got to control yourself."

John said nothing. He just sat there blinking at me while he thought. I knew how threatening it could be for him to think about exercising some control over himself. I couldn't help wondering if, on his darkest level, he had tried to set up a situation in which someone would step in and take charge of

him. Did he want Yoko to order him back to the Dakota because he could not behave without her? I wondered. Did I
have to start hiding the liquor bottles? Was John going to insist that I start playing mother? I did not want to become
Yoko; I wanted John to stand on his own two feet and I was
trying to learn to be independent myself.

John lay back, and I lay by his side. He reached over and
pulled me tightly to him. We were lying there clinging tightly
to each other when the phone rang. We both knew it was
Yoko. Another day had officially begun.

10

"Listen, May," said Yoko as soon as she heard my voice. "I've already heard about what happened. You know you're not supposed to give him liquor."

"I didn't give him any liquor!" I exclaimed.

"It's your job to take care of him. If you were taking care of him, there wouldn't be liquor in the house. Why aren't you taking care of him?"

"I am taking care of him."

"Then he wouldn't have gotten near a drink in the studio. I'm surprised at you. I didn't know you weren't doing your job."

Nothing I said could dissuade Yoko from blaming me for John's behavior. She had an answer for everything. And finally, in exasperation, I gave the phone to John.

"I'm all right, I'm all right," he told her. Then he said, "I know what you told me." When he got off the phone, John looked at me sheepishly. "Yoko did warn me about Phil," he said quietly.

Yoko called repeatedly throughout the day. Her concern grew with each call. She was worried about the shape John was in, the way I was taking care of him, and that his album could reflect the fact that both he and Spector were out of control.

In between her phone calls everyone else called, too. John took all the phone calls himself, reassuring everyone that he was fine. It was a bad dream that had passed, he said.

As we were getting ready for the session that night, John pointed out that a chemical change occurred in his body as soon as he drank any alcohol at all. After a drink or two, he would usually run wild, never remembering anything that had happened while he had been drinking. John wondered out loud if all the psychedelic drugs that he had taken during the 1960's had affected his nervous system. Perhaps his earlier overindulgence was responsible for those fits as well as the memory loss that followed them.

"You said you drink because you're nervous," I replied gently. "Drinking lets you get your anger out. When you're sober, you always look away. You push everything to one side. John, I'll help you. Let's start dealing with things as they occur."

He cocked his head to one side and thought for a second but did not respond. "It's time to go," he said brusquely.

All of the musicians stared at John when he walked into the studio. They had all heard about what had happened and they were curious to see how John would respond to Spector. When Spector arrived, he had a huge black eye. John was extremely apologetic. Spector kept nursing his wound and reminding John that he was responsible for it. He kept up the joke for quite a while before he told us that he had hired one of the best makeup men in Hollywood to create the black eye. John burst into laughter, and the session, though hectic, proceeded without incident.

Four more sessions were scheduled for the month of October. At the first of them Spector appeared dressed in an elaborate karate outfit. As soon as they saw him, the musicians broke into laughter and applause. Spector broke out his bottle of brandy and took a big swig. The session was off and running.

Whenever a break was called, everyone poured into the control booth; bottles were passed from musician to musician, and at the end of each break the studio assistant had to mop up the liquor that had been recklessly spilled over the recording equipment. The word had spread throughout Hollywood that the sessions were the best parties in town. Los Angeles is a town that usually shuts down by midnight; after midnight, celebrities with time on their hands are always eager to find someplace to go. Those sessions were it. At the first of the four, Joni Mitchell pranced in with Jack Nicholson on her arm.

"Joni has a trophy," John whispered to me after Mitchell made her entrance.

Joni returned for the second session, and later in the evening Mick Jagger made an unexpected appearance. He just walked into the studio and stood there quietly. When John spotted him, he walked over to greet him. Friends for years, their reunion was relaxed and low-key. Unlike his public image, Mick, like John, seemed essentially shy and unpretentious.

"Hello, May," he said sweetly after John introduced us. "I'm delighted to meet you." Then he told John, "I don't want to be in the way. I'll see you later." Mick went into the control booth and watched quietly. He had absolutely no need to make his presence felt. Essentially quiet and self-assured, Jagger neither craved nor required the star treatment. After about an hour of quiet observation, he said good night as sweetly as he had said hello and left.

At the third session Harry Nilsson paid a visit. "I'm a real fan of his!" John exclaimed when he spotted him. "I love his singing voice." John and Harry had met in England and they too had a warm reunion. Harry also watched quietly. Later that evening Joni Mitchell appeared. That time her escort was Warren Beatty.

"Yet another of Joni's trophies," John observed.

Mitchell and Beatty went into the control booth. Spector was in a particularly feisty mood that night, and as he was about to signal for a take Mitchell said, "Phil, do you have change of a dollar?"

The interruption was all Spector needed. Instantly he was up and running. "Lock the doors!" he screamed. "Bring me the key!" The key was placed in his hand. He dangled it in the air. "I may eat this!" he bellowed. Spector ranted for twenty minutes. "There are too many visitors," he roared. "Visitors bring other visitors. How dare these people come to my sessions? What's the matter with them?" He stared at Joni Mitchell and Warren Beatty and then launched into a tirade about how nauseating he found groupies.

Throughout Spector's explosion Joni Mitchell stood there with a neutral expression on her face. Beatty, however, looked stunned. I wondered if anyone had ever spoken to him like that before. John, who thankfully was in control, was visibly shaken by Spector's outburst. To his credit John tried to treat everybody gently and could not bear to see people needlessly embarrassed, even if they had done something as annoying as interrupting a take. John tried to calm down Spector, but Spector could not be silenced.

John took my hand. "I'm gettin' out of here." He walked up to the doors and tried them, and they opened. They hadn't been locked after all.

We went to the car. "What about Arlene?" I said. John marched back to the studio. "Arlene, come with us," he shouted. Arlene got up and ran. As we left, Spector was still yelling, and Joni Mitchell and Warren Beatty were still standing there.

By the end of those evenings almost everyone was roaring drunk. At three in the morning, when the sessions were dismissed, the A & M parking lot resembled an alcoholics ward on a binge. That night the incident with Mitchell and Beatty had been so tense that the musicians were even more drunk than usual. One of them jumped into his car and roared from the lot. We learned in the morning that he had wound up in a severe car crash on his way home and had been taken to the hospital.

At the next session that musician appeared with his head swathed in bandages. As soon as he saw John he said, "I need a drink, man." John didn't want to give him any liquor. The musician followed him around the studio, hounding him. "I know you've got liquor. You always do. Can't you see I need a drink?"

"Go to May," John said. "She'll take care of you."

"What do you want me to do?" I asked.

"Give 'im somethin' to drink. I can't stand people beggin' at me."

I was overwhelmed by the ugliness of the sessions. I had never before experienced such self-indulgence and basic disrespect for human values. Keeping John calm was my main concern during each of them. I knew I couldn't stop John's drinking—the conflicts he felt were too deep. When he did drink, he did not allow himself to lose his head again—at least for a while.

As dreadful as the nights of recording had been, our days remained wonderful—despite Yoko's endless calls. Every day we woke up happy. We made love almost every morning, and often twice a day; we were happiest lying in each other's arms.

I took the driving test, got my license, and occasionally we borrowed a car and took long drives up and down the coast, spending the day alone together, wandering on deserted beaches. We visited Lou Adler in Malibu and stayed long enough to watch a dazzling sunset over the Pacific Ocean. We also went to Rodeo Drive in Beverly Hills to shop. More precisely, since our funds were limited, we window-shopped. We would tour the most expensive boutiques and press our noses against the windows like kids at a candy store, ogling all the goodies, while buying almost nothing at all. We joked about the things we'd buy if the Spector album turned out to be a hit. Sometimes we could not resist buying clothes. John was very skinny and we both wore the same size. We liked to buy matching clothes and dress like twins. John bought me a pair of leather pants, which he liked to wear as well. When we passed a camera shop, I stopped to look at an SX-70 Polaroid camera, a model John already owned. The camera was to be one of my surprise birthday presents, and from the moment I got it I began to snap candid pictures of our life together.

One night after he had had a few drinks, Tony King told us he had made a tape of himself impersonating the Queen of England. He played it for us. It was very funny. John and he decided to film a commercial for *Mind Games* featuring Tony dressed as the queen. Tony asked John's permission to bring Elton John to the shooting of the commercial, which was scheduled for October 24, the day of my twenty-third birthday.

On the morning of the twenty-fourth John was up before me. "Happy birthday," he said when I woke up. He gave me a big kiss. Then he handed me a pair of car keys. "Go down to the garage," he told me, an impish grin on his face. I dashed out of the house. In front of the garage was a rust-colored 1968 Plymouth Barracuda. John stood on the steps. "Now we have our own car," he shouted. "No more Elliot Mintz." I ran back and threw my arms around him.

"I love it! I love it!" I exclaimed.

"I know you needed one," said John. "Practice on this one for now."

The car had cost $800, and I was proud of it. Others did not have the same reaction. In Los Angeles people seemed to judge you only by how much you spent. How expensive was your car? How big was your house? How much did you spend on clothes? Those people were shocked that a man as rich as John would buy me a secondhand car and then enjoy being driven around in it. They couldn't understand that our comfort did not depend upon having an expensive new car. John had given me a sensible present, a present that he could afford, based on his commitment to living economically. I did not want to practice on a brand-new Mercedes-Benz. Like John, I wanted to make our $10,000 loan last.

Later that morning we went to the television studio to watch the filming of the commercial. When we got to the studio, Tony was already dressed as the queen. Tony greeted John, then introduced him to Elton John. The two men shook hands. I don't know how the meeting would have progressed under more formal circumstances, but Tony's hilarious getup broke the ice. John and Elton were both very witty men and they began to tease Tony about his scepter, his crown, his dress. Both of them genially tried to outdo each other as they raked over their "queen." They laughed and quipped with each other for an hour, and at the end of an hour they were friends. Then they began to talk seriously about music and about the problems of celebrity.

"You know, I'm going through my Beatles period now," Elton told John. "I don't know what I'm going to do when it's over. You stopped at the top, John. You never ran down."

"At least you're aware that you'll peak. It's going to happen, and I'm tellin' you to be prepared. It's advice nobody gave me," John replied.

John invited Elton to a recording session, and Elton promised to go. Each told Tony how much he had liked the other. Tony explained to me that because they were both English, John and Elton were instantly capable of sizing each other up. They had a clear sense of each other's roots and could speak directly to each other without pretense. It was as if they were old, familiar friends even though they had never met before.

Then Elliot Mintz told us that David Cassidy, who was at the height of his fame as the co-star of *The Partridge Family* and was a good friend of Elliot's, wanted to meet John. John was in such good spirits that he uncharacteristically agreed to a lunch. A date was set. Elliot and David were to arrive at our house around noon to take John, Arlene, and me to a nearby restaurant. I remembered that we had a recording session that night, but the thought of canceling the lunch made John nervous. He didn't want Cassidy to think he was unfriendly, so, despite the session, we decided to go.

Half an hour before they were due to arrive, Yoko called. She was opening at Kenny's Castaways that night and had a list of opening-night problems to go over with John. The call went on and on. Convinced she would receive enormous press coverage, she wanted to remind John again and again that if asked why she was appearing without John, she would say that she had thrown him out.

I became restless, so Arlene and I went out for a walk. While we were outside, Elliot's car pulled up and Elliot stepped out, followed by David Cassidy. We were introduced, and I took David into the house to meet John. The minute John spotted Cassidy he became the public John and began to cascade the television star with witticisms and wisecracks.

After we chatted for a while, we went to an Italian restaurant on Sunset Boulevard. The chatter continued during lunch, interrupted only by a woman who approached the table. Ignoring John, she asked David Cassidy for an autograph. John did not seem to mind.

After lunch Elliot invited us back to his house high on Laurel Canyon. Elliot's house was built on stilts and had a breathtaking view of Los Angeles, a view that both John and I found fascinating. John stretched out on the couch and gazed out at the city. Arlene began to study the Hollywood hills through Elliot's telescope. I continued to chat with Elliot and David Cassidy. Everyone was tranquil and relaxed. Suddenly John got up and stalked out of the room. I headed after him. "Are you all right?" I asked.

John was distant. Something was bothering him but he refused to discuss it. "I want to go home," he said sharply. John remained quiet during the drive home and ignored me for the remainder of the afternoon. He did talk repeatedly to Yoko, who kept telling John how nervous she was.

On the way to the studio that night John remained unresponsive. He had a drink or two and came to life briefly only when Elton John made a surprise visit. The two spoke animatedly to each other. Elton watched for a while and then left. A few minutes later Harry Nilsson wandered into the studio, then Cher arrived. Spector was working on "Love Comes Knocking." While everyone waited she sat with Spector, reminiscing about the days when she had sung backup for him. Cher decided she wanted to sing backup on this new record. She told Spector, but he refused to allow her to sing. "I can sing this, Phil, you know I can sing this," she pleaded.

"No!" replied the producer.

"Please let me sing."

"No!" snapped Spector again.

The exchange between the two of them was so irritating, I got up and left the studio and sat outside for a while. When I returned, John was gone.

"Where did John go?" I asked Spector.

"He walked out."

I got into the Barracuda and headed after him. By the time I got to the house John had had a few more drinks.

"John, please tell me what the matter is," I said as soon as I walked through the door.

John said nothing and stared angrily at me. I walked over to him and tried to put my arms around him, but he pushed me away. I stared at him. "Please, what did I do?" I approached him again, and he shoved me even harder. Then he reached out and grabbed my hair and pulled it so hard, my head snapped back involuntarily.

"John!" I screamed. "What's wrong?"

Finally he let go of my hair and began to pace back and forth. Then he stopped and glared at me again. His eyes were filled with anger. I knew at any second he might explode; he looked as if he might even hit me.

"You know what you did!" he finally snapped.

"I don't! I don't!" I cried out.

John took a big swallow of vodka. "You flirted with David Cassidy."

I was stunned. "What are you talking about?"

John began to circle me. "You were waitin' outside for him when he came to the house today. Then you ordered the same thing he ordered in the restaurant."

"What does that mean?"

"It means that I always knew you'd cheat on me and now I have the proof!" he screamed. "You were flirtin' with David Cassidy."

"Your imagination is running away with you, John. I love you. I don't want to cheat. I don't want David Cassidy."

"Don't lie to me. I can't stand being lied to!"

"I'm not lying," I replied.

"You're a liar!" he screamed. "Don't you know who *I* am? I'm John Lennon." Then John exploded. He reached out and wrenched my glasses from my face, threw them on the floor, and trampled them. On the coffee table he found the camera he had bought me and smashed it angrily against the tabletop. He ran around the house smashing anything that seemed to be in his way. Vases and lamps flew across the room. He attacked the furniture, overturned tables, and knocked down chairs. I stood stunned and terrified by the outburst.

Suddenly the doorbell rang. "Are you all right?" Arlene called out.

John looked at me, shaking with rage. "Tell Arlene to go away," he shouted. "I want to be alone with you."

"I can't send her away. She lives here."

"Send her away! I don't want anyone in this house but you and me."

I stood there not knowing what to do.

John ran to me, wrenched my shoulder bag from me, dumped it on the floor, and rummaged around until he found the car keys. "Send her away, or I'll smash the car. Tell Arlene to drive the car away, or else I'll smash it."

I took the car keys and went to the front door and opened it. "I heard what was going on in here and I was afraid to use my key," Arlene said when she saw me. "Are you all right?"

For an instant I wanted to drive away with her. Still, I knew I had to stay with John and somehow try to calm him down. Leaving would only convince him that I had been flirting with David Cassidy and that I really didn't care about him. Even though I was frightened I knew that remaining in the house was a chance I had to take. I handed Arlene the car keys. "Go for a little drive," I told her. "Stay at somebody else's house tonight."

"He sounds very dangerous. Are you sure you don't need any help."

"Arlene, please. Just go."

We looked at each other and said nothing. I knew Arlene wanted me to leave with her. I also knew that she knew that I wouldn't.

"I'll call you," she said, and she left.

When I went back into the living room, John was on the phone. "I'm callin' Yoko," he screamed. "I'm going to tell her everything."

John caught Yoko backstage at Kenny's Castaways, minutes before her opening-night show. When she came to the phone, he shouted, "You were right, Yoko. You were right." Then he ordered me to pick up the extension at the other end of the living room.

"May, are you there?" she asked.

"Yes."

"Listen, May, I told you not to give him any alcohol. You know by now what happens when he drinks."

"You were right, Yoko. You were right," John said again.

"John," Yoko replied, "you are drunk. You must calm down. Now I have to give my show. I'll call you later." She hung up.

For the following half hour John kept up a stream of in-sults and accusations. "You are only interested in me money," he said. "Did you know, the day you left for Los Angeles, Yoko stopped your salary? You don't have any money. What do you think of that?"

"I love you, John. That's why I'm here. Haven't I tried to help you save money?"

"Before I left, Yoko told me not to spend·more than a thousand dollars on you. She was right! You're a fortune hunt-er. That's all you are."

I got up and began to pace. John followed after me, kick-ing his way through the rubble in the living room, repeating everything he had said before.

"Where did you get these crazy ideas?"

He wouldn't let up, and seemed to be enjoying his own anger, and his anger seemed to be giving him energy. Again he was a victim, yet now he believed he was *my* victim. The more helpless he felt, the more furious he became.

Finally the phone rang. John picked it up. It was Yoko. She had just concluded her show. "Take the other phone," he ordered me again. I picked it up.

"Yoko, tell her that you told me that she would cheat," he screamed.

Yoko said nothing.

"Tell her that you told me that she was only after me be-cause I was famous."

Yoko did not reply.

"You were right, Yoko—she *doesn't* treat me like a star. Tell her that you told me she was a fortune hunter who was only after me for me money."

She giggled nervously.

I didn't know what to do. I knew how complex and para-noid John was; I knew how complex and unpredictable Yoko could be. I was no match for either of them. Yoko told John things as a way of maintaining her authority over him. Perhaps I should have suspected that she would tell John things about me—things that weren't true but that John would still believe in order to keep his idealized image of Yoko intact. I knew John *had* to believe Yoko was perfect; it was his way of insuring that he always had the ultimate security blanket to which he could turn in case he needed help. Still, Yoko *had* discarded John. To manipulate him like that after she had discarded him was to put *me* in danger. I was stunned and sickened by her actions.

"Tell her that you told me that all she wanted was me money. Tell her, Yoko," John shouted again.

Yoko giggled some more. "May, you know how people say things when they're drunk."

"Tell her. Tell her that you told me that all she wanted to do was use me."

"You see what happens when you feed him liquor," she said.

"Yoko, you've probably never seen him like this," I replied evenly. "And if you have, I'm sure you had someone with you to help you. I am here alone, and you know John can become dangerous. He could hurt himself and he could hurt me. This is not the moment for you to blame me for things you know I didn't do."

"Tell her you told me she would cheat," urged John. "You were right, Yoko. She wants to cheat. She wants to cheat with David Cassidy."

"John, you're just drunk," Yoko replied disdainfully.

John scowled. "Own up to it, Yoko. Say it. Say you said it. Tell her you told me she would cheat."

She said nothing.

"You lied to me, Yoko," John screamed. "*You* lied to me, and *May* is a cheat!" John slammed down the phone. He was wild-eyed.

A few seconds later the phone rang and John grabbed it. "Yoko," he shouted into it, "you lied to me." He hung up again.

John and Yoko began to trade calls, but it appeared that Yoko did not have too much patience with John. She was more concerned about describing to him her opening-night triumph. John grew more upset. Finally I picked up the extension. "Don't call us again," I told her. "You're only making it worse."

Yoko called back every fifteen minutes for the following two hours. I wanted to take the phone off the hook, but John wouldn't let me. "Let it ring!" he screamed. He looked at the phone. Then he kicked it. "That bitch!"

John could not sit still and kept wandering around the house, and he ranted at me every so often. Eventually he went upstairs and collapsed on the bed. The house suddenly became very quiet. I sat there trying to make sense of what had happened. How had something so promising and sweet become such a nightmare? It was too much for me, and I began to sob. I sat up for the rest of the night, crying quietly. I was exhausted and I felt sick. At least, I thought, when John wakes up, he won't remember a thing.

The phone rang early the next morning, too early for it to have been Yoko. It was Arlene. "I'm staying at Jimmy Iovine's," she told me. "Are you all right? Are you all right?" she kept asking.

"I'm doing the best I can."

Arlene promised to check in every half hour.

An hour later John was up. He walked down the stairs and stared angrily at me. "We're goin' back to New York. Make the arrangements." I opened my mouth to speak, but he wouldn't let me. "It's over!" he shouted.

"John . . ."

"It's over! It's over!"

I went to the phone, called the airline, and booked our passage. Then I called Arlene and told her that we were going back to New York. She volunteered to drive us to the airport. Arlene could hear from my voice how distressed I was. "I'll hurry," she said.

I told John about the arrangements, then I started to cry. He looked at me. "It's over," he repeated.

An hour later Arlene and Jimmy Iovine arrived to take us to the airport. The ride was extremely tense. John and I were both silent. Jimmy made lots of silly jokes, but no one laughed. The flight was equally as tense. Whenever I tried to say anything to John, the only thing he would say was, "That's it. It's over." He must have said it thirty or forty times.

Cynthia and Richard Ross were waiting at the airport for us. Richard, the owner of the restaurant Home, was a friend of mine whom John had grown to like.

"We booked you a suite at the Stanhope Hotel," Cynthia told us.

"Take me to the Dakota," John ordered.

Once again we rode in silence. John was dropped at the Dakota, and I was taken to the Stanhope. Cynthia and Richard helped me check in. "What's going on?" asked Cynthia after the bellman left the room. "I don't want to make matters worse, but you look awful. You look like you haven't slept in days."

I sat there and could hardly speak. Then I began to cry. Cynthia hugged me. "What's going on?" she asked again. I described the album sessions and the night that John had been tied up, as well as the David Cassidy incident that had occurred on the previous night.

"I don't know what to do," I sobbed. "I'm trying to do the best I can."

Cynthia volunteered to stay with me. "You need a nurse," she said. "You need some food and some sleep and some laughs." She refused to leave me and ate with me and sat in a chair watching me until I finally fell asleep.

At eleven that night Yoko called from backstage at Kenny's Castaways.

"How is he?" I asked.

"Everything's all right," she replied soothingly. "John is fine. He's at the apartment, asleep. Don't worry about a thing."

"Are you sure everything's all right?"

"Listen, May, you don't have a thing to worry about. I'm not going to fuck him."

I was appalled.

"I'll have him call you in the morning." She hung up.

John did call in the morning, and we spoke quietly to each other. "I don't know what came over me," he said gently.

"Whatever it was, it's over now," I replied.

We talked some more and then John asked, "Would you go back to California with me?"

An hour later John arrived at the hotel. "Fung Yee, I couldn't bear seein' you talk to someone else, that's why I did it. I was just so jealous. I couldn't help meself. I'm so sorry now."

"John, this is a question you've got to answer. Tell me the truth. Do you want me to go back with you because Yoko told you to take me back or because you really want me to be with you?"

"This is my decision."

"John, I'm going back to Los Angeles because I love you and you know I love you. But I can't go through another scene like the one last night. So I want you to tell me that you know I don't want to cheat and that I'm not going with you because you're rich and famous. I want you to say the words to me. It's very important for me to hear them coming from your mouth."

John cocked his head to one side. "I know you don't want to cheat," he said softly, "and I know you're not goin' with me because I'm rich and famous."

As quickly as we arrived in New York, that's how quickly we left. Two hours after John got to the hotel, we were on a flight back to L.A.

11

There were two more sessions in early November, each as wild as the earlier ones. Then abruptly everything was suspended because Phil and John did not know what they wanted to record.

For the next two weeks we relaxed and saw our friends. Spector was at the house a few times, and John and he began to write together, and John composed some new material of his own. John also had a series of meetings with his lawyers, who wanted to bring him up to date concerning the maneuvers to dissolve the Apple partnership. We were also fielding Yoko's calls a little more successfully. I began to unplug the extension in the bedroom so that when the phone rang downstairs, we wouldn't hear it upstairs.

Then one night we decided to go to the Roxy. While we were waiting in front of the club a pleasant-looking man approached us. "Hello, John. How are you?" he asked.

"I'm fine."

The man was Dr. Arthur Janov. Janov was the psychologist who had discovered primal therapy and had practiced it on John and Yoko. John and Janov chatted for a few minutes, then John said with a smile, "Well, Yoko beat you, didn't she? She won out."

When we went into the club, John explained that Yoko had fought Janov throughout the therapy; they each had thought that they knew what was best for John. "Janov was very tough," John observed, "but he was no match for Yoko. She watched everything he did. She figured it all out and she learned to do it better."

I remembered what Yoko had told me the very first day I went to work at the Dakota, and the memory made me sick.

A few days later Yoko suddenly announced that she was flying immediately to Los Angeles to see how we were doing, and almost before we knew it we were on our way to her expensive bungalow at the Beverly Hills Hotel to take her to lunch. I wondered if trouble was in store.

Yoko registered genuine surprise when she saw Arlene, whom we had asked to join us. It was the first time Yoko learned that we had disobeyed her edict to live in isolation. She said nothing, however. Later she told John and me that any problems we had were caused by allowing Arlene to move in with us. By having someone with us, she said, we had allowed ourselves to be distracted from the job of growing closer.

At lunch, however, Yoko told me, "I'm pleased to see that he's calmed down and that you're both getting along." That night John visited her at the hotel and spent an hour or two with her. When he returned he was cheerful about the visit and was pleased to find her in such good spirits about everything. Yoko flew back to New York a few days later.

After Yoko left, things were calm and pleasant, and John was in wonderful spirits for the next ten days. When he wanted to, John could be an avid reader, and he decided to read every book in the house. In the afternoons we sat by the pool and read quietly.

John became obsessed by two books Tony King had given him as gifts, Hunter Thompson's *Fear and Loathing in Las Vegas* and Nigel Nicholson's *Portrait of a Marriage*, which Tony said would remind John of his marriage to Yoko. John loved the Thompson book, a seamy study of a drug-involved journalist investigating the underbelly of America, and became obsessed with the notion of starring in a film version of the book. On the other hand *Portrait of a Marriage* really disturbed him. The book was an account of the fifty-year marriage of Vita Sackville-West and Harold Nicholson, both of whom were bisexual and continually unfaithful to each other, yet were able to evolve a relationship of great depth and longevity despite the incompleteness of their marriage. John was very distressed by the theme of sexual incompatibility in the midst of great emotional attraction and the fact that no matter how hard one tries, a marriage may always remain incomplete.

It appeared that the nightmares of October had passed. John suggested that we go to San Francisco, and we invited Tony King, Mike Hazelwood, and Arlene to join us. When Yoko called, John told her about the San Francisco trip. She called back to suggest that we look up Jerry Rubin, who was staying in San Francisco, as well as Steve Marish, a young psychic whose powers impressed her.

John loved the idea of going to San Francisco. He joked about visiting Rubin and Marish. "Yoko's goin' to have them check up on us, you know," he said merrily. He seemed in wonderful spirits and appeared not to have a care in the world.

The day before our San Francisco trip, when John awoke, he sat up, looked at me, and frowned. I sat on the edge of the bed, talking to him, but he said nothing. I knew something was bothering him.

"John, what are we going to do today?" I asked.

There was a long pause. Finally he said, "I want to take a drive to the beach."

While we were getting dressed I turned to him and said, "Come on, John, tell me what it is."

He looked blankly at me. Then he said, "I thought it would be better to tell you on the beach. But maybe it's better if I say it quickly without delayin' it. I think it's time for us to break up."

I was stunned. "Why?" I asked. "Why?"

"I think it's time. It's just time." He could offer no other explanation.

"Are you sure?"

"Yeah."

I could see that he was serious.

"When do you want me out?"

"Well, you know, whenever you get yourself together."

It made no sense. John made no sense. We had never been happier. Things had never gone as smoothly. I felt as if I had just been smashed across the face for no reason at all. All I wanted was to get out of there quickly. I got my suitcase and began to throw my things into it. While I packed, John stared at me and said nothing, and I said nothing to him. Then he got up and went to speak with Arlene. He told her that we had broken up and that he wanted her to stay with me. He even offered us a trip to Europe.

Arlene walked into the bedroom and threw her arms around me. "Don't worry, I'll take care of you," she said softly.

I was in shock and could hardly speak. "I want to get out of here—now," I stammered.

"I'm going with you."

In less than half an hour Arlene and I were both packed and ready to go. We carried our suitcases to the car. I went to John. "Here's your key," I said. I handed it to him and ran from the house.

Arlene and I had nowhere to go, so we checked into a motel on Sunset Boulevard. We sat in the motel room and tried to make sense of things. Neither of us had any money. We didn't have jobs. We didn't have a place to live. John suddenly, inexplicably, had pulled the rug out from under us, and I was hurt and upset and felt very panicky.

We learned the next day that John had gone to the Roxy on the previous night, accompanied by a black girl who was a well-known groupie. I became even more upset. I felt so devastated, I was numb for a week.

Finally I realized I had no choice. It was time for me to go home to New York to start my life again. The next day Arlene and I booked a flight and flew to New York, and I returned to my apartment. For the next few days I was miserable and lonely. All I thought about was John. I hated to admit it, but he had a dark side that terrified me and, worse, a side that only Yoko understood. By Sunday, at the end of my first week in New York, I decided to call her.

"It's May," I said when she picked up the phone.

"Yes, May."

"Yoko, I didn't mean to disturb you." She said nothing, so I went on. "I forgot how cold it gets here this early in the year."

"You're not in Los Angeles?"

"I'm in New York."

"Come over now. Come over right away. Quick. I must see you."

Half an hour later I was at Yoko's door. She greeted me warmly, and we sat down in the living room. "Are you all right?" she asked.

"I'm still in shock," I replied.

"What happened? Tell me the whole story."

She listened intently, smiling knowingly as I discussed John's erratic behavior. By the time I was finished she could not contain her laughter. "It's okay, it's okay," she said. "Don't worry about a thing." She smiled at me and said, "You know Michael Brecker likes you. I'll try to set it up."

I couldn't believe it. Her solution to my problem was to offer to fix me up with a musician in her backup band. "I don't want Michael Brecker," I said evenly.

"Maybe we'll try Rick Marotta." Marotta was another of her musicians.

"I don't want Rick Marotta either."

"May," she said, "don't worry about a thing. You can still work for me. Stay here! Why don't you use the second phone line for all your calls! Give out the number to your friends and have them call you here. Make this apartment your new home. I want you to work for me."

"*Fuckin' amazin'!*" John's evaluation of her ripped through my mind. I had always found Yoko to be unpredictable, and at that moment she was more unpredictable than ever. As I look back on it I realize that Yoko's unpredictability and intensity enabled her to spin intricate webs and to convince anyone that whatever she did was essential to some greater plan. I was in love with John. I would need Yoko's help—and she seemed willing to give it to me! Her maneuvers were fascinating and confusing, and I knew that at any moment they might be turned against me, unless, somehow, John decided to really free himself from her spell.

I spent the rest of that day and the early evening at the Dakota. Occasionally Yoko would look in on me, doing her best to make me feel relaxed and happy. I spent Tuesday at the Dakota also. That night we went out to dinner. At dinner she said, "You know, I spoke to John."

"Oh, really?" I replied coolly. "How is he?"

"He's okay. He was hanging out with that black chick. It's nothing. He told me he never had a black chick before and he wanted to try one out. After he had her, he threw her out."

Yoko invited me to sleep at the Dakota, but I refused, telling her instead that I would stay with her until she fell asleep. I sensed that she was lonely. She had just finished her engagement at Kenny's Castaways. What Yoko liked best was fame. Then, after a brief moment of being in the limelight, of being famous, she had to cope with the anxiety she felt whenever she wasn't in the public eye. We talked for a while, then Yoko became sleepy. She got up and changed into her nightgown. I sat on the edge of her bed and talked gently to her until she began to doze off. Then I got up and let myself out of the apartment.

The next day, while I was at the Dakota, the phone rang, and I picked it up. John said, "Hello, Yoko."

"One minute, John," I replied, and I went and got her. "John is on the phone," I said. Yoko looked at the astonished expression on my face and laughed. She took John's call, then walked into the living room and sat beside me. "He also freaked out when he heard your voice," she told me merrily. "Don't worry about a thing."

From that moment on she began to trade endless calls with John.

"Listen, May," she said the next day, "John needs someone with him. It's time for Julian to visit him, and he's getting paranoid about seeing his son. You know, he hasn't seen Julian in almost three years. I can't be there. I don't get along with Julian."

"I'm trying to take care of myself," I replied. "I could go back to him if *he* wanted me, but not because *you* want me to."

Yoko shrugged. "It's John we must think of, May. In order for John to take care of Julian, someone must take care of

John. That's all there is to it. John is already getting crazy. You don't want him to go crazy again, do you? As soon as Julian goes you can leave. It will only be for two weeks."

I wanted to go back, but not in the role of surrogate mother. I said so to Yoko, but she would have none of it. She marshaled all of her considerable powers of persuasion, and for two long hours I jousted with her.

Finally we both grew silent. I told her calmly, "I need a few days to collect myself."

"I'll tell John." She got up to make the call. When she returned, she said, "May, you must go tonight. John said to me, 'Yoko, I need someone here tonight. You know how I get.' May, you know what that means. You *do* know how he gets. You've got to go now."

It was seven o'clock. Yoko booked me on a late flight. Urging me not to worry, she hustled me to the door. I returned to my apartment, threw my things together, and headed for the airport. Seven hours later, at four in the morning, I was back in Los Angeles. During the flight I had tried to collect myself, and it seemed to come down to the fact that I wanted to be with John. I also knew that even if our affair resumed, I could not count on John's being able to control the irrational part of his personality.

During my absence John had moved back to Harold Seider's apartment in West Hollywood. There was no answer when I got there. I tried the door, and it opened. "John," I called out. "John." The apartment was deserted.

John did not turn up until six the next night. After demanding that I go to him immediately, he had stayed away for more than twelve hours.

I was in the bedroom when he bounded up the stairs. As soon as he saw me, he jumped onto the bed, pulled me to him, and clutched me tightly. He said nothing, just rocked me in his arms. Then he whispered, "I'm sorry, Fung Yee. I'm sorry. I missed you so much."

"John," I said, "why weren't you here when I returned?"

He launched into an explanation. "I got nervous waitin' for you. A bunch of us went out and we met up with some people. This girl and I ended up in a hotel. I didn't want to make it with her. I kept tellin' her that me nurse was comin' back to L.A. I told her I only wanted me nurse; I wanted me lady. When she saw that I wasn't goin' to make it with her, she called some more people, and we went up to Mulholland Drive and took some acid."

I looked at him, and he smiled gently. "When I woke up that day I realized how much I loved you. It frightened me. I was so afraid of gettin' close to you, I got scared. That's why I asked you to leave."

He began to smother me with kisses. Then he said, "I certainly fooled Yoko." John started to laugh. "I got on the phone and I kept tellin' her that I would freak out unless I had someone here. I knew I could get her to send you back to me, and she did. I couldn't tell her that I missed you, could I?"

Other men would have called directly—other men could have told Yoko the truth—but John couldn't.

"I see, John," I said softly. I wanted to be with John and I knew then that even that part of him—the part of him that loved me—was still tied to his game with Yoko. My hope was that as time went on I could encourage his love for me to grow. Nonetheless it appeared inevitable that I would never know from moment to moment where I stood. It was awful, but I believed it was worth it. It was worth it because I loved him so much.

12

After John had had his coffee the following morning, he said to me, "You know Julian is comin'."

"Yoko told me."

"I'm nervous. I don't know what he likes. I don't know how it's goin' to be."

It was something he would repeat often. In reality, John dreaded the visit of Cynthia and Julian. He had not seen his son in more than two years. The very concept of fatherhood unnerved him terribly. How could he play the role of father when he felt it was essential for his survival that someone always be there to take care of him? In addition, the fact that he had ignored Julian made him feel guilty. His preference at that point was never to see Julian and, therefore, to avoid the bad feelings his own behavior conjured.

He also did not want to see Cynthia, whom he had not seen in four years. She reminded him of difficult decisions he had made: to leave the Beatles, to divorce her, and to marry Yoko, as well as to abandon his son. After John had made a hard decision, he never wanted to be reminded of that decision or the fact that he had once had a choice. When something was over, it was over for good.

I sat with John and talked about the visit. We discussed my childhood, and I told him again how awful it had been for me to know that my father did not want me. "John, can you imagine how hard it must be for Julian to be the son of someone as famous as you and to have the world know that this famous, beloved father has chosen to stay away from him? Julian is only ten, you're thirty-three. You can try to handle your feelings, Julian can't. Despite the way you feel, you've got to be as kind and as warm to Julian as you can possibly be."

"It's hard, Fung Yee. I don't know what to do. I'm tryin' to deal with it." John started to pout again. Then he snapped, "I just don't want to see Cynthia."

"She's going to be there, so you might as well accept it."

The more we talked, the more agitated John became, despite the fact that he agreed with me in concept. "Do you want to cancel the visit?" I finally asked.

"No."

Still, he was so terribly uneasy that I decided to organize the visit myself, making it go as smoothly as possible, hoping John would get caught up in the preparations once they began. He did, but he would get nervous and balk, then he'd jump in again.

It was decided that Cynthia and Julian would arrive right after Christmas and stay through New Year's. With John's consent I reserved a suite at the Beverly Hills Hotel for them. "Come on, John," I said. "Julian deserves the kick of staying in a nice place and seeing celebrities."

Harold Seider suggested we take Julian to Disneyland and on tours of the movie studios. He had his office make arrangements so that we would get VIP treatment and not have to wait on line.

John kept Yoko up to date on all the arrangements. After one call, he hung up and said, "You know Cynthia's still in love with me. She'll do anything to get me back."

"John, you and Yoko haven't seen Cynthia in four years. Are you mind readers? How do you know what's going on in her head? And even if it's true, what can she do to get you back if you don't want to go? What are you worried about?"

John shrugged and tried to laugh it off, but it was quite clear to me that he was still under Yoko's spell, and she had chosen, for some mysterious reason of her own, to get him agitated and upset about Cynthia. Even I, in my vulnerable position, recognized before I met her that Cynthia meant John no harm. Nevertheless Yoko kept working at it. The next day, after one of her phone calls, John repeated what he had said the day before. Again I tried to joke him out of it, but he kept repeating those ridiculous statements, and every time he repeated them he grew more anxious about the visit and more convinced that he did not want to see Cynthia. I think at that point more than any other I began to fear the power of Yoko's influence over John: To turn John against Cynthia was to make sure that John would *never* see Julian.

A few days after my return to L.A., I talked to Arlene, who had remained in New York City. Arlene didn't have a job. She and Yoko liked each other, and I suggested she might want to work for Yoko. Arlene was pleased with the idea. I told John. "I'll suggest it to Yoko," he said. "If she thinks it's your idea, she won't do it."

When Yoko called, John made the recommendation, and Yoko welcomed it. The next day Arlene went to work for Yoko. Paid on an hourly basis, she was to serve as Yoko's companion, making herself available whenever Yoko needed her.

As soon as Arlene arrived Yoko told her that she was to help her create a new piece of art for Charlotte Moorman's exhibition. Moorman, an old friend of Yoko's, had made her mark in avant-garde art circles by giving a number of concerts in which she played the cello topless. Occasionally a meter was hooked up to her nipples to measure the electricity that flowed through her body while she played. Moorman had been given the use of a train in Grand Central Station and had assigned a train car to each of her avant-garde artist friends to use as the setting for a new piece of artwork.

Yoko couldn't make up her mind about what she wanted to do with her train car. Finally she told Arlene she was going to do something about life and death. Arlene was dispatched to have a Lucite coffin built. "I need it by tomorrow morning," Yoko told her.

The next day the coffin, as well as a Lucite flower pot and an antique phonograph player, were taken to Grand Central Station and set up in Yoko's train car. Arlene, dressed completely in black, her fingernails painted black as well, spent the day sitting in front of the coffin in the railroad car, smiling enigmatically at the crowd.

Arlene and Yoko had an extremely pleasant time together. Yoko often cooked for Arlene, and they took walks and went to the movies together. Arlene was also put in charge of the limousine. John didn't care about limousines, and when one was ordered, he preferred to have a sedan model, which he found less pretentious. Yoko told Arlene, "You must always get a stretch." The stretch limousine was the biggest model. Yoko wanted Arlene to make sure that a stretch would be available at a moment's notice, and she took one everywhere. Whenever anything was delivered to the Dakota, Yoko also liked it to arrive via stretch limousine. Despite Harold Seider's attempts to rein Yoko's spending, the limousine bills were enormous.

Most of all Arlene and Yoko shopped together. Even though Yoko had been told to end those shopping binges, she realized she could not stop herself. "Why do I spend all this money?" Yoko asked Arlene.

"Some people go to psychiatrists," Arlene replied. "Your therapy is shopping."

Yoko agreed and increased her therapeutic shopping, spending thousands of dollars more on clothes she never planned to wear. She and Arlene went to Henri Bendel, and Yoko bought a pigskin suede coat with a fox collar and a fox lining, a silver fox coat, a mouton reversible jacket, and four designer dresses. The cost of those items was $23,000. On the way out of the store Yoko spotted some plastic bracelets. "May likes these," she said. "I'll get them for her for Christmas." That purchase added fifteen dollars to her bill.

Arlene essentially found Yoko to be generous. Whenever they went shopping, Yoko always bought Arlene a present. Arlene took her to a boutique on the Upper East Side, where they discovered that the salesperson was also a medium. Yoko hustled the salesperson out of the store to her limousine and brought her back to the Dakota, where the salesperson proceeded to fill a glass with water and then look into it and report a number of visions. Yoko was entranced.

A few days later Yoko and Arlene visited another woman spiritualist who performed "spiritual cleaning." Yoko had the woman remove all of the bad vibrations she felt were surrounding her.

Yoko frequently dispatched Arlene to David Spinozza's apartment house to leave articles and gifts for him with the doorman. Yoko was also trying to figure out what to give Spinozza for Christmas. "He hates the fact that I get my lipstick on everything," she told Arlene. She sat down and made Spinozza a lipstick piece. She took a coffee cup, covered it with lipstick, and put it in a Lucite box. After the gift was wrapped, Arlene delivered it to Spinozza's building. I had never seen Yoko wear lipstick, so I found this story very strange.

Yoko never mentioned my relationship with John to Arlene. She told Arlene that she could get John back at any time, but that she didn't want him. She explained that when she married John, she had expected to have a quiet, rich, easy life and to devote herself to doing her work, but that John had grown increasingly difficult to live with. She also felt that she had become sufficiently famous in her own right and did not want to share her fame with John anymore. John stood in the way of her career, and she was determined to continue on her own.

When Yoko told Spinozza that John was in her way, that she was the real songwriter in the family anyway, Spinozza asked her, if she was the real songwriter, why she put John's picture on every album she made. He suggested that she move out of the Dakota, refuse to take any more of John's money, and record an album on her own with no support at all from John. That, he explained, would enable her to find her own public and prove herself on her own terms. Yoko accused him of not being creative.

I repeated none of that to John. It reminded me of *Rashomon,* a Japanese movie I once saw, in which four people told the same story differently, each insisting that his version was the truth.

Meanwhile, as we continued to plan the visit of Julian and Cynthia, we had other problems to deal with. Not the least of them was Phil Spector, who was embroiled in a custody battle with his wife, Ronnie; Spector faced a hearing in January. No matter what anyone said to him about anything, Spector only wanted to discuss the custody hearing. "Do you know what the judge will do? Do you know what Ronnie will do?" was all he could say.

To ask him about John's album was to be asked about the hearing; he asked those questions if you asked him the time of day. It was all John needed as Cynthia and Julian's arrival neared.

All of that weighed against the troubled Spector sessions, with a few more scheduled for early December. By then, because of the riotous nature of the sessions, we had been kicked off the A & M lot and had moved to the Record Plant. John continued to drink at sessions, but he did not run wild. At one point, provoked by a comment, Spector pulled his gun from his holster and waved it in the air. Suddenly he pointed the gun over his head and fired it. The sound could be heard in the next room. I got up and ran into the adjacent game room, where Mal Evans and John stood staring at Phil. John rubbed his ears. Finally he said sternly, "Listen, Phil, if you're goin' to kill me, kill me. But don't fuck with me ears. I need 'em."

The next night we had dinner with Mal. "I've got the bullet," he told us.

"What bullet?" asked John.

Evans showed him the bullet, which had lodged in the roof of the Record Plant.

John was astonished. "I think it's a real fuckin' bullet!" he exclaimed. "I think it's *real*."

Eventually the sessions were suspended again. Still, despite all of John's preoccupations, whenever we were alone together we were calm and content. In addition, from the moment I had returned, our physical desire for each other was even more intense. Lovemaking was an intrinsic part of our relationship. We craved each other physically and found enormous pleasure, excitement, and emotional release in making love.

While we waited for Cynthia and Julian we also continued to participate in the Los Angeles high life. We had started to enjoy the parties and we both got an enormous kick out of seeing stars. John was a legend and he knew it, but it did not stop him from being a star-struck kid at heart. Whenever we went out in Hollywood, we always wondered about the stars we might see. The one John wanted to run into the most was Brigitte Bardot. We both agreed that Bardot probably wouldn't be caught dead in Beverly Hills.

It appeared to us that Los Angeles was filled with rich, famous, and powerful people. It seemed to me that all of those people might as well have been kids stuck in a small town, phoning each other, trying to drum up some excitement. At night stars would cruise up and down the streets, looking for things to do. That's why so many of them dropped into our recording sessions. Finally there was a place for them to go.

On one typical night we joined Cher and Harry Nilsson for dinner at an elegant Chinese restaurant near the Beverly Wilshire Hotel. I always got a kick out of eating Chinese food in Hollywood. Those elaborate dishes were nothing like the food my mother made.

After dinner, we all drove around looking for something to do. Cher suggested we drive to the Playboy Mansion West.

"Don't you need an invitation?" I asked.

"*We* don't need an invitation," Cher replied. She drove up to the gate, reached out, and picked up the phone in the call box. "It's Cher," she announced. The gate to the Playboy Mansion flew open.

A few Bunnies came down to meet us. Since our visit was unexpected, the Bunnies were dressed in street clothes and not in any of their abbreviated party clothes. They weren't wearing fur ears or tails made of cotton; they were dressed in slacks and blouses. "Mr. Hefner will join you shortly," they told us. "Why don't you make yourselves at home."

We roamed over the vast grounds. Whenever we ran into a Bunny, she kept suggesting that we visit Mr. Hefner's zoo and see his llamas. Finally we went into the Mansion and Hefner came down from his bedroom. He was wearing pajamas and was surrounded by Bunnies—one on each arm, with others trailing behind him. "Welcome," he said. "All of the facilities are yours. Make yourselves at home."

We went to the Grotto, the large, steamy Jacuzzi that Hefner had built for nude bathing. Everyone kept wondering which of us would undress and swim in the nude. I knew I wouldn't. John suddenly got the idea that it was time for Harry to take a bath. Like a mischievous kid, he whispered in our ears that on the count of three we should all toss Harry into the water. John whispered, "One . . . two . . . three!" and suddenly we pounced on him and tossed him in. Harry splashed around happily. Then Cher climbed to the top of the rocks.

"It's so steamy in here," she said. "I've lost an eyelash."

We all got on our hands and knees and crawled around in the dark, looking for Cher's false eyelash. When it was finally retrieved, Cher clamped it back on. Then she waded in the pool while John and I watched. After her swim we all went into the Mansion. Hefner showed us around, pointing out each and every lavish accoutrement that made his home the symbol of making fantasy living a reality. After we left, John remarked wryly, "I was very impressed. I never met a man who had so many ashtrays. I never met a man with so many ashtrays who made sure to have a pipe in every one of them." Then he said, "I want to go to the studio. I don't want to go home yet."

L.A. was so dull and desolate, it was impossible for John— for so many of those famous music stars—to get enough excitement.

On the following Sunday afternoon Mick Jagger called to ask us what we were doing. We had no plans. We called Jim Keltner, who had no plans either. "The Jim Keltner Fan Club Hour" had been a credit on George Harrison's *All Things Must Pass* album, given to a group of musicians who had participated in a jam led by Jim. John decided to stage another Jim Keltner Fan Club Hour session that evening, using any musicians who were available to play.

During the afternoon musicians phoned each other, eager to round up an illustrious crew for the jam, and that night a dazzling group assembled for the session. Mick said he would be the lead vocalist, with Harry Nilsson singing backup. Jesse Ed Davis and Danny Kortchmar were going to play guitar, with Jim Keltner on drums, Bobby Keys and Trevor Lawrence on horns, and Al Kooper on keyboards. Jack Bruce was in another studio and he came in to play bass. An army of girls were gathered in the studio. They were invited to sing backup with Harry.

Jagger found a single he loved called "Too Many Cooks." No one had ever heard it before, and before anyone had a chance to ask a question he persuaded everyone that they *had* to do it. Mick was a natural leader. He seemed to get pleasure in doing the work in an organized fashion, and he knew exactly how to get what he wanted from everyone. There was also an air of mysteriousness about him. He'd look at you and wink, and his wink seemed to be saying, "You may think you can pull the wool over my eyes, but I'm just letting you get away with it. You'll never know what I'm really thinking." This was a genuinely mischievous man.

After Mick played the record and copied down the lyrics, he gathered the musicians together. John decided he wanted to produce the session and not perform on it, and he went into the control booth to get proper levels on the microphones. The musicians listened to the record a few times, then quickly worked up an arrangement. Mick rehearsed the group a couple of times, making a few suggestions along the way. The musicians also contributed their own ideas. When John put echo on Mick's voice, Mick said, "John, I hate echo. Please take it off," and John obeyed. Unlike John, Mick liked his singing voice and did not insist that it be adorned with special effects. At the end of half an hour they were ready to begin. They did three or four takes, with John producing.

Everyone listened intently to the playback. The singing and playing sounded terrific, and John had expertly produced the track. "Too Many Cooks" had been arranged, rehearsed, and recorded in little more than an hour, a far cry from the Spector sessions.

Everyone was delighted by the result, which had been achieved in such an easygoing, professional, and economical manner.

For the remainder of the evening some of the musicians jammed together while the rest hung out, talking and relaxing. There was some drinking and some smoking of marijuana, but the evening was really about professionals getting together to do the thing they loved most—making music—and being in the company of others who felt the same way.

That edition of The Jim Keltner Fan Club Hour turned out to be a lovely evening—so much more fun and so much easier than the Spector sessions. That particular configuration of musicians never met again, but the tape of their performance—documenting a night in which John and Mick made music together with their friends and had a wonderful time doing it—still exists.

As Cynthia and Julian's visit neared, Yoko increased her calls. One day I counted twenty-three. The average, however, was fifteen. By the time the month ended she had run up a long-distance phone bill of $3,000. Her calls continued to keep John on edge. On the night that I had allowed her to convince me to return to John, she had told me that I would only have to stay with him for two weeks. Three had gone by. She kept hinting that I had been back for more than the allotted two weeks, but I did not respond to her hints. When she quizzed John about our relationship, he did not say very much either. She didn't precisely know how John and I were getting along and, hoping to find out, she kept calling and calling.

A day before the arrival of Cynthia and Julian, John slammed the phone down angrily. He was livid. "Fung Yee," he shouted, "something terrible has happened."

I looked at him. His eyes flashed with anger. "What's the matter?" I asked.

John wouldn't respond.

"What did she tell you?"

Still, he wouldn't answer, but with Cynthia and Julian due to arrive in less than twenty-four hours, John suddenly had the look in his eye that meant a rampage might be imminent.

"All right, then, don't tell me. But at least listen," I said firmly. "I've never asked for very much. But I'm asking you for something now. Your son hasn't seen you in years. No matter what you've heard, you've got to be nice to Julian tomorrow."

John did not reply. Lost in thought, he paced back and forth until bedtime. That night I could not sleep and did not go to bed. John walked into the living room to ask me what the matter was.

"I can't stand the fact that you might hurt Julian. It reminds me of all the times that I was hurt as a kid and couldn't do anything about it."

John suddenly switched gears. "Yoko's just being paranoid," he said with a laugh. "She's afraid that I'll go back with Cynthia and divorce her and she'll get a small divorce settlement, just like Cynthia did."

John smiled at me, but it was short-lived. Suddenly he frowned and said nothing. I realized he was trapped between his anxieties and his sense of what was right.

When he got up the next morning, he was so nervous, he began to chain-smoke and to pace incessantly. We had rented a limousine to take us to the airport. When it pulled up in front of our apartment, John told the driver to wait. He paced and smoked some more but did not take a drink. Eventually he made up his mind. "Let's go," he said, and he bolted out the door.

John was consumed by nervousness in the limousine and at the airport while we waited for the plane to land.

Julian spotted John as soon as he and Cynthia passed through the exit gate. The child burst into a huge grin. "Dad . . . Dad," he called out as he ran to John.

John scooped his son into his arms and hugged him tightly. Then he said hello to Cynthia and gave her a polite kiss on the cheek. "Hello, May," she said, extending her hand.

"Do you remember May from England?" John asked Julian. I was pleased that Julian did remember that we had spent time together at Tittenhurst. We led them to the limousine. The ride began as a silent one; then John asked Julian about the flight. Julian's excited chatter broke the ice, and we were all more at ease by the time we arrived at the hotel.

When we were in their suite, John and Cynthia fell into a brief conversation about old times, and I played with Julian. John, however, quickly became restless. "We've got to go," he said.

"We'll all have brunch tomorrow," I added.

"What a lovely idea," exclaimed Cynthia.

John headed for the door, and I followed. John had spent less than half an hour with his son; it was all John could handle on the first day.

The next day John proved capable of spending two hours with Cynthia and Julian before his nervousness overwhelmed him.

The following day, during which we planned to take Julian to Disneyland, would be the real test. John wanted to leave Cynthia behind. Julian, however, hid behind a couch and would not go unless his mother could go along, and John finally relented. During the drive Julian alternated between shyness and ease with his father. He said to John, "I can't believe I can talk to you whenever I want to now." John was puzzled. "Do you remember in England when I used to come visit you? I was allowed to speak to you only once or twice a day. Otherwise I couldn't speak to you at all," Julian told him.

John started to relax. He asked Julian about school and his friends; he asked him about the music he liked and whether he was studying any musical instruments. Cynthia had a natural English reserve about her, yet she was friendly and perfectly cordial to me. It was obvious that she had real affection for John. It was equally obvious that she had not traveled to the United States to steal him from Yoko. Cynthia believed that because they had once spent so much time together, they should be able to have an easy conversation. Her entire demeanor made it clear that she expected nothing from John, and John responded to her cordiality. Everything was going a lot better than I had hoped.

Before we got to Disneyland, John said firmly, "We have to watch out for photographers. I don't believe in having a kid's picture taken just because he has a famous dad. I hate all those stars using their families to get free publicity by having themselves photographed with their children. If I see a photographer, I'll break his fuckin' camera."

Once we got inside, Julian became very excited. He dashed from attraction to attraction, urging John to keep after him. John trotted after his son, and they both appeared to be having a merry time. Cynthia turned to me as John and Julian ran ahead. "When I found out about you and John, I was so happy. I knew Julian could see his father again. Really," she said in her English fashion, "whatever happened between John and me, he shouldn't want to divorce his son."

Cynthia smiled warmly at me, and we fell into a conversation about our childhoods. I knew that the meeting between John's first wife and his mistress was peculiar, but Cynthia had no feelings of jealousy. I told Cynthia that we were happy—that we had problems only when John drank.

"John has always drunk when he feels insecure," she replied. "When he was nineteen, he desperately wanted to make it as a musician and he was afraid he wouldn't. He'd drink, we'd go to a dance, and he'd always find someone to pick a fight with. When he was drunk, someone always got beat up."

John was pleased with the excursion and he adored Julian. "He's like a little man," he kept telling me. "He's able to have conversations. He can think, he can discuss things. He amazes me."

Two days later we joined Cynthia at Mal Evans's house for dinner. Everyone had a few drinks, and after dinner we all sat on the floor, listening as Cynthia and John had a long, funny talk about the good old days. They regaled us with stories about their stay at the Maharishi Mahesh Yogi's ashram in India. Toward the end of the conversation Cynthia remarked, "You know, John, I always wanted to have another child."

"With whom?" John asked, glaring at her.

Cynthia paused. "With you," she replied offhandedly.

"I can't have another child, I'm sterile."

"I don't understand," Cynthia replied.

"I have proof I can't have another child. I've been checked out medically and I have a low sperm count because of the drugs I've taken."

Soon afterward John decided to leave.

On the way home he brooded about Cynthia's comment that she had wanted another child. As soon as we returned to the apartment he phoned Yoko. "You were right, Yoko," he said. "She still loves me and she'll do anything to get me back."

A few nights later John and I decided to go to the Troubadour. John had been looking forward to the evening for quite some time. He loved Ann Peebles's performance of "I Can't Stand the Rain," and was eager to attend Peebles's opening night at the Troubadour. We joined Jim Keltner and his wife, Cynthia, and Jesse Ed Davis and his girl friend, Patti, for dinner before the show. Jesse brought along a friend of his, a quiet hippy type who was never introduced and who rarely spoke. When we arrived at the restaurant, I noticed right away that Jesse was behaving strangely.

Jesse, like Phil Spector, enjoyed making things happen. They were the kind of people John chose as friends. He enjoyed following their lead, but unfortunately, when he was around them, John's self-destructive tendencies usually emerged.

As soon as the waiter appeared John orderd a drink that he had just discovered and loved: a brandy alexander. Even though John was a vodka drinker, he loved drinks made with cream and sweet liqueurs. They tasted just like milk shakes, and he could down them quickly and easily. John used alcohol as a medicine to calm his nerves. Like a child, he preferred a sweet-tasting medicine that did not taste like medicine at all.

"I'm hungry," I said. "Let's order some food."

"No, not yet," said Jesse.

The waiter was summoned and another round was ordered. It was followed by a third round of doubles. Finally they let the waiter take our dinner orders. By then John was already getting high and a little out of control. I knew a tricky night was ahead.

During dinner John got up to go downstairs to use the bathroom. While he was there he rummaged through a supply closet and found a box of sanitary napkins. Somehow he had attached one of the sanitary pads to his forehead. John thought it was hilarious; of course, so did Jesse. The Keltners and I did our best to get him to take it off, but the more we pleaded, the more adamant he became. "I like it," he said. "I like it."

John and Jesse ordered some more drinks and grew so noisy that the manager told us we would have to leave unless we quieted down. Right then was the time to get him home, but I was afraid that attempting to take him home without seeing Ann Peebles might make him even more rambunctious. Either way I knew I was in for a rough evening.

John insisted on wearing the sanitary pad to the Troubadour. "Attaboy, John," Jesse said. "You got to do what you want to do."

When we got to the Troubadour, the club was packed. Finally a waitress appeared to take our drink orders. She had a large station and it was obvious that she was under a lot of pressure. Rather than simply tell her what he wanted, John teased and hassled her. "This is John Lennon. Do you know this is John Lennon?" Jesse told her. John grinned at her. The waitress didn't respond; she just looked aside angrily. John teased her some more. Finally the orders were taken, and the drinks were served. During Ann Peebles's performance, John called out obscenities. His voice cut through the room.

Some people laughed, others booed, and a few turned to shush him. All of the reactions met with the same response from John—another barrage of obscenities delivered even more loudly. The audience did not want the show interrupted. At the same time they were fascinated that it was John who was doing the calling out.

John continued to let loose, and the audience grew even more restive; finally we were asked to leave. When we were in the parking lot the Keltners said good night and left.

Jim Keltner, a mild-mannered man, had remained in good humor throughout the evening. At a later date he told me that he once heard that in the Beatles' days in Hamburg, at the end of their shows, John sometimes got drunk and then, pretending he was German, would go out and roll English sailors, who would subsequently blame the Germans for the beatings and robberies. Jim had always believed that contrary to their public image there was a rough side to the Beatles, and he was not surprised by John's drunken behavior.

After the Keltners left, John, still wearing his strange headgear, insisted that Jesse, Patti, and Jesse's silent friend join us at the apartment.

"No, John," I said. "Enough is enough."

"We'd love to go," Jesse said firmly.

"Don't be rude to our guests," said John.

As I drove back to West Harper Avenue John suddenly said, "I want to get out of the car."

"We're almost home, John," I told him.

"I want to get out now." Even though the car was moving, John threw open the door and fell out onto the road. I put the car in reverse, drove backward, and reached out for him. He was so strong, he nearly pulled me out. Finally, with his cooperation, I was able to haul him in.

When we got into the apartment, John looked around, giggled, and said, "It's too bright in here." He picked up a frying pan and smashed the kitchen light. Jesse and he broke down laughing.

Patti and I sat in the living room, watching John and Jesse. One or the other would say something silly, then they both would dissolve into more hysterical laughter. I got up to go to the bathroom. Before I went upstairs I asked Patti to watch them. Suddenly I heard a loud thump. Then I heard Patti scream, "You've killed him!"

I ran downstairs. Jesse was lying on the kitchen floor.

"You've killed him! You've killed him!" Patti was screaming.

"No, I haven't!" John took a container of orange juice from the refrigerator and dumped it on Jesse. Jesse stirred.

John grinned. "You see, he's not dead at all."

John explained that he had gone into the kitchen to get a Coke. Jesse had followed after him, and John had taken the Coke bottle and bashed Jesse over the head, and Jesse had collapsed on the floor.

"You've killed him!" Patti shrieked again.

"He's all right," I reassured Patti.

"John's killed him!" she bellowed.

I did my best to help Jesse get to his feet. "You've killed him!" Patti screamed, even when she saw Jesse stumbling across the floor to the couch. "He's dead!" Patti called out, even though Jesse was sitting up and laughing.

Just then there was a knock at the door. "Who is it?" I asked.

"This is the police."

I looked through the peephole. I could see the uniforms. "Who is it?" I said again.

"The Los Angeles Police Department," a gruff voice replied.

"Shit!" exclaimed John. He had an automatic fear of the police. The sight of them always took him back to the time he and Yoko had been busted for possession of drugs in 1968. He bolted up the stairs and hid in the bedroom. The police knocked again. I tried to open the door. Someone had locked it from the inside and had taken the key from the lock. It was impossible to open the door without the key.

The police knocked again.

"Just one minute," I said. "This is a dead-bolt lock, and I've got to find the key." I roamed around the apartment, searching for the key. While I frantically looked for it the knocking continued. Patti didn't have it, John didn't have it, Jesse didn't have it. I kept calling out, "Who took the key?" Then I would run back to the door to talk to the police.

"Are you looking for this?" It was Jesse's friend, who had not spoken all night. He gave me the key, and I ran to the door and opened it.

Shotguns were pointed in my face as well as a bright flashlight. "There's been a complaint that someone's been shot in this apartment," an officer said. They continued to point the guns as they stepped past me into the apartment.

"Look around," I said. "We've just been drinking and fooling around, but we haven't killed anybody."

The police could smell the liquor, and they did not put down their guns. They roamed around downstairs. Finding nothing, a cop said, "What about upstairs."

"Just a minute," I said. I went upstairs. A policeman with a drawn gun followed after me. He did a double take when he saw John.

"John, you've got to come downstairs," I said quietly.

"No." He was as tense as I'd ever seen him.

"You've got to come down," I repeated evenly. "If they come up and get you, it will be worse."

"Shit." John slowly followed me past the policeman and down the stairs. All of the police were amazed to see him. Still, they kept their guns and their flashlights aimed at him. John smiled at them.

The youngest cop asked reverently, "Do you think the Beatles will ever get back together again?"

"You never know," John replied nervously. "You never know."

The police did not have a search warrant, yet they took a careful look around, probably for drugs. Then they told us not to make any more noise and left. Their visit had a sobering effect on Jesse, and he and Patti decided to leave soon afterward, taking their silent friend with them; I walked them to their car. As I stood on the street I heard John scream, "I hate Roman Polanski. He's no fuckin' good." His voice was filled with equal parts of anger and anguish. He sounded just as he had on the night Spector had tied him up.

I dashed back to the apartment. John was upstairs. Shaking with rage, he had attacked the four-poster bed and was doing his best to break loose one of the posts. "It's Roman Polanski's fault!" he screamed. "Roman Polanski is to blame for everything." We had met Roman Polanski at a few parties, but John had never expressed any anger toward him. I watched as he systematically began to demolish the room. His fury was terrifying as he set about trying to destroy every object he could get his hands on. He picked up the television and hurled it against the wall. He used a lamp to smash the mirror and then hammered the lamp against a chair. He dumped a bureau drawer onto the floor and then began to shred the clothes with his hands. I did my best to calm him, but when I approached him, he reached out and pulled my jade necklace from my throat—the necklace John knew I had promised my mother I would wear every day for my entire life—threw it on the floor and trampled it.

Nothing I said could stop the rampage. John was furious because he had allowed himself to be manipulated by Jesse, and he had been humiliated by the actions of the police. Then, once again, it was his turn. The best I could do was keep out of his way. I tried to remain calm, but in that state John was a very dangerous man, and I was terrified.

I knew I needed help, and I did not know whom to wake

up then. I thought for a moment and decided to call Yoko. After all, I had allowed her to persuade me to return; I believed she deserved a clear picture of what I had been persuaded to return to.

While I spoke to her, she could hear the sounds of destruction in the background. She wanted no part of it. "Call Elliot Mintz," she said abruptly and hung up.

As soon as I hung up I called Elliot, who said he'd be right over.

"Elliot," roared John. "I don't want that Jew bastard in my house. I'll kill him if he comes through the door."

I went downstairs and sat there doing my best to stay calm while I waited for Elliot, and John continued to wreck the upstairs. Occasionally John came to the top of the stairs to scream, "I'll kill that Jew bastard the minute I see him." But John did not come down, and eventually the noises stopped. I assumed he had passed out and I got up and slowly walked upstairs, ready to run if John was still awake. The entire room had been reduced to rubble, and John had passed out on the collapsed bed. I looked at him and became so upset, I started to cry. Elliot never arrived.

When he woke up in the morning, John looked around. "Did I do it again?" he asked, once again not remembering a thing. "What happened?"

I rubbed my eyes; my voice was trembling as I described what had happened.

John picked up his smashed Martin guitar. The television had fallen on it. "This is the first time in all these years I ever destroyed anything that belonged to me." He turned and looked sadly at me. "You're not wearing your necklace," he said. I showed it to him. "I'm sorry. I'm sorry," he said quietly. Then he said, "I don't want Julian to know anything about this."

I got up and made coffee. Then Yoko called. She gave John three explanations for the night's events and John repeated them to me: John had exploded because I had not done my job, because Cynthia wanted him back, and because he had seen Julian despite the fact that it hurt her because she could not see her daughter, Kyoko, who Yoko insisted had been kidnapped by the child's father, Yoko's second husband, Tony Cox.

Elliot Mintz called soon afterward. He said that he had come to the front door. When he heard John screaming that he was going to kill him, he decided not to come in.

"He's a very brave man," John observed sardonically when I got off the phone. Then we phoned Julian and had a pleasant chat; neither he nor Cynthia seemed to have any knowledge of what had happened, and John was very relieved.

In the afternoon we left the apartment and found a small crowd in front of the building. As we went to the car they chased after us. We did not know then that we were front-page news. Stories detailing the "Kotex incident" at the Troubadour had become front-page news, and the waitress at the club had been quoted as saying that John had insisted upon telling her that he was John Lennon—which was untrue—and that she had replied by saying "What you are is an asshole with a Kotex on your head"—which I had never heard her say. The newspaper accounts also described the visit the police had made to our apartment and had printed our address. That explained why there were people milling around in front. As the day went on the crowd continued to grow larger. The phone rang incessantly with reporters wanting firsthand information about the previous evening.

John felt trapped. He didn't want to go out and face the crowd, but he couldn't stand being holed up.

"We've got to get out of here," he said. "Let's move to a hotel."

"How will we pay for it?" I asked.

John thought. "We'll charge it to the budget of the album. Let's go."

We packed our things and moved to the Beverly Wilshire Hotel. In three months we had moved in and out of Harold Seider's apartment twice, in and out of Lou Adler's house, and flown to New York on one day and back to Los Angeles on the next. While we were registering at the Beverly Wilshire, John turned to me and said, "I should give my occupation as gypsy."

The next day we saw Cynthia and Julian. Even though

they had read about it in the newspapers, they never mentioned the Kotex incident and neither did we. Julian's visit was almost over, and John endeavored to make those last few days as pleasant as he could for his son. Because Julian liked it so much, we even went back to Disneyland two more times.

On the day of their departure we took Cynthia and Julian to the airport. "I want to come again to see you on my next holiday," Julian told John before he got on the plane.

When we returned to the car, John leaned back and breathed a long sigh of relief.

"You've got to make me a promise," I said on the way home.

"What is it?"

"I want *you* to call Julian once a week. It would be terrible for him after this time with you if you disappointed him by disappearing again. You're a real person to him now and you've got to keep in touch."

John hemmed and hawed. Then he said, "It is the right thing to do. I promise you, Fung Yee." He was silent for a while, then John said suddenly, "I really would like to keep in touch with me son."

13

After Julian's departure, our attention naturally turned back to Spector, who was only concerned with one thing: the custody hearing. "The hearing is tomorrow and I need you to go with me. I need you in the courtroom with me. I need you to sit beside me."

We decided to go. John really wanted to help. But the minute Spector spotted his estranged wife, Ronnie, at the courthouse, he jumped up and began to scream obscenities across the room at her. John did his best to get Spector to sit down, and they wound up arguing with each other.

"I thought for once you'd be calm," John said finally. "I can't believe you're goin' to go into the courtroom this afternoon and raise hell in front of the judge."

Spector launched into another angry, abusive tirade. John sighed. "Phil . . ." he said wearily, "Phil . . ." and John once again tried heroically to reason with him, but Spector could not be stopped.

"I'm disgusted. I can't stand it anymore." John took my hand. We got up, leaving Spector in midsentence. We did not learn the outcome of the hearing. John did not want to call him, and Spector did not call us.

A few days after that, Harold Seider told us that he wanted to go over all of the Apple negotiations with John. "These matters are just too complicated to do over the phone. It's best that we deal with this face to face."

Since John's team of lawyers was based in New York, Seider suggested that we return to New York for a week to meet with all of them at once.

Seider's call came at a time when work on the Spector album had ground to a total halt and Spector refused to return our calls. In any normal situation an album like that could have been completed in a month's time. It was over three months since we had begun recording, and the end was nowhere in sight.

"We'll go to New York for a week and at least clear up the legal matters," John said. He asked Mal Evans to meet us at Harold Seider's apartment. We had not been back there since John had demolished it after the Kotex incident. John and Mal sat in the middle of the rubble. "Mal, we'll be gone for a week. I want everything in this apartment repaired or replaced while we're away. When we get back, I want everything to be like new."

"Leave everything to me," Mal replied.

"I also want you to make sure to have my guitar repaired."

"It will be like new."

John gave Mal my jade necklace. "This is the most important of all. I want it fixed and I want it fixed perfectly."

Mal took the necklace. "I'll do it the first thing in the morning."

We decided that when we went to New York, we would stay in my studio apartment, which John had always found cozy and attractive. For the previous five months I had had the rent bill forwarded to me and had paid the $195 rent out of my savings. I never wanted anything from John, but it made me nervous to realize that in five months I had gone through the $1,200 it had taken me three years to save.

When I told John that I could not afford to pay the rent anymore, he said, "I want to make sure we always have a place to stay when we're in New York." I did not want to lose an apartment in New York City that I knew I could always afford.

He advised me to have my rent bill forwarded to his accountant.

Then John called Yoko and told her we were coming. "You can get us at May's if you need us," he added. We packed and left the next day.

When we got to my New York apartment, John collapsed on the bed. "It's good to be back! I always feel better in New York!" He wasn't kidding. Almost immediately a startling transformation occurred, and our life in New York became ultranormal, closely resembling the time we had spent together at the end of the previous summer when Yoko was in Chicago. We got up early and went to bed as soon as the Johnny Carson show was over. In the mornings we had coffee, read the newspapers, and made our phone calls. John, who had disliked walking at the beginning of our relationship, loved to prowl around Manhattan on foot, and in the afternoons we usually took long walks. We especially loved strolling down Fifth Avenue and looking in the store windows. While we walked, people would sometimes look and nudge each other when they spotted John, but they prided themselves on leaving him alone.

We discovered a little Mexican restaurant in my neighborhood and dropped in at all hours to gorge on Mexican combination plates. Most of all, however, John loved Whoppers. Whenever the urge came over us, we went on Whopper binges, buying bags full of them and taking them home with us. In the evenings we sometimes went to the movies, standing in line like everyone else. The movie we loved most was *The Way We Were*.

At night John also liked to go to Richard Ross's restaurant, Home, to eat and drink. Richard, whom I had introduced to John, loved to fawn over him. Whenever Richard heard from us, he would drop everything to devote himself to pleasing John just for the privilege of hanging out with him. John knew that we had to have friends. He felt comfortable in public only with musician friends; other than that he relied on people like Ross and Elliot Mintz. It was an easy way out, but John always believed that strangers would have expectations of him, expectations he might not fulfill, and that was why he feared them. He knew that he could never disappoint Richard; just the sight of John was enough to send Ross into a tizzy. It sometimes took that much slavish devotion before John could relax with other people in public.

John did overdrink a few nights at Home, and also got drunk on sake one night at a Japanese restaurant, but drunk was different from crazy, and John did not get crazy.

Besides John's good mood, there were other indications that he was in fine shape. He had desperately wanted to write new songs but nothing had come to him during the previous four months. Almost from the moment we arrived in New York, as he was drifting off to sleep he would jot down words, phrases, and images on the pad he always kept at his bedside. In the mornings he would stare with delight at the pad.

Each day he grew a little bolder. At the end of our first week in New York, I became ill, and we had no food in the house. To my amazement John volunteered to go to the supermarket on his own. "What would you like?" he asked.

"I'll do it," I said.

"No, I've got money. I can go."

We made up a grocery list, and John went to the store. He came back half an hour later, carrying two shopping bags full of food. He was exultant. "I haven't gone to the store for anyone since I was a kid. I loved it," he exclaimed. A trip to the supermarket may seem trivial, but it was an enormous step for John, who normally would never have done anything that practical and public on his own. He was eager to go to the supermarket again and he did, too. Soon he got into the habit of choosing what he wanted to eat rather than eating what he was fed. He also felt comfortable about making his own change at the register; in Los Angeles he had liked other people to pay for him, because counting his own change, like dialing the phone, proved annoying. I wanted John to function independently and I viewed those excursions to the supermarket as a major step in that direction—a step that made me very, very happy.

John even began to handle Yoko's calls with ease. They had begun the night we had returned. Unaffected by whatever she told him, he had no desire to spend too much time talking to her; often he would be off the phone after a three- or four-minute conversation. The day after we returned, John went to the Dakota for a brief visit. It was a courtesy call, and he was back an hour after he left. Yoko, sensing John's unresponsiveness, eventually began to call less frequently and seemed to be losing interest in monitoring and controlling our moves.

A day or two after we arrived a date was set for John to begin his meetings with his lawyers. The meetings were conducted by Harold Seider, David Dolgenos, and Michael Graham.

Whenever a Beatle made a solo album, such as John's *Mind Games,* the monies from those albums poured into Apple. The royalties were frozen by the English courts. Convinced now that he was going to make the most successful solo albums, Paul McCartney was determined to have his solo royalties flow directly to him. The best way to achieve that was to effect a satisfactory formula to dissolve the Apple partnership. Paul, of all the Beatles, was the one who was most insistent.

The unwinding of Apple brought other problems with it. There was the suit with Allen Klein. Klein was suing John, Ringo, and George for breach of contract. He was also suing Apple Corps, since the Beatles' corporation was also a signatory to the Klein management agreement. Even though Paul was a partner in Apple Corps—and, as a partner, was being sued by Klein—he was determined not to give Klein any monies from his solo albums. He insisted that the other Beatles indemnify him against any monies from his solo albums that he might owe Klein if Klein won his lawsuit against Apple Corps.

It was amazing to see how many complications were involved in dissolving the corporation. For example, the assets of Apple Corps included the Beatles' homes. Decisions had to be made about how to divide up the property as well as anything else the corporation owned.

In addition, all of John's and Yoko's New York expenses had been charged to Apple Corps. John told me that the expenses had been estimated at two million dollars. The Beatles did not want to pick up the expenses, and they certainly did not want to pick up the cost of Yoko's albums. There was a demand for John to agree to pay those monies back to the corporation.

Altogether there seemed to be an unending list of negotiating points for John to go over. He listened intently during the meetings, occasionally asking a number of pointed questions. His main concern, however, was extremely basic: He was concerned about the "bottom line." John believed that no matter what happened he would always have to give somebody something in order to resolve an issue. "How much money will I have to give them? Do I have to give away any albums or songs?" he would ask bluntly. The answers to those questions were his primary concern, and he did not want anyone to get his hands on what he believed rightfully belonged to him.

At the end of the week as one of the meetings was drawing to a close, David Dolgenos looked nervously at me. I could see that he wanted to discuss something privately with John. John also sensed Dolgenos's desire to be alone with him. Dolgenos, however, did not ask me to leave; nor did John. Finally the lawyer said, "There's another matter we ought to begin discussing." He grew more uncomfortable. Then he looked at John and said, "I'm concerned because Yoko is asking for a lawyer to handle her divorce."

Surprise flickered on John's face. He suppressed it quickly, however, and smiled benignly. It was the smile he used when he did not want anybody to know what he was thinking. There was a heavy silence in the room, and Dolgenos did not know whether to go on. John threw me a piercing look. I knew he wanted me to leave the room.

I got up, excused myself, walked out of the room, and sat down in the reception room.

I must admit I was as surprised as John was. The news had caught us both off guard. My first thought was that she was up to something—something that I didn't understand and didn't trust. John had been acting with real independence. I wondered if Yoko was trying to undermine his newfound self-confidence.

I knew I would be thrilled if Yoko really did want to divorce John, but that would be too easy. Of course, I wanted John to marry me, but it seemed impossible that he would ever totally free himself from his need for Yoko. To dream about marrying him seemed to me to guarantee that I would inevitably be hurt, so whenever I thought about marrying John, I quickly pushed the thought out of my mind.

How would John respond to Yoko's news? I wondered. Would he become so frightened that he would begin to drink and run riot in New York as he had done in Los Angeles? Not since that day when she had suggested that I go out with John had I felt so dislocated.

I waited nervously in the outer office, not knowing what to expect when John came out, hoping that if he was really upset, he would not erupt and then turn his fear and anger against me. The wait took half an hour, and my mind whirled during every second of it.

When John finally emerged from the meeting, of all things he was smiling sweetly. He came over and kissed me on the cheek. "I've just called Yoko," he said. "I'm goin' over there now. I want to see exactly what's on her mind." Surprisingly, *I* was the nervous one, and John, sensing my nervousness, gave me a hug. Arm in arm, we left the office. During the cab ride home he was in an exuberant mood. Yoko's news seemed to be making him happy. I knew how fascinated he could be by her games, and I assumed that the fascination was the source of his pleasure. I did not allow myself to think that it was he who really wanted a divorce.

"I'll be back in an hour," he said when the cab pulled up at the apartment. He gave me another kiss before I got out, then he went on to the Dakota.

The phone was ringing when I got upstairs. It was Yoko. When I picked up the phone, she did not even say hello.

"May, what mood is John in?" she asked.

"He seems fine," I replied.

"You know I'm afraid of him. I'm really afraid of him," she said sharply.

"I don't think you've got anything to worry about," I replied evenly.

"Are you sure he's all right? I could call a locksmith before he gets here and have him change all the locks. I don't want him to come over here and do anything to me."

"You'll be fine, Yoko. Just fine."

She slammed down the phone.

Two hours later John came back with a beautiful raccoon coat on his arm. He handed it to me, and I took it and put it on.

"Where did you get that?" I asked.

John chuckled. "Let me tell you the story. Yoko never wears this coat, and I told her we needed it. Right now, we couldn't afford to buy you a winter coat. She said, 'Let me try it on first to see if it fits.' It didn't, and she said, 'I'll give you this coat on one condition: that you tell May it's from me.'"

John laughed out loud. "I have a coat just like this. Yoko told me Arlene had borrowed it and she would have to get Arlene to return it." He paused, then he smiled at me. "You know, Fung Yee, I'll be a free man by June."

I looked searchingly at him. "Is this Yoko's idea or yours?" I asked.

"We discussed it, and it's just not workin' out—the two of us. And it's best that we are apart, even though we care for each other."

"Is this what you really want?"

"Whatever's best."

He came over and kissed me. "Now, why don't you call Yoko and thank her for the coat. We might as well keep the peace."

I was still wary, but I couldn't deny how excited I was by John's news. He wrapped his arm around my shoulder while I dialed Yoko's number.

"Yoko, it's May," I said. "John just got home and gave me the coat. It's beautiful. Thank you for thinking of me. Thank you very much."

"I'm glad you like it. I've been thinking all day about how much I wanted you to have it," she replied sweetly. "May, I don't want you to be cold, and now you'll be warm. That makes me very happy."

"Thank you," I repeated.

"May, I want you to be happy." Yoko was silent for a moment, then she said, "I'm going to go through the rest of my wardrobe and see what else I can give you. As soon as I'm done I'll call you back."

When I repeated Yoko's promise to John, he looked skeptically at me. From that moment on Yoko increased her calls, but she wanted only to speak to me. The calls were "sisterly" calls: My big sister wanted to gossip with me about John's reaction to the divorce. "How is he today? . . . How is he taking the news? . . . Has he said anything? . . . What is his mood like? . . ."

I resented the gossipy, adolescent tone of those calls and kept insisting that Yoko speak directly to John; that only made her more determined to wring information from me. She seemed to be having difficulty accepting the fact that John was cheerful and calm, in good spirits about the divorce, even amused by her endless attempts to get me to entrust her with my perceptions of his state of mind.

I did not permit myself to think about any of it. Deep down I was really convinced that if push came to shove, Yoko would not divorce John, and I did not want to let myself plan on that future happiness. Their divorce presented a possibility that I was afraid would be snatched away. All I wanted to do was live from day to day, and the fact that John was calm and happy was enough for me. In addition, I was encouraged by the fact that his dependence on Yoko seemed to be really diminishing.

A few days later Yoko called to tell us that she wanted to give a party and that she was going to invite Mick Jagger. She wanted us both to attend; if anyone asked any questions, she told John, she planned to tell Mick as well as her other guests that she had thrown John out and that John had not left of his own accord.

"Why does anything have to be said?" I asked John. "Everyone will see that you're with me and she's alone. No matter what she says, you're the one who decided to change his life, and you have."

"She's my best friend," John replied. "I don't give a shit, but these things matter a lot to her. I don't give a damn."

However, John had been annoyed by her phone call. "I don't want to go to the party," he declared. "I don't want to play her games. I don't want to do what she wants me to do."

A series of calls began, all of them focused on getting

John to agree to go to the party and to agree to Yoko's story that she had thrown him out, and John had to promise to make especially sure that Mick Jagger never learned that John had left Yoko of his own accord.

The calls went on for four days, but John remained determined not to go to the party. Finally he lost his temper and shouted into the phone, "I don't give a damn what you tell Mick. All I know is that you are tryin' to play games with me and I've had enough. If you want the fuckin' divorce, do it fast."

I said nothing. I knew that anything I said then would make him more upset. "We're not going to the party, and that's that," he shouted.

After John's outburst, Yoko lay low for a few days. Then something else happened to interrupt our serenity.

My downstairs bell rang. I went to the intercom and asked who it was.

"This is Davey Blotter. John invited me to come to New York City with him." I would learn later that Blotter was a Los Angeles street person, someone John had tripped with after he had asked me to leave our Los Angeles home.

Instantly John got up and dashed into the bathroom. "Davey Blotter? Get rid of him. Make sure that he doesn't know I'm here," he shouted from behind the door.

"John's not here," I said into the intercom.

He did not respond.

A few minutes later my doorbell rang, and I looked through the peephole. Somehow Davey Blotter had gotten into the building. He and his young son, Blotter, were standing in front of my door. John had told me about the demented look in the eyes of some of his fans; the look in Davey Blotter's eyes fitted John's description exactly.

"I want to see John," he said again.

"He isn't here. I'll pass on the message when I hear from him."

"John invited me to New York."

"Are you sure he invited you?"

Davey ignored the question. "I must see John. Now."

"Please go away."

He grinned at me. "Blotter and I made friends with your upstairs neighbors, and they're letting me stay with them. Now, I always see you when you come and go. Maybe I'll catch John when he's coming up or down the stairs."

Then Davey and his son went upstairs. He had been telling the truth. Somehow he had talked himself into staying in the apartment on the floor above us. From his door he could look down the stairs, and it would be very easy for him to see us coming and going. I was dumbstruck. John and I had been able to live in an apartment complex in West Hollywood and had not had any problems until John's outbursts; there had been no problems in my apartment until now.

John was frantic. "I've got so many crazy fans. You know, all I need is one of them, one of them who really is me fan and who really loves me but has a screw loose, and do you know what he'll do? He'll probably get me. That's what he'll do."

"Do you really believe that?"

"Damn it, I do. I do."

John was so nervous, he refused to go out that afternoon or night. In the morning he said, "Let's get out of here." Money didn't matter at that point. I immediately called the Pierre Hotel and reserved a suite. Then we packed our bags, dashed from the apartment, ran to Third Avenue, hailed a cab, and sped away to the Pierre, never to hear from Davey Blotter again.

John calmed down as soon as we moved into the hotel. Even though he told Yoko that we had moved, he did not want to talk to her when she called. Whenever he did take the phone, she once again would tell him that she was still planning to give her party, wanted us to come, and wanted John to agree to her version of the story of their split-up. John's response usually was the same: "I'm not goin'." He would hang up and Yoko would call again.

John also kept asking Yoko for his fur coat, and she kept telling him that Arlene had not returned it. Finally I called Arlene. "I gave it back to her the day after she asked me for it," Arlene told me. "I saw her hang it in the closet."

John shrugged when I told him. He did not want to confront Yoko. "We're not stayin' long enough to worry about it," he explained, and he never asked Yoko about the coat again, although she continued to complain that Arlene had not given it back.

It appeared that Yoko eventually did give the party without us. Arlene told me that Yoko had made some phone calls and had invited guests to the Dakota, Mick Jagger among them. But she had hired neither a bartender nor a caterer and had ordered no refreshments, even though there was nothing to eat or drink in the apartment. "That's the way she is. She probably didn't think about it," John observed.

Our week in New York stretched to almost a month. Finally John's meetings were almost over. He understood thoroughly what was being done on his behalf with reference to his problems with the other Beatles and Allen Klein; the lawyers would then do their work. John could not bear leaving the Spector album unfinished and he decided that it was time to go back to Los Angeles.

Our plan was to stay for Yoko's forty-first birthday on February 18 and then to leave for Los Angeles a day or two later.

On her birthday Yoko refused to come out with us but invited us to the Dakota. The apartment was deserted. Yoko, dressed in a nightgown, had decided to spend her birthday resting in bed. We followed her into the bedroom and then watched while she climbed under the covers and pulled them up to her chin.

John sat on the edge of the bed. "Happy birthday, Yoko," he said cheerfully, and he bent over and kissed her cheek.

"Happy birthday, Yoko," I echoed.

Yoko pursed her lips into a thin smile. She looked like the brave victim of a terminal disease.

"How do you feel?" John asked.

She said nothing.

"Yoko, are you all right?"

She managed another brave smile. "Fine," she whispered. "I've never been happier."

We did our best to cheer her up, and she kept reassuring

us that she was very happy, but her tone remained funereal and finally her morbidity overwhelmed both of us.

"I'm not upset that I'm forty-one," she said softly, looking pleadingly at us as if she had just been sentenced to execution and we were the only ones who could pardon her.

John began to pace. Then he said, "Let's go," and he headed for the door. Our birthday visit had lasted only twenty minutes.

Two days after that, on the day of our departure for Los Angeles, John told me that he wanted to go to the Dakota to say good-bye to Yoko before we left for the airport. He went ahead while I finished packing. John always liked to take limousines to and from airports, and when I was ready, I had the driver take me to the Dakota. I called up for John. A few minutes later he came downstairs.

During the ride to the airport he was strangely silent. "How was she?" I asked. "Is she feeling better? Has her mood improved?"

"She's fine." Even though there was no emotion in John's eyes, I sensed that his mind was whirling. It was apparent that Yoko had told him something, something that had darkened his mood. We had had a happy month in New York. Nonetheless it appeared that in the space of half an hour John's anxiety had suddenly been fueled.

"Whenever you get that expression on your face, it means you're brooding about something—something Yoko has told you, something she's told you about me. What did she say?"

"Nothing."

"Are you sure?"

"Yes!"

As soon as the plane took off John ordered a vodka. He gulped down the drink and then ordered another. The second drink was followed by a third and then a fourth. I felt panicky. I knew I could not control John's drinking, and I was afraid that he might become agitated enough to run riot on the plane, even attempting to dismantle it in the same way he had attacked Harold Seider's bedroom.

"You've had enough," I said quietly. "Please tell me what's on your mind."

John turned and stared at me. There was a furious glint in his eyes. "How could you do this to me?" he shouted.

"What did I do?"

"I know I shouldn't bring this up. I know it's none of my business, but I can't help it. I can't tell you how much you've hurt me."

He ordered another drink. There was a pained expression on his face.

"How could you do this to me?" he repeated as he gulped the drink. Then he put the drink down and turned slowly to me. He grabbed my arm and slowly began to twist it. He was like a child playing with a toy, a toy he had suddenly decided he wanted to break. I let out a scream and tried to pull away. He twisted even harder. I froze and did not move. "I have no right to bring this up," he said again.

"Say it! Please say it!"

John opened his mouth to speak, but the words wouldn't come. Instead he dropped my arm and grabbed my hair, yanking my head back against the seat. He looked very confused. It was the look that overcame him when he was drunk. All the seats in the first-class section were taken. I thought I might escape to the tourist section, yet I was afraid that if I got up, John would really explode. Those were the moments with John that filled me with real terror. So I sat perfectly still, not knowing what he would do next.

Then he suddenly screamed, "Yoko told me something about you, something awful."

"What did she tell you?"

Finally John told me that Yoko had discovered the name of someone I had once gone out with—a man John also knew—and she had described my affair with this man to John. "The guy said that your libido wasn't that great," John snapped, wrenching my head back again. John, who was an insanely jealous man, was always deeply threatened by the thought that any woman he loved had ever been with, or had even considered being with, another man.

I looked around. The people near us were pretending they weren't listening, but it was obvious that they were. I turned back to him.

"That was three years ago. Three years ago you and I never dreamed we would be together."

John yanked at my hair. "Yoko told me that you only slept with him once and you didn't have enough libido."

"I didn't love him the way I love you," I pleaded. "I felt awkward and I probably didn't satisfy him."

I couldn't look John straight in the eyes, not because I was embarrassed, but because I couldn't bear seeing the deranged look on his face.

"Yoko wanted to know how I could be happy with a woman who didn't have enough libido. I defended you to Yoko. I told her you had enough libido for me. I told her your libido was fine. I had to defend you to Yoko. I had to keep defendin' you."

I looked at John. My words, as logical as they were, had not gotten through, and automatically I thought back to that moment when Yoko told me she knew where his deepest fears lay.

John had to know that a woman responds differently to different men; he had to know that I found him a wonderful lover. I could not remember a day that we had been together that we had not made love, even during the most awful moments in Los Angeles. Still, once again John preferred to ignore the truth in order to drown himself in self-pity. I felt sick and sad as I watched him continue to swig vodka, stopping to scream at me or to attack me physically. No one on the plane said or did anything, ignoring us even though they were aware of what was going on. The stewardesses patrolled the aisles, refilling John's glass, looking the other way while John yanked my hair and twisted my arms.

"I'm hurt. . . .What you did hurt me. . . .You hurt me. . . . I'm hurt," he wailed as he grew progressively drunker. "Because of what you did, I had to defend you to Yoko."

The more he said it, the worse I felt, not because of what I had done three years before but because his conversation with Yoko had been able to erase in twenty minutes the pleasures of the weeks that had just passed. John raged on for an hour, and as his anger mounted in ferocity I realized that at any second he might really hurt me or rise from his feet to attempt to do damage to the plane. My concern, my fear, and my sadness made me dizzy. My stomach began to throb.

Then John wrenched back, leaned forward, and began to vomit. I grabbed for the vomit bag and put it underneath him. He heaved and heaved, literally seeming to be vomiting up his guts. When he was finished, he collapsed against his seat, white-faced, sick, and in pain.

A stewardess approached us, smiled, and said, "Can I get him another drink?"

At that moment even the stewardess seemed insane.

"No. Get us some napkins, a cloth, and some more vomit bags."

The stewardess returned with them, and I did the best I could to clean John off. Holding his stomach, he moaned, "I'm hurt. I'm really hurt." Finally he passed out.

I had an awful headache and I held my head in my hands. There was the smell of vomit in the air. I was so upset and my stomach was so jumpy that the smell got to me and I wanted to retch also, but I couldn't. By the time the plane reached Los Angeles we both looked like corpses.

Mal Evans was waiting for us at the airport. During the ride to Harold Seider's apartment John turned to me and asked, "What happened on the plane?" He remembered nothing. I quietly described what had occurred.

"I had no right to do that. That was way before me," he said in disbelief.

"Please, let's forget it." I was still too shaken by the incident to want to discuss it.

"I was just so hurt by what Yoko said, by the way she threw it in me face. I'm very, very sorry."

Changing the subject, I asked, "Mal, how is the apartment coming along?"

"It's almost done."

"Is me guitar fixed?" John asked.

Mal hesitated. "No. I brought it in yesterday."

"And May's necklace?"

"What necklace?"

John tensed. "I'll buy you another," he said to me. "I promise. I'll buy you another."

At the *Sgt. Pepper's* opening. PHOTO: RON GALELLA

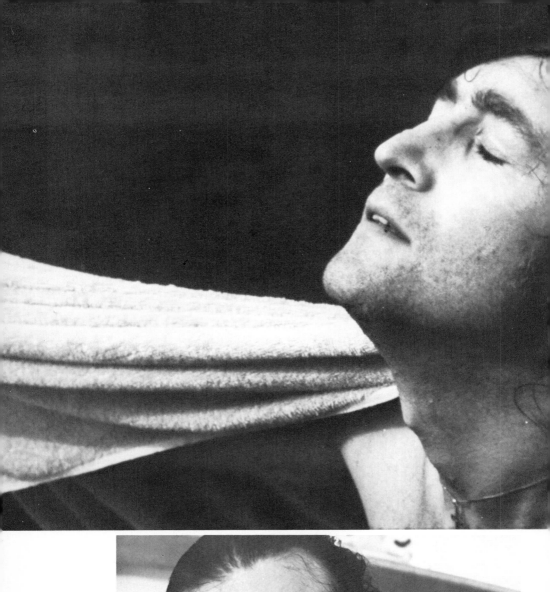

Summer 1974,
off Long Island.

Julian, summer 1974.

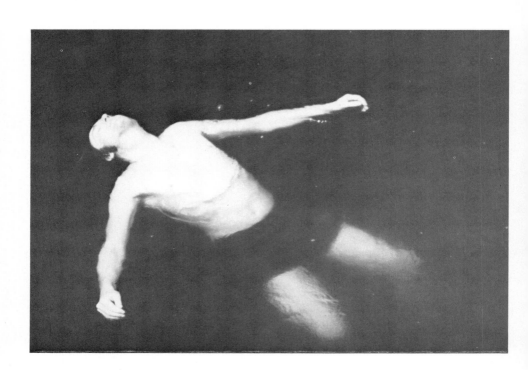

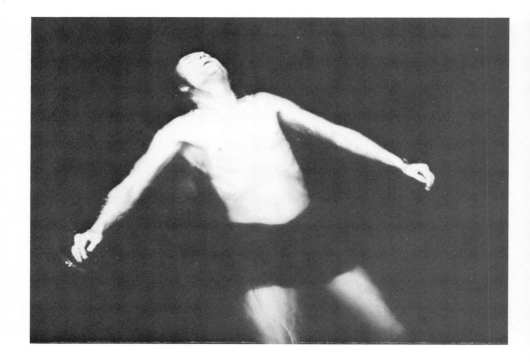

Long
Island,
1974.

In Elton John's suite at the Sherry Netherland,
New York, 1974. PHOTOS: MIKE HEWITSON

With Ringo and Tony King, Hollywood, 1974.

Aunt Mimi at her house in Bournemouth, England, 1975.

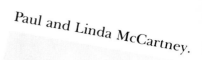
Paul and Linda McCartney.

The entrance to
our E. 52nd St.
apartment.

Mick Jagger and friend.

David Bowie and friend.

Greetings and likenesses.

May's last message from John, a fan's greeting that he rerouted
to her from Capetown, South Africa.

1974.

When we got to the apartment, I opened the door. I was relieved to find that most of the damage had been repaired. Upstairs, however, we discovered that the bed was still broken and cinder blocks had been put underneath it to hold it up. John had the capacity to forget anything, and until that reminder of the Kotex incident, he had totally forgotten that he had literally tried to rip Harold's apartment to shreds.

He sat down on the broken bed. I could tell that he was filled with remorse. "I'm sorry. I can't tell you how sorry I am. It was so hard for me to hear that there had been anyone else but me. I was so hurt. It made me crazy."

I sat beside him and took his hand. "We're back, and there's plenty we've got to do. What happened on the plane is over. Please forget it."

"I can't forget it. I'm sorry. I want you to know how sorry I am."

"I'm sorry it happened, too. But we've gone a whole month without an incident like this and we've seen that we can have a month that's fun and happy. Let's go to sleep, and tomorrow we'll begin again."

John looked gratefully at me. "You understand everything. You're the first woman I've ever met who'll put up with me."

"John, being with you is much, much better than I ever thought anything could be. I can live with the bad moments. I hate them and I wish they wouldn't happen, but I don't know how to stop them."

"I'm sorry. I'm sorry. I'm sorry." As he said it tears came to his eyes and John began to weep. Then he began to push his head against me as if somehow he would climb back into the womb. I put my arms around him and held him tight, amazed how at moments like that John could regress into infancy, regress to the moment of birth, even attempt to make himself unborn. I cradled him in my arms and rocked him gently until the sobbing finally subsided. Then I got some Kleenex and wiped away his tears. Finally he calmed down, and we undressed and went to sleep on the broken bed, holding each other gently throughout the night.

The next morning the phone rang. John was sound

asleep. Without any hesitation at all I picked it up. "Good morning, Yoko," I said. Before she had a chance to reply I said, "You told John things yesterday that were none of his business or yours."

"May," she replied with a giggle, "you hear things and sometimes you just can't help repeating them. You know how those things are." She sounded genuinely surprised, and I realized that even she did not know when John would or would not repeat what she had told him.

"I don't know how these things are," I said coldly.

"Oh, May, I didn't know he would repeat them." She giggled again.

"It's not John's fault for repeating them. It's your fault for prying information out of people and then repeating what you hear."

She knew she was caught and she responded by giggling some more.

"There's nothing harmless about making other people unhappy," I told her.

Yoko giggled some more.

"It's not your job to give John any information about me. The information about me comes from *me*. Yoko, you're not doing your job!"

This time it was I who slammed down the phone.

When John woke up, he asked, "Is everything all right?"

"Yes." I didn't know whether or not everything was all right at all. All I wanted to do was forge on. "You better call Yoko back," I said. Then I went into the kitchen and began to make coffee.

14

That afternoon we once again began placing calls to Phil Spector. None of them was returned.

"I'll get the tapes, book the studio time, and I'll finish the fuckin' tracks meself," said John.

We called the Record Plant and learned that at the end of each session Spector had taken the tapes with him. If we could find Spector, we could get the tapes.

"We could cut some new songs," I suggested.

"I'm not ready to do something new. I want to finish what I've got," John said with finality. He was still afraid to work on his own. So we continued to call Spector. Finally we were told that he had been in an automobile accident and was in seclusion in a sanatorium in Palm Springs.

Then we called Harold Seider to ask for his help in retrieving the missing tapes and to find out what our legal position was with reference to Spector. We also called Capitol Records to explain why the album had ground to a halt.

John's mood was extremely dark. He had come back to Los Angeles to make music, and that album was the only music he felt he was ready to make. Yet, there was nothing he could do, so he did his best to push his distress out of his mind.

Within a day or two after we returned we learned from the rock 'n' roll grapevine that Ringo was in town. John loved Ringo very much and still felt very brotherly and protective toward him, so we began to see him every day, along with Ringo's close friend Harry Nilsson. Harry proved himself a brilliant nonstop talker, and John grew fascinated with Harry's chatter as well as his compulsive search for excitement.

I must admit that I was as fascinated with Harry as John was. He was a truly funny, bright man. He also could hold his liquor—something John could not do. With each drink Harry took, he actually seemed to grow more in control, while John became sloppier and sloppier. Again it was one of those situations in which John preferred surrendering to a stronger personality.

For all their hell-raising, nothing terrible happened at first. Then Ringo told us he was leaving town and suggested that we move into his duplex apartment at the Beverly Wilshire and take the upstairs bedroom, while his manager, Hilary Gerrard, remained downstairs. John and I loved the idea. Ten days after we returned to Los Angeles, we packed up and moved once again.

A few days later Harry suggested that we all go to Las Vegas. We had a lot of fun together, and after we returned, John said to Harry, "I think I'd like to produce an album with you."

Harry was a wonderful singer, writer, and arranger, and he, like John, was eager to make a hit album. The two of them needed a focus; I hoped this album would be it.

Harry loved the idea. "What should we do?" he asked.

"What would you like to do?"

"I'd like to do my favorite golden oldies."

"No. You've got to do your songs. We can make it half originals, half of your favorites."

We saw Harry every day, and the minute John and he got together they would begin to talk about the album. They were both wildly enthusiastic and began throwing song titles back and forth. John would pick up his guitar and strum each of the songs to see if they really wanted to do it. When they agreed on a tune, like Bob Dylan's "Subterranean Homesick Blues" or one of John's all-time favorites, "Save the Last Dance for Me," they'd discuss the approach they wanted to take. John would play the song in a number of different tempos. "How does it feel? How does it feel?" he'd keep asking me, wanting to know if the approach made me feel happy or sad or gave me a sexy feeling. Harry also played us a number of his new songs. There was not a happy tune in the lot. At that point in his life Harry's songs seemed focused on losing—losing in life as well as losing in love. They seemed a startling contrast to the more upbeat golden oldies like "Rock Around the Clock," which John and Harry planned to do.

While Harry and John were busy discussing material, Bruce Grakal, the lawyer Harry shared with Ringo, took over the job of organizing the production end of the album. Grakal was a professional, and things quickly began to fall into place. Dates were set in early April to begin recording at the Record Plant.

At the end of the week Ringo returned to Los Angeles. When he learned about the album, he declared, "I wouldn't miss this for the world." John also asked Jim Keltner to play drums along with Ringo and had his favorite bass player, Klaus Voormann, and Klaus's girl friend, Cynthia Webb, fly to Los Angeles from England to play on the album. Bobby Keys and Trevor Lawrence were asked to play horns, and Kenny Ascher was invited to play keyboards. John also asked Jesse Ed Davis to play guitar.

Harry's friends seemed to include every hard drinker who happened to live in or was passing through Los Angeles. Among them was Keith Moon, with whom he had once shared an apartment in London. Moon was also staying at the Beverly Wilshire Hotel.

"John, I'd like to play on the album, too," Keith said one day when we ran into him in the lobby of the hotel.

"It will be me pleasure," John replied. Then we had three drummers: Ringo, Jim Keltner, and Moon.

Whenever we ran into Moon, I found him to have wonderful manners and a surprising amount of gentleness. The world of rock was filled with stories about Keith's wild behavior, one of the strangest of which Mick Jagger told us over our favorite kind of dinner, Chinese food, a few nights later.

"A few nights ago, I heard noises in my suite," said Mick. (The Jaggers were also staying at the Wilshire.) "I thought there was a burglar. The only weapon I could find was a lamp.

I picked it up and tiptoed into the living room. I was going to bash the burglar over the head. The 'burglar' was Keith. He had broken into my suite."

"How did he get in?" John asked.

"You won't believe it. He had climbed onto the terrace of his apartment and had made his way across the wall of the building, going from terrace to terrace. He climbed all the way around the building. Can you imagine him hanging off the side of the hotel at four in the morning? Can you imagine anyone doing that? He could have fallen off and killed himself. It's the sort of thing you only do in movies.

"What would have happened if I had had a gun? I could have jumped up and shot him in the dark."

It was turning into a charged time. Just as Keith and Mick had surfaced out of nowhere, suddenly Elton John reappeared to tell us about a birthday party for Ricci Martin, Dean Martin's son. The party was to be held at the home of Martin's estranged wife, Jeanne, and the guest list included Elizabeth Taylor.

John was very excited. "I've never met Elizabeth," he said. "I'm dyin' to go."

The party took place in a lavish Beverly Hills mansion, and there was a large buffet table and a bar. John and I stood in one corner, searching for stars we had never seen in person before. While we looked over the crowd, everyone was busy staring at us. Even though John always liked to meet really famous people, he was still the most famous person in the room. We slowly made our way through the house, chatting with whoever approached us.

"Where's Elizabeth?" John asked. "I want to see Elizabeth."

Forty minutes after we arrived, Elizabeth Taylor sailed into the room. The party stopped dead while everyone turned to stare at her. There was a star! I was surprised to see how small she was, because everything about her was larger than life. Her hair was teased up in an elaborate hairdo that towered above her head. Her extraordinary violet eyes were lined in thick beads of violet eyeshadow. She made no concession to her weight and she was costumed in a paneled paisley dress, each panel a different shade of pink. Around her neck she wore one huge diamond surrounded by a cluster of large emeralds. She was dazzling.

Like teenage boys, John and Elton nervously approached her. She beamed when she saw them. "Oh," she said, "I'm so pleased to meet you." John and Elton responded to her genuine delight. They both did their best to amuse her. She laughed merrily at their lines and threw in a number of her own.

When David Bowie arrived, she seized his arm and said, "David, do you know John?"

"No, but I've always wanted to meet him." Bowie flashed his bright smile at John. There was a look of genuine admiration in his eyes. John, who found Bowie's music fascinating, was very cordial. David had great charm and was also very funny. The dialogue began to flow even more quickly.

The group finally broke up, and David announced, "I've got to go. I've got to go." He turned to leave. Later in the evening we found him in deep conversation with Elizabeth Taylor on a couch in a deserted room at the back of the house. John and I stared at them. The screen goddess and the porcelain-faced, orange-haired rock star made a startling-looking couple. Yet, sitting there, gazing into each other's eyes, they seemed to be long-lost friends, sharing their most intimate secrets. "May, John, join us," Elizabeth called out when she spotted us, and we sat down beside them. In a few minutes all of the remaining guests had crowded into the little back room, and once again we were surrounded by onlookers.

On the way home John and I talked about how much we had liked Elizabeth Taylor. "She's not rock 'n' roll," said John. "She's not like us. She comes from another school. We get crazy as we get older. She's been trained to deal with things."

Each day John and Harry grew more enthusiastic about the album they planned to make; they had already agreed upon most of the material, and John was in wonderful spirits.

The informal way in which they worked seemed to be producing results, and I was delighted by the lack of secrecy and confusion that had typified the meetings with Spector.

When Yoko called, John told her about the album, but he did not respond at all to her questions and comments. Once, when he got off the phone, he turned to me and said, "Guess what Yoko told me Spinozza gave her?"

I shrugged my shoulders.

"Yoko said he gave her a good fuck." John smiled happily. "Isn't it wonderful? I was beginning to worry she wasn't going to get it."

At night Harry and John and I still continued to pal around together, and John continued to drink, but even though Harry continued to prod him, John did not get out of control.

Still, I felt better when Harry was not around; too soon there came an evening that would bear out my fears: the appearance of the Smothers Brothers at the Troubadour.

The engagement was designed as a comeback, an attempt to relaunch Dick's and Tommy's television careers by allowing them to demonstrate their comedic skills. Every major television executive in Los Angeles had been invited to their opening, as well as a multitude of celebrities who were friends and fans of the Smothers Brothers and who were eager to lend their support on that strategic evening.

Harry joined us, and before we went off to the second show, he and John had a few drinks. When we got to the club, hordes of photographers were milling around. I parked the car in the Troubadour parking lot, and we made our way to the entrance. As soon as the photographers spotted John, they began to click away. By then John and I knew that if we just maintained neutral expressions, the photographers would concentrate on him and then ignore me.

Finally we got inside the Troubadour to find the entire club buzzing with anticipation about the return of the Smothers Brothers. We were ushered into the VIP section. The right-hand side of the club was always reserved for celebrities, and we were seated at a long table in a group that included Peter Lawford, Pam Grier, Jack Haley, Jr., writer Gwen Davis, and *Welcome Back, Kotter* producer Alan Sacks. We were introduced to everyone, and everyone was very friendly. The small talk was pleasant, and everyone seemed eager to see the Smothers Brothers.

"John, we're at a table of fans," I said.

He smiled. "I'm a fan, too."

I began to chat with Peter Lawford about my favorite MGM movie musicals when the waitress approached the table to take our drink orders.

John stared at her. "Yeah, right," he said. "I'm the fuckin' asshole with the Kotex on me head."

It took only that remark for me to realize that John might be in the mood to let go; Harry sensed it also. Someone suggested we order "milk shakes," double brandy alexanders, and John did. He downed the drink as soon as it arrived.

"Let's have another," John said, and another round was ordered.

While waiting for the drinks John began to hum one of his favorite rhythm and blues songs, "I Can't Stand the Rain." I took his humming as an omen; that was the song he had wanted to hear the night of the Kotex incident at the very same club. Then Harry joined in, and the two of them began to sing out loud, banging spoons and knives against glasses and salt cellars to create an instant rhythm section. The people at our table seemed fascinated by the music John and Harry were making; yet, it was obvious they felt that it was not the time or the place for it. "That's really wonderful," said Lawford. "You'd be a great opening act for the Smothers Brothers." He smiled at John; John smiled back.

Peter Lawford was also drinking brandy alexanders. John reached for Lawford's glass and gulped down his drink.

Harry sang louder. As they continued to sing a silence pervaded the room; everyone was listening. Suddenly our table was surrounded by photographers. At one point John reached over and smiled at me. "Do you know I love you?" he said softly.

"I love you."

John grabbed me and started to kiss me. The photographers went wild, and flashbulbs began to explode in our faces. "John, everyone is going to know."

"I don't care." He squeezed my hand and he kissed me harder.

Reporters began to call out questions: "Who is she? What's her name?" They had a scoop and they knew it.

I never wanted the press to find out about us; neither did John, and we had agreed to be discreet in public, so that even if we were photographed together, there would be no evidence that we were involved. The following week a picture of us would appear in *Time*, announcing our relationship to the entire world. In that one moment John had undone all of the public secrecy we had maintained during the previous seven months—had undone it in front of the entire Hollywood press corps.

"The secret is out," he said drunkenly. "Let's have another drink." He had two more doubles before the show began.

The lights started to dim as a signal that the show was about to begin. The Smothers Brothers were announced, but if anything Harry and John sang even louder. When Dick and Tommy made their entrance, there was a huge ovation. When it died down, John and Harry could still be heard singing. The comedians began their act and realized that two shows were going on: theirs and the one in the audience.

"They love you, John!" Harry said.

John sang louder. Harry joined in again and they banged the table and continued to gulp down drinks.

The Smothers Brothers forged on, like the professionals they were. Occasionally John stopped singing, and I thought I was in safe territory. I was wrong. John and Harry loved Tommy but hated Dick Smothers. John looked up at the stage when Dick began to speak, smiled drunkenly, and shouted out, "Hey, Smothers Brother, fuck a cow." Then he began to sing again. Then he stopped again to yell, "Fuck you, Smothers Brother," at Dick Smothers. Harry yelled too, and John would try to top him with an even louder "Fuck you."

"Harry, tell John to stop it," I hissed at Harry. "Tell him to stop it or I'm going to kill you."

"They love it," Harry replied. Then he turned to John. "Hey, man, they really love you."

John screamed out another "Fuck you."

From the stage Tommy Smothers said gently, "Is that my good friend Harry out there?"

By that time our table was in an uproar. So was everyone else. From all parts of the room people began to hiss and jeer. "Lennon, shut up," people began to call out.

"They love you," Harry told John. "Do you see how they love you?"

John smiled benignly. "Fuck 'em all."

"Hey, man, Tommy's a friend of mine," Alan Sacks said to John.

"Fuck you, man," John replied.

Peter Lawford glared at John. "Look," he said, "I didn't come to see you. I came to see the Smothers Brothers." He rose and stormed away from the table.

As John grew noisier so did the audience. "The Smothers Brothers are on the right side," a woman called out.

"They were fucked over, and now you're fucking them over," someone else shouted.

"They're on your side. They need your support," screamed someone else.

Then someone yelled, "How will *you* sleep after what you're doing to two guys who need your help?"

Those comments had no effect. The singing and the cursing went on and on.

Then the Smothers Brothers' manager, Ken Fritz, approached our table. "Look," he screamed, "we've worked hard for this, and I'm not going to let you fuck it up." He grabbed John's shoulder, and John, his sudden strength surfacing, rose in a rage. As he stood up he overturned the table. At that moment Peter Lawford charged from the bar area, leading the Troubadour bartenders into the battle. From nowhere people reached out and began to take swings at John. They had become enraged and felt betrayed by him.

For a moment everyone began to throw wild punches at each other. The bartenders as well as the Troubadour bouncers surrounded Harry and John, forming a wedge as they hurled them away through the angry crowd. "May—May—where are you?" John screamed. He was in a total panic.

"I'm right behind you," I screamed back.

Finally all of us were hurled through the Troubadour doors onto Santa Monica Boulevard. There was a mob of photographers waiting in front of the club, and suddenly one of them began to scream, "Lennon's hit me! He's hit me!" Surrounded by the Troubadour staff, John was incapable of hitting anybody, and I suspect the photographer had been slammed by the doors when they were flung open.

"He hit me, he hit me," the photographer continued to yell.

"Sure, lady, sure!" I screamed.

Followed by the crowd, we were shoved toward the parking lot. When we got there, John suddenly leaped onto the parking attendant and wrestled him to the ground. The attendant, a young man, was astonished suddenly to find himself with John Lennon on top of him. Pinned to the ground by John, he looked up and smiled lovingly at him. It was obvious that it was the most unbelievable and magical moment of his life. John was momentarily calmed by the love in that young man's eyes, and he allowed the stunned attendant to wriggle loose.

When we finally got our car, Harry insisted that we go with him to another party. "I don't want to go," said John.

"Then I'll go with May." Harry grabbed me.

"Get your fucking hands off me," I screamed.

Harry had never heard me curse. Astonished, he let go. I drove, and Harry insisted on giving us directions, and John insisted that I listen to Harry, and we wound up in the Hollywood hills at a party in the house of some people none of us had ever met. For an hour John and Harry serenaded a surprised roomful of strangers. Then I drove Harry back to his apartment. John did not want to go home, but I couldn't deal with any of it anymore. I had had enough. "Get out," I told John. "I'll pick you up in the morning."

I left John and Harry in front of Harry's apartment house.

Early in the morning Yoko called me at the hotel. She was

furious. Her phone had been ringing off the hook all night and she hadn't been able to reach John to square their stories to the press. "Where is he?" she asked angrily.

"He's sleeping it off at Harry's."

She asked for Harry's number. Then she said, "How could you do this?"

"I didn't do it," I said. "They did."

Yoko didn't listen. "How could you let this happen?"

"Yoko, I did my best to stop it."

"This is your fault."

I said nothing. I was too exhausted to argue.

"You do know this is your fault, don't you?" I kept quiet. "What you've done amazes me." I didn't say a word. Finally, when she realized that I was not going to respond, she slammed down the phone.

After her call I went down to the hotel lobby and picked up the morning papers. There were headlines and huge photographs of John and me splashed over the front pages. I read the news stories. The press had learned my name and had described me as "John's private secretary" and "the new mystery woman in his life." When I saw the coverage, I knew why Yoko was so angry. I told the front desk that we weren't taking any calls. Then I went back upstairs and called John at Harry's apartment. "Have you seen the papers?" I asked.

"Yes. I couldn't have done all this," he replied.

"You did, John, you did." John asked me to send telegrams of apology and flowers to the Smothers Brothers, Ken Fritz, Peter Lawford, and Jack Haley, Jr., which I did.

"Yoko called," he continued. "She was very upset."

"She called me, too. John," I asked, "are you ready to come back to the hotel?"

"Yes."

When I got to Harry's apartment, Harry's phone was ringing nonstop. I took a few of the calls. The press wanted to know why John had left Yoko, how long we had been together, whether John was planning to get divorced, and whether we planned to marry. They were calling everybody. I learned that after his show Tommy Smothers had gone to Peter Lawford's house and had walked into Lawford's living room wearing John's glasses, which Tommy's wife had grabbed during the melee. Despite the uproar caused by John, Lawford's guests were fascinated. They had spent the rest of the evening trying on John's glasses to get the feel of what it was like to be *John Lennon*. I also learned that we had been discussed by Rona Barrett on *Good Morning America*.

As soon as I got John back to the hotel the phone rang. It was Yoko, whom the operator had put through. She wanted to speak to John, and when he got on the phone, I could tell by his answers that she was insisting that somehow what had happened had been all my doing. Exasperated, John got off the phone, but Yoko persisted in calling all afternoon.

"We have to be more careful," John said between her calls. Then he added, "I have to be more careful." Then he shrugged. "It's too fuckin' late now."

That night we were scheduled to go to the American Film Institute dinner at the Century Plaza Hotel, honoring James Cagney. It was an event we had been looking forward to for weeks, since Cagney was one of our all-time favorite movie stars.

The press went wild when they saw us. They screamed at us and grabbed at us, and we literally had to battle our way through them into the hotel.

"May, May," they screamed. "May, how about a picture?"

"John, hug her."

"Kiss her for us."

When we finally got inside, John caught his breath and said, "I can't believe it. That was more press than I got when I was a Beatle."

I didn't want the attention. I wasn't used to it and I didn't know how to handle it; I also suspected it would drive Yoko into a frenzy. That suspicion was the worst of all.

At the end of March, John was presented with a bill for our one-month stay at the Beverly Wilshire Hotel. The bill came to around ten thousand dollars. The bill had been run up not only by us but also by Ringo, Hilary, Harry, and their guests. Even though it was being charged to Apple, John was upset by the extravagance. The part of him that wanted to live reasonably was angered by the fact that the part of him that had no control had run wild once again.

He was also worried about Harry. While John continued to drink and carouse with him, John was not the *singer* on the album. Now, with recording about to start, on top of everything, Harry had contracted the flu and with it a terrible cough. Together, we all hit on the idea of going to Palm Springs the following weekend—ostensibly to "dry out in the desert." Harry handled the arrangements, and we found ourselves at a quiet, cozy, sleepy place at the base of a mountain with accommodations for only forty guests. Behind it was a small swimming pool as well as a Jacuzzi.

"I can't wait until tomorrow. I'm going to lie in the sun all day," I told John.

John smiled. "So am I."

The weather that Saturday was gorgeous, and after a lazy day and a glorious sunset, Harry said, "There's a good restaurant on the top of the mountain. Let's go there and have a nightcap."

We got into our car and drove to the aerial tram, which took people to the top of the mountain, and parked near it. The tram consisted of one small car that could hold no more than thirty people. There were no seats on the tram, and when it was full, the occupants had to stand crammed next to each other. As it moved slowly up the mountain we stood watching the view from one of the windows.

The restaurant at the top of the mountain was charming. Harry ordered coffee and brandy for all of us. I was so relaxed, I even drank a brandy myself.

"It's time for another round," Harry announced.

"Not for me," I said.

Harry ordered the drinks. When John finished his, I could see that he had become a little tipsy. It had also suddenly become very chilly.

We talked some more, then Harry looked at John and said, "Let's go." We all got up.

As we walked to the tram we stared up at the stars. It was a remarkable night. The sky seemed black, making the light of the stars appear even more intense.

The tram, the last of the evening, was very crowded, and quite a few people on it were drunk and noisy. They waved to John, and John waved back.

During the ride down the mountain the current failed on the tram and the lights blacked out. Everyone laughed. Then people around us began to neck. Suddenly I felt a hand on my rear end. I jumped. Then I saw another hand reach over to grope John. There was another hand on me, fondling my breasts. It was very dark, but not that dark. I could see hands crawling over Harry. The entire tram had come to life with people who wanted to grope John and anyone who traveled with him because we presumably had been touched by the magic of a Beatle. I stood there paralyzed while hands investigated all of us, watching while strangers attempted to masturbate John and Harry.

John looked at me and said quietly, "It's nothing. This has always happened whenever we've gone out in public."

"What do I do?" I asked.

"Enjoy it," he replied sardonically.

Then a woman who must have been in her fifties pushed her way to us, looked at John, and said, "Squeeze my tits. Please squeeze my tits." More women continued to rub against John and Harry. Everyone wanted the thrill of rubbing their private parts against all of us.

It was astonishing, very funny, and horrible all at the same time. When we finally got to the ground, we made a run for it. We dashed to our car, pursued by the crowd, which was anxious for one last moment of physical contact before we left. John laughed it off. The experience once again reminded me of how unnatural life had been for John, whose fame was so extraordinary that it had been virtually impossible for him during a major portion of his life even to venture into the real world.

When we got back to the hotel, Harry said, "Let's take a Jacuzzi," and, as usual, following his lead, we changed into our bathing suits. When we met at the Jacuzzi, we found that Harry had brought a bottle of liquor with him, despite the fact that we were supposed to be drying out.

"To our health," he said, took a slug, and passed the bottle around. John took a drink. "Have another one," Harry told John.

"John's had enough," I said.

John looked at me and frowned. He was having fun and did not want me to interfere with it. Harry gave John the bottle, and John took another gulp. Half the bottle was emptied before Harry said, "Now it's time for the Jacuzzi."

He got into the water; so did John. As he was about to pass John the bottle I slipped in between them. My intention was not to stop John from getting the bottle, but it appeared that way to him. He turned and looked at me, a hurt expression on his face. He was drunk and looked very confused. Slowly he reached out, put his hands to my throat, and began to strangle me. As his hands closed tighter I screamed out and tried to pull away, but he was incredibly strong. Everyone froze. It seemed as if no one could believe what they were seeing. It couldn't have been more than a few seconds, but it seemed an eternity with John's hands around my neck. Finally Harry snapped to life and pulled John off me. I must say I believe Harry Nilsson saved my life that night. I dashed from the Jacuzzi into our hotel room.

Later everyone came in. Harry reached for the bottle and I shook my head. John looked at me and smiled sweetly. By then he was so drunk, he looked as if he could not see me at all. Slowly he walked over to me, picked me up, and hurled me across the room. I landed with a thud against the wall. I picked myself up, ran into the bathroom, and locked the door.

I turned on the light and looked at myself in the bathroom mirror. There were finger marks on my throat and bruises on my back. I really wasn't calm at all: I was in shock. For the first time I thought about leaving John. I knew he did not know what he was doing, but I also realized that being drunk does not make you another person; it allows whatever is inside to come to the surface. I had to accept the fact that the murderous rage that was in John had always been there and was a permanent part of his personality. People who had seen him drunk agreed that he was the worst drunk they had ever seen and were amazed by the physical strength that emerged when he drank. How could I stay with someone who was so dangerous?

I was heartbroken. I was so much in love with John, it was very hard for me to blame him for what had happened. But I was enraged. So what I did was blame Harry, who was not the cause of John's behavior but certainly was his partner in it. I hated people like Harry who exploited the hideous part of John.

I also know I must have been crazy to have put up with incidents like those. I realized that in my own way, I too became a child then, just as John did. I became Little May, the serious, duty-driven child who had seen my father continually hit my mother and who had also been beaten often by him. From what I had seen it was expected that you would be beaten when you lived with and loved a man. In my family, believe it or not, behavior like this was thought to be unpleasant but was not considered extraordinary.

Still, I had also been away from that life for a long time, and that was not the way a man and woman had a relationship. My mother had always wanted to arrange a marriage for me, the way hers had been. I may have been living with John Lennon, but I thought John would help me escape the path my parents had trained me to follow. I saw I was instead being cast in the mold I had always quietly but determinedly resisted. I was very angry.

For the next half hour I heard screams and giggles. I hated to think about what was going on. Finally, the noise subsided, and I heard everyone leave the room.

I opened the door and stepped back into the living room. Then I looked outside. There was no one there either. I left our room and went to Mal Evans's room to ask if I could sleep there. Just as I got to his door I saw Harry and John walking around the corner of the hotel. Harry was naked. Palm Springs at night was extremely still, and John and Harry were noisy enough to awaken the entire town, but there was nothing I could do. I ducked into another room and slept on the couch.

I was still there the next morning when John came in, all

smiles and sunshine. "You're up early this morning, me little Fung Yee."

"John, sit down," I said. He did. Then I described the evening to him. He looked at my throat and back. Then he knelt beside me and started to cry. "You've been so good to me. Why did I do this? Please tell me you forgive me. Tell me you forgive me," he said through his tears.

Still stunned by what had occurred, I said very little. Awhile later we learned that during the night the hotel manager had caught John and Harry frolicking on the hotel lawn. He had quietly asked them to leave in the morning. He did not call the police; he just wanted to preserve the peaceful atmosphere.

Throughout the ride back to Los Angeles I did my best to disguise my wounds, but I was a nervous wreck.

The next few days passed very quietly, and John was gentle and sweet to me. Then he had a brainstorm.

"There should be an asylum somewhere for aged rock 'n' rollers. Then we can all be put in padded cells where we belong." He thought for a second. "Let's open an asylum. We should all rent a house and live together. Then we can watch Harry, save money, and make sure all the musicians get to the studio on time when we begin to work on Harry's album."

I shuddered. Meanwhile John told Harry, who naturally loved the idea, and Harry, always the organizer, had Bruce Grakal look for a house. Before I knew it John and Harry had invited Ringo, Keith Moon, Hilary Gerrard, and Klaus Voormann and his girl friend, Cynthia Webb, to live with us.

John loved the ocean and wanted to live near it, and in a day or two a large house on Santa Monica Beach had been located—a house that had five bedrooms. We drove out to look at it. It was a large, airy, two-storied house with a pool behind it, and it had direct access to the beach. The kitchen, a mirrored dining room, and a small study were on the first floor, as well as a large living room that housed a piano and a billiard table. A spiral staircase led to the bedrooms and a den. The rental agent told us that it had been built by Louis B. Mayer and had once been Peter Lawford's house. The rumor was that it was the house in which Marilyn Monroe's affairs with Jack and Bobby Kennedy had taken place. John was intrigued to learn that we would be sleeping in the same bedroom in which those alleged assignations had occurred.

On the night before we moved I turned to John and said, "You know, John, March was a little frantic. I hope April will be a little calmer."

He laughed. "What are you going to do when we all go crazy at the same time?"

My face must have turned an ashen white. John put his arm around me and said quietly, "Don't worry. I'm not goin' to go crazy this time. What I'm gonna do is make fuckin' sure Harry's album gets done."

15

No matter what John had told me beforehand, I was convinced that I was moving into an insane asylum. I discovered, however, that the inmates in our beach house may have been insane, but only at night. Stunned by the daylight, they remained calm and quiet until sundown. In the early evenings we would all head out to the studio and record until eleven or twelve. By midnight Harry, Keith, and Ringo would be bursting with energy and they would set out for the Rainbow or On the Rox—usually to straggle back just before sunrise.

John, however, did not go with them and therefore never allowed himself to get out of control. My life on the beach was much, much easier than I had ever expected it would be.

John may have been insecure about his own singing and playing and disappointed about the fact that he had not yet produced a number-one solo album of his own, but he was still always at his happiest and best in the studio. The Nilsson sessions were no exception. John made sure every musician understood what he was aiming for and exactly what was expected. During those sessions, although the material was uneven at best, John was in total command. Everyone was so happy that no one seemed to sense that the results were not at all what they could have been—not even John. The fact that John was feeling fine and working at capacity but was unaware that the album was deficient puzzled me. I assumed something was on his mind; he did not offer a clue. Somehow, I told my-self, with musicians as capable as these, the album would have to work out.

Because everyone loved John and was delighted to be liv-ing with him, a good feeling also prevailed in our house. When we moved in, John and I took the master bedroom, Keith took the tiny cubicle next to the master bedroom, and Klaus Voor-mann and Cynthia Webb moved into the equally tiny bedroom next to Keith's, while Harry and Hilary moved into the two small bedrooms at the other end of the floor. Ringo, however, wanted a bedroom with a bath attached, so we converted the den across the hall from us into a bedroom for him. The only decoration in the den was a framed photograph of John F. Kennedy. Ringo, who disliked daylight, kept his blinds drawn at all times. I jokingly labeled his bedroom "the den of dark-ness."

The house came with full-time help, a Mexican couple named Armando and Nita. I was delighted; otherwise I knew I would wind up not only taking care of John but everybody else as well. Armando and Nita did not speak much English but had had plenty of experience taking care of large houses. There was a lot of work for them to do, for, like John, all of the guests were accustomed to living in hotels or to being waited on at home. They never hung up their clothes. Nor did they ever make their beds or even think of doing their own laundry or boiling their own water for a cup of coffee. They were used to maid service and room service around the clock as being an automatic part of their lives, and they expected their rooms to be tidied up, their laundry to be done, and meals ready to be served to them at any time of day or night.

Armando and Nita became the equivalent of hotel room service. "I'm hungry, Armando" was all you had to say, and Armando instantly whipped up a plate of pork chops with a hot chili sauce or delicious Mexican sausage and eggs. The couple seemed to enjoy feeding the men, and the men, who never thought about food until they got hungry, were glad that there was someone there to feed them.

On a typical day Klaus and Cynthia were up first. They

were vegetarians, so they made their own food. After they fixed breakfast, they would keep to themselves and spend the morning swimming in the pool.

I was up next, usually around ten, followed by John an hour later. Ringo and Harry would be next. They always came down in their bathrobes and always wore dark sunglasses. Ringo would look up, blink behind his glasses, and say, "Daylight hurts." After they had coffee, they'd totter out to the pool and sit there quietly, trying to shake off their hangovers. Finally, when Keith joined them, more than anything else our asylum resembled a rock 'n' roll rest home.

Keith Moon's entrance was always the most flamboyant. Wearing nothing underneath, he would throw on a long brown leather coat split up to the backside, so that when he turned around his naked rear was always in full view. Then he would put on ankle-high boots and a flowing white scarf. He also parted his hair in the middle and slicked it down. Carrying a briefcase, he would descend the stairs.

As soon as John spotted him, John would rise ceremoniously. "The Baron's up. How are you today, Baron von Moon?"

"Splendid, Mr. Lennon, absolutely splendid." Then Moonie would greet whoever else was up and go right back upstairs to change into jeans. When he reappeared, dressed and stoked, he'd already be talking a mile a minute.

"Mr. Lennon, did I ever tell you about the day I decided my hotel room would look better with the furniture nailed to the ceiling?" Baron von Moon asked.

"Tell us," John demanded.

"It was a major undertaking, Mr. Lennon. I got the roadies, and we started with the bed. We got some ladders. First we tied the mattress to the bed. Then we glued down the pillows, sheets, and blankets. We turned the bed upside down, hoisted it up on our shoulders, and drove some big spikes through it into the ceiling. It was a true joy to behold."

"Then what did you do?"

"We did the bureau next—of course, we took the drawers out first. We glued the lampshade to the lamp before we glued that to the bureau. We also had to glue the chairs. They proved the most slippery and difficult. But we did not stop until the job was done. It was such an improvement."

John just shook his head in amazement.

Our first session was scheduled for the day after we moved in, and it went beautifully—so beautifully, that it took only four hours to lay down the basic instrumental and vocal tracks of "Subterranean Homesick Blues." When the tracks were finished, the musicians did not want to go home, so they hung out, jamming with each other or practicing their own licks. At midnight, however, Ringo and Keith left. It was time for them to hit the town.

The jam continued for another half hour, then visitors arrived. The visitors were Paul and Linda McCartney. I thought it uncanny that they had chosen to turn up on the very first night of recording. Later Paul and Linda would insist that it had been a coincidence, but that was hard to believe, because everyone on the rock 'n' roll grapevine knew we were going to start recording that night.

Paul headed straight for John. "Hello, John," he said eagerly.

John, however, was a study in casualness. "How are you, Paul?" he replied softly.

"Fine. How about you?"

"Okay."

"Hi, duckie," Linda said to John, kissing him on the cheek.

"Hello, Linda."

John and Paul made small talk as if they had been speaking on the phone two or three times a day and had spoken just a few hours earlier. It was one of the most casual conversations I had ever heard. They couldn't be the two men who not only had been trading vicious attacks with each other in public but also had squadrons of lawyers poised in battle against each other while they carved up their multimillion-dollar empire. They looked like any pair of old friends having a pleasant low-key reunion.

"How nice to meet you," Linda said when we were introduced. "I've read all about you in the English newspapers." I was surprised by Linda's English accent. I had never heard one quite so "British."

The small talk continued; then Paul, like a man possessed, suddenly bounced up and headed straight for Ringo's drum kit and began to bash the drums. "Let's play!" he exclaimed.

Linda immediately headed for the organ. "Let's play," she echoed. They couldn't be stopped.

John strapped on his guitar and began to play "Midnight Special," one of the numbers the Beatles used to jam on when they first began to play together. So did Jesse Ed Davis and Danny "Kootch" Kortchmar, while Harry sang along.

Then we had another visitor, Stevie Wonder, who was also recording at the Record Plant. "Stevie, Paul is here, and we're goin' to jam," John called out.

"Okay," said Stevie. He went to the electric piano.

"Let's record it," said John.

"Yeah," Paul agreed.

John suddenly became very enthusiastic. There was no bass player in our studio; he and I set out to find one. "We need a bass player," he told the startled producer in the control booth of the studio next to ours. "Paul and I are jammin' together."

"I play bass!" the producer exclaimed. He dashed from his session to join ours.

"Fung Yee, I want you to play," John told me when we returned to our studio. "Grab a tambourine."

I got up and joined the musicians.

"Let it rip," said John.

That was the first time John and Paul had played together since *Abbey Road* in 1969, and it sounded wonderful. The team of Lennon and McCartney had been reunited with amazing ease. After they'd run down the song, John turned to Paul. "Could you please tell your organist to turn down the volume? I can't hear Mr. Wonder," he told him.

John and Paul played it again, and it sounded even better. They made joyous music together that night. Like the Lennon-Jagger "Too Many Cooks," the tape of "Midnight Special"—

the one and only time John and Paul, backed by Stevie Wonder and Harry Nilsson, played together after the breakup of the Beatles—still exists.

When they were through playing, John and Paul once again picked up their casual conversation. It was as if they had not played at all. Then John said, "Why don't you come visit us?"

"Where do you live?" asked Paul, and I gave Linda the directions.

I was buzzing with excitement during the ride home. "I can't believe how easily it went. It's as if you had never stopped playing together. Did you like playing with him again?"

"It was interestin'," John replied.

"Were you surprised when they came through the door?"

He remained silent. The neutral expression on his face could have meant a million things. One thing I knew it meant was that he didn't want to hear another question about it.

We did not see Ringo at all the next day until he arrived at the session that night. He walked in and went straight to his drums. He fiddled with them, then stopped, then fiddled with them some more. "Somebody did something to my snare drum," he said irritably.

"Paul was here last night. He played 'em," explained John.

"He's always fuckin' around with me things!" It sounded as though Ringo were back in Liverpool and that all of them were still teenagers and that nothing in their lives had changed since the day they had played together for the very first time. I realized then that no matter what might happen among them, this was the way they would always relate to each other.

A few days after that, Paul and Linda arrived at the house to spend the afternoon with us. They brought their three girls with them: Mary, who was five at that time; Stella, who must have been around three; and Heather, twelve, Linda's daughter by her first marriage.

The children were adorable, and I asked Armando to

make sure they had drinks and had something to eat if they got hungry.

We showed Paul and Linda the house and then sat down in the living room to talk. While we talked Paul kept staring at the piano. He couldn't stand it anymore and got up and headed for it. The minute John saw Paul go to the piano he ducked out of the room, and Linda followed after him. Ringo also made a quick exit.

John told me later that Linda had questioned him about me. She wanted to know who I was, where I came from, and what we were planning to do with our futures. She also wanted to feel John out about business. Her questioning had made John very uncomfortable.

I remained in the living room while Paul began to sing and play a group of 1930's standards. While he was playing, his five-year-old, Mary, said, "Daddy, are you some sort of pop star or something?" Everyone burst out laughing.

The concert continued, and Harry and Keith began to sing along with Paul.

When Linda returned, I noticed she was wearing platform shoes. Our house, like so many houses in Southern California, was shag carpeted, and I noticed that she kept tripping on the rug. "Linda, why don't you take your shoes off? Make yourself comfortable," I told her.

"I'm fine. After all, these shoes are British-made," she replied in her ultraprecise English accent.

Later we all went for a walk on the beach and then sat by the pool, taking in the sun, while the girls went for a dip. The conversation remained casual, since John and Paul did not discuss any controversial issues; there was not much gossip, and the afternoon went by pleasantly. After a late lunch, Linda launched into a long paean to the joys of living in England. When she was finished, she turned to John and said, "Don't you miss England?"

"Frankly," John replied, "I miss Paris."

The girls had begun to yawn, and it was getting late. Paul and Linda gathered their belongings. "Let's see each other again," Paul said right before they left.

"Let's," John replied.

"Good-bye, duckie," Linda said to John.

We walked them to their car, waved good-bye as they pulled away, and then went back into the house. "I had a good time," I told John.

"It was interestin'."

"Do you think anything is on Paul's mind?"

John didn't answer.

"That's some English accent Linda has."

John smiled. "Not bad for a JAP," he said wryly. Then he turned and went upstairs.

The next week continued to center on recording, and led to a fantastic jam one night among Ringo, Keith, and Jim Keltner, all drumming together on "Rock Around the Clock."

Everything was going so well—until Harry's voice kicked up. Harry desperately wanted to sing his best, and going for it, he had, we now realized, strained his vocal chords after doing innumerable takes. The worse the strain, the more compulsive he became, endlessly insisting on repeating his vocals even though each performance sounded scratchier than the one before it. It was as if he believed that somehow, if he just kept singing, the much-admired Nilsson sound would once again somehow magically emerge. After he did the vocal on a song of his called "Old Forgotten Soldier," John turned to me and said, "I don't want to use it. It hurts me to listen to it."

Meanwhile Harry insisted on repeating the song; John did not have the heart to stop him. It was a dark, desperate song about loneliness, aging, and failure. The combination of Harry's agonized sounds and the depressing lyrics was unbearable. Harry sang it again and again and again. We were all horrified. "Come on," said John. He was so upset, he made me take him home.

"Harry's voice is still all fucked up with strain and coughin'," John said to me that night. "We'll have to do all the vocals again."

During that month Yoko continued to call frequently. Her conversations with John were friendly, and nothing she said upset him. Nonetheless, as the month began to draw to a close, John's behavior began to change. Each day he grew a little quieter, going to bed one night at ten o'clock and sleeping until late the next morning.

"John, are you all right?" I asked.

"Yes. Yes."

The next day he was up even before I was, and I found him outside, reading. "Would you like some breakfast?" I asked.

He did not respond. Finally he got up and walked inside. As soon as he was through eating he went back outside, sat by himself, and continued to read. In the afternoon, when everyone went to the pool, he got up and walked inside again.

Later I went into the bedroom. "Is anything wrong?" I asked.

"I have to be by meself." He turned away.

That pattern continued for another few days. Even though John seemed to be pulling away from me, the physical passion between us did not diminish at all. John was very mercurial, and it was obvious that he had suddenly begun to separate himself from his friends and to separate himself from me in mind but not in body. I did not know what was really going on, and as the days of silence continued, I grew more frustrated and nervous.

Suddenly John stopped drinking and refused all offers of drugs. All he wanted to do was read and be by himself.

"Have I done anything?" I asked.

"I have to be by meself!"

His grim expression said it all.

That night, however, when we returned to the studio, he finally opened up.

"Harry told me he's been coughin' up blood. Must have been that fuckin' flu, and then singin' so hard on top of it. I should have stopped him instead of lettin' him go on. I should've given him a rest."

John looked at me. He was really scared. "I don't want to be fucked up," he said. "It scares the hell out of me."

We talked quietly for an hour that night before going to bed. I thought that I understood why John had been brooding and was pleased that he was finally willing to talk about what was on his mind. We made gentle love and then went to sleep.

In the morning, however, John was silent again. He remained silent for the next few days. Once again I grew nervous and uneasy. Everyone else in the house seemed unaware of the change in John, and I had no one to talk to, which only added to my feelings of uncertainty.

I was sitting at the pool by myself when Klaus and Cynthia joined me. "We hear John's going to New York," Klaus said casually during the conversation.

I got up and found John. "Are we leaving for New York?" I asked.

"I'm leavin'. You're not."

"What do you mean?"

"I'm goin' to take Harry to New York. If I can get him and me out of Los Angeles, I'll have a better chance of gettin' him to do the vocals."

"John, I don't want to stay here by myself."

"I need time alone. You can't come with me," he replied sharply.

"How long are you going to be away?"

"I don't know. I'll call you."

We stared at each other but neither of us said another word, and that was the end of our conversation. I went back to the pool and sat down, doing my best not to cry. John could have suggested that I go home to my apartment instead of leaving me in Los Angeles by myself. He could have asked if I had enough money to keep going on my own. Once again my welfare seemed to mean absolutely nothing to him. I was very hurt, but I was so much in love that I did not even allow myself to express the anger I really felt. I just decided to put up a brave front and keep to myself.

On Sunday night John left for New York; Harry was to follow a few days later. Our parting was a cold one. John kissed me briefly, then he got into the limousine. At the beginning of the month I had been afraid that John would run riot in the house. How ironic! He had sobered up totally and had suddenly decided to move on without me. After John left, I thought about how I felt. There was no denying it: I was hurt and angry and very confused, and no matter how hard I thought, I could not figure out why John had decided to abandon me.

16

I asked myself if perhaps it was the end. I hated to consider it, but with John, *any* moment could be the end. I decided to give him two weeks. If things did not work out, I would use the thousand dollars that remained of our loan from Capitol Records to return to New York and to start rebuilding my new life.

I couldn't wait for the weeks to pass. From the moment John left I noticed a change of attitude toward me in our house. I realized that I had been perceived only as John's girl; without his presence, I had begun to go totally unnoticed. Only Moon found the time to sit and talk to me, treating me not as though I were invisible or just another chick but as a fellow human being.

One day, while Keith and I were driving along, he said, "You know, May, I'm glad you're with John."

"Why, Moonie?" I asked.

"Because he's been his old self once again. No one could believe how he had suddenly abandoned all of his old friends. It's been a miracle to see him friendly and happy and eager to work again."

It was a miracle—a miracle that had inexplicably ceased to be. Each day I missed John more; at the same time without him around I was becoming more independent. As my independence grew I began to like myself more. Still, I really hoped John would call. I was in love, and John meant more to me than anything else. Just before the two weeks ended he did call. Even though he had to have known that I would be there for him if he wanted me, his insecurity was so great that he found it essential during the phone call to determine for himself if I still cared for him. After rejecting me, it was *John* who was afraid of being rejected. I sensed he was testing the waters, testing them by being as casual as possible while he tried to determine where he stood with me.

"How was your day?" he began.

I described the day. "How was yours?"

He told me about Harry's album. He was very enthusiastic. "I'd love you to hear it," he said after he had told a story or two about the sessions in New York.

We talked for a few more minutes, then John suddenly announced, "Do you hear the bangin' on the door? Harry and I are sharin' a suite. He always forgets his key. He always does this to me. I'm not goin' to answer it. But he keeps bangin'." The banging grew louder and louder. Finally John couldn't stand it. "Hang on, let me go and open the door." After the interruption, he seemed uneasy and had difficulty picking up the conversation. Apparently just the sight of Harry had darkened John's mood. After a few moments hesitation, he said, "I'll talk to you tomorrow."

He called the following evening, and we were both more relaxed. John began to sketch the story of the previous two weeks, telling me that Harry had gotten him to drink again. Of course, John remembered nothing that occurred when he was drunk, while Harry remembered it all.

The next night when John called, he told me that, once again, he had stopped drinking. "I'm just so tired of bein' crazy all the time." Then he told me about an incident that had the night before convinced him he had to stop. He had asked Paul Simon and Art Garfunkel to go to the studio to jam with Harry and him. By the time Simon and Garfunkel arrived, John was so drunk, he could hardly hold his guitar.

"Paul and Art turned up and they were both draggin' their asses," John told me. "God, were they serious! Dennis brought them in, and we said our hellos, and I said, 'Do you want to jam?' 'Sure.' So Harry and I started, and I told Paul I'd tell him when to fuckin' come in. We just started to play. Paul started to play also. I turned around and I said, 'I told you to wait.' So this went on and on and on, and he kept comin' in when he wasn't supposed to. And finally I fuckin' told him to stop playin'. He was just so impatient. He went into the fuckin' control booth, and I could see him fuckin' around in there. I could see him mumblin' to himself. Dennis told me he was so pissed off, he says, 'He may be one of the Beatles, but I'm *Paul Simon.*'

"I fuckin' went in there because I could see Dennis gettin' a little uptight and I could see Paul gettin' uptight, and I wanted to smooth it out—to clear the air—and I asked him what was wrong. The man was just fumin'. He said, 'I'm not doing *anything.*' Then I told him he was a fuckin' twerp!"

"You didn't!" I exclaimed.

"Well, he *was* a fuckin' twerp."

"Then what happened?"

"Then Harry comes walkin' in, not knowin' a thing. And I turned around and told him what just happened."

"What did he do?"

"Harry caught the tail end of this and Harry fuckin' told 'em to get out. Then there was this screamin' match. Then Art, who's been stargazing at me all night, comes over and says, 'Well, good night. It's been a nice evening.' They head for the door. Paul's still cursin' and carryin' on. I just couldn't fuckin' believe it! Can you imagine this scene, man. All these people cursin' away. I couldn't fuckin' believe it."

John was still irritated by Simon's behavior, realizing, perhaps, that Paul Simon, unlike almost everyone who entered John's orbit, had a powerful sense of himself and could actually refuse to be treated badly.

"I got so fuckin' tired from the thing, I left." John added, "Today I'm still tired. That's why I'm not gonna drink anymore."

John called again the following evening. Each night for a week and a half we talked for hours on the phone. During these conversations John played me tracks from *Pussycats*—

Harry's album—and we discussed the mixes. He also told me that he'd been seeing Yoko.

"How is she?" I asked.

"She's fine. She's on this fast because she doesn't like the way Harry and I look. She's all right. I'm just on my best behavior because I don't want people to think that now that I'm no longer livin' with her, they don't have to treat her with respect. You know how her ego is. It's important for her to have people know that I may be still around, even if I'm really not. You know how easily her feelings can be hurt."

During the second week of calls John began to flirt with me over the telephone.

"How do you look?" he asked.

"My tan's getting darker. I'm getting darker and darker every day," I teased him.

"That sounds very nice. I think I'd like to see that tan."

"Would you?"

"You know I would. How else do you look?"

"John, you know how I look."

We both laughed.

By then my anger had passed, and those calls were making me very happy. During the third week John began to call the first thing in the morning, then again at night. At the end of the fourth week—it was almost June—John called at seven in the morning. When he asked about what was going on, I told him about the birthday party we were planning to give Mal Evans that day. He called again four hours later and suddenly said, "How would you like to take a trip?"

"To where?"

"Don't you want to come home?"

"Sure I would," I said excitedly.

"I want you to come home. Find out when you can get here. As soon as possible."

I was ecstatic. I got off the phone and packed my bags, taking with me everything that was mine. I didn't know what was going to happen in New York, but whatever it was, I figured I could handle it. What I did know was that I couldn't wait to get out of Los Angeles *and* I couldn't wait to see John. When I got to the airport, I took the first plane out. It would bring me into New York at midnight. Before I boarded it I called John; he wasn't in, and I left him a message telling him my arrival time.

That night, when I reached the Pierre in New York City, I called John's room from the desk phone. There was no answer. By then I had learned that whenever I flew to John, I could not expect him to be there when I arrived. Neither surprised nor angry, I sat down in the lobby to wait. After half an hour I spotted Harry staggering through the revolving doors. There was a beautiful girl on his arm, and they were both drunk.

"Good evening, Mr. Nilsson," said the doorman.

"Good evening, Mr. Nilsson," said the desk man as Harry lurched up to the desk to pick up his messages.

Then Harry noticed me. "May!" he shouted, launching into a loud, bawdy description of all the sexual things he wanted to do to me.

The desk clerk averted his eyes, and so did the bell captain. "Where's John?" I demanded.

"Isn't he upstairs?"

Harry explained that the suite had two bedrooms. He suspected that John, who had begun to go to bed early again, was asleep in his bedroom and was probably having his calls put through to Harry's room. We went upstairs. "There's John's bedroom," said Harry, pointing his finger at a closed door. I approached it nervously. What if John was in there with another girl? With John *anything* was possible, but I banged on the door.

"Who's that?" asked a sleepy John.

"It's May."

He ran to the door and opened it. "You bugger, you! I thought you weren't goin' to come until tomorrow." He had misunderstood my message and thought I was arriving at noon the following day. "Come over here. Let me see what you look like." He turned on the light. "My God, I'm so glad you're here."

John began to kiss me, and it was the kind of moment in which our passion for each other overwhelmed everything, a moment I could have had with no one else.

The next day, after we had our morning coffee, John reached over and kissed me. "The pressure was too great," he explained, "so I just had to leave. I couldn't stand bein' in L.A. It was makin' me crazy. I don't want to drink anymore, because everyone sees me as a crazy person." He squeezed my hand. John said excitedly, "We've got to get a place for ourselves, because when Julian comes, we've got to have a place for 'im to stay. And I'm ready to make an album of all new stuff. Fuck the Spector stuff until I see it."

"That all sounds wonderful."

"You've got to promise me that you are not goin' to go near Harry," he continued. I saw the flicker of jealousy in his eyes. He did not like the fact that I had spent even a minute alone with Harry the night before.

"Don't worry. You don't have to beg me to make that promise."

"Now, don't answer the phone. When I was talkin' to Yoko a few days ago, I told her I was thinkin' of bringin' you back and I wanted you to come home. She just looked at me and she said, 'Are you sure?' I said, 'Yes,' but I didn't tell her when. How was I supposed to know I was goin' to ring you up ten minutes after I told her?"

For the first time, I realized, it had been John's idea and John's idea alone to get us together. This time he had not acted under Yoko's instructions. It had taken a month, but John had finally decided that *he* wanted to be with me.

It was the best news so far.

17

John was still involved in meeting with his lawyers, and his attitude remained the same: "I want to settle all of this, but I still have to know what everyone wants from me and what I have to give away. And I don't want to give up *anything* that's mine."

Thankfully he had at least put *Pussycats* behind him. "I gave my heart to that album, and this is absolutely the best I could do based on the way I felt when I made it."

Then he brightened. "The truth of it is, I needed something to get me ready to do me own album."

He reached for his guitar. "Want to hear some new stuff, Fung Yee?"

John pulled out a bunch of papers. There were phrases scribbled on some, whole lyrics on others. On other pieces of paper he had written down chords that indicated melodies that had come to him for which he did not have lyrics. Those notes were the core of John's new album, an album he would name *Walls and Bridges.*

John worked by instinct. Songs ran through his head just before he fell asleep and while he was sleeping. Not until he had finished *Walls and Bridges* did John realize that he had put together the album to tell Yoko what had happened, to tell her about the pain and the sorrow he felt after they had parted. At that time he told me, "I guess I wanted her to know how frightened I was. You know, you can have this really great love and you can't believe that it will end—and it does. . . ." He said he also realized he had written the album to me as well. "I wanted to tell you about the surprise you feel when time goes by and suddenly—unbelievably—you fall in love with somebody else."

On the day of his decision to make the album, however, none of that had yet been clear to John. All he could say was, "I want to put a song on the album for Yoko and I want a song for you." My song was "Surprise, Surprise," a song John had begun to write the day after we made love for the first time. John played it for me, looking caringly at me while he sang, "I was blind she blew my mind . . . I love her."

When he finished, he asked, "Do you like it?"

Tears were streaming down my cheeks. "Of course I do."

"Do you really like it?"

"I really do." I put my arms around him and kissed him. "John . . ."

"Yeah?"

"Thank you. Thank you very much. This song is the nicest present you could ever give me."

John seemed very pleased. Then he played me the song he had written for Yoko, a tender ballad that he called "Bless You."

"Do you think she'll like it?" he asked when he was done.

"It's a beautiful song. She's going to love it."

Then John ran through the rest of his songs, explaining each before he played it. One in particular, "Scared," left me very quiet.

John seemed to know exactly what I was thinking. "Do you know which song of all me old ones I like the best? . . . 'Help!'" He paused. "I'd like to redo 'Help!' someday. The way we did it, it never told all of the truth." John wanted to do a more soulful, mellow version of the song. He was convinced that that kind of rendition would give "Help!" much greater emotional impact. What he was most interested in was feeling: John wanted people to have intense emotional experiences when they listened to the songs he wrote.

"Some of these songs are as raw as any you've ever written—but you're also writing very tenderly," I told him.

"I just wanted to get me feelings down. These songs are about the past eight months. They're about growin' up."

He looked at me, and I could see that he wanted an overall reaction to what I had heard. I was overwhelmed by his burst of creativity. "Your confidence is back!" I exclaimed. "I can hear *you* in these songs. John, I like what I hear. I'm very happy."

He put down his guitar, reached out, pulled me to him, and began to kiss me tenderly. Then he said, "Are you ready to go to work?"

"Ready!"

John wanted to start recording in two weeks, and he wanted Jim Keltner, Jesse Ed Davis, Klaus Voormann, and Nicky Hopkins brought from Los Angeles to play on the album, along with some New York musicians. He wanted to record at the Record Plant in New York, and he wanted Roy Cicala and Jimmy Iovine to engineer the LP. He also wanted to write the entire album before he started recording so that he could rehearse the musicians before he went into the studio. That time he was determined to do it right!

John had never been more enthusiastic. We set June 17 to start recording, which gave me two weeks to organize the production end of the album while John finished writing it. There were musicians to hire, and I decided to call them immediately.

John told me he wanted to make sure all the needs of each of the players were satisfied. He wanted the sessions to be happy occasions. He also told me to have everybody bring his wife or girl friend with him to New York. Wives and girl friends had usually not been welcome at John's sessions before. Yoko had said, "The studio is a place to work." The result of her dictum had been an unofficial rule banning all women except her, and myself, from the studio while recording was going on.

During the next two hours I reached each of the musicians John wanted. "Wait until you hear these songs," I told them excitedly. "You'll love them. John is writing better than ever."

Everyone was delighted to get the news. The players loved John and his music and couldn't wait to begin, and they were all extremely cooperative about their travel arrangements. I sensed that it was the beginning of a charmed experience. I booked their flights, then booked the studio time and the rented rehearsal space for the two-day rehearsal period before we were to begin recording. By the time I was finished, I was giddy with excitement.

Then John picked up the phone, called Yoko, and bluntly told her that I was back. Later that day she called, and we had a polite chat. During our talk I looked up to see John sitting cross-legged on the bed, his pad in front of him; he was playing his guitar, stopping at times to jot down a phrase or a line. Occasionally he bounced up and walked over to me to sing me a chorus and to get my reaction. "I haven't written this quickly in years," he said excitedly. "I can't remember when I felt this good."

He refused to allow anything to interfere with that happiness. That was why, even though Harry was still in New York, John made sure not to spend too much time with him. One morning John told me, "Before Harry goes back to Los Angeles, we have to go to RCA."

When John wished to disengage himself from a relationship, he liked first to put on a public display of great love and respect. He couldn't bear anyone he loved perceiving him as a bad guy. Despite the many real problems with *Pussycats,* John was proud of it. He believed it *was* the best work he could have done under the circumstances. His feeling for the album and his desire to give Harry a real good-bye led him to one last meeting at RCA, where Harry was in the process of negotiating a new recording contract. Fully aware of his own charisma and the effect his words had when he was speaking bluntly, John said, "This album is terrific work. You've got a terrific artist here. It's insane to lose him when he can do work like this."

Shortly thereafter Harry left for Los Angeles, and later he called from California to tell John that a new contract had been signed.

After Harry's departure, we continued to work furiously to prepare for the June 17 start of recording. Then, just a few days before we were to begin, Al Coury, Capitol's head of promotion in California, invaded our planning meeting at the Record Plant.

"I've got them!" he announced. "They're here." Coury was referring to the Spector tapes, which had been missing for months.

"I don't believe it!" John exclaimed.

Sure enough, the Spector tapes were piled in front of him. An amazed John circled them. "I didn't know there were so many. I can't believe all these boxes." Then he shrugged his shoulders. "Got to put 'em away until I can decide what to do with 'em."

We had been trying like crazy for five months to get those tapes from Spector's offices, only to find ourselves so busy with the new album that we had to lock them up in the Record Plant safe for the time being.

That night, when we went back to the hotel, Ringo called John from Los Angeles.

"You can't believe how well it's goin'," John told him.

Ringo was delighted. Nonetheless he told John that he was nervous about his new recording project, to be produced by Richard Perry, who had produced the extremely successful *Ringo* in 1973.

"I'm desperate for some good material," Ringo told John. John had written the best-selling "I'm the Greatest" for the *Ringo* album.

"Don't worry, mate, I'll see what I can do."

When John got off the phone, he told me he was going to send Ringo "Goodnight Vienna," a song he had been holding for him. "I'll get the band to do a demo of the song for Ringo when we're in the studio," he declared.

All of the songs for John's new album were written except for one. John had decided to take the orchestral arrangement he had made up for "Many Rivers to Cross" on Harry's album, set words to it, and use it on his new album. He had a three-word opening line: "So long ago . . ." and that's all he had. This was the last song John had to finish.

"Have you finished 'So Long Ago'?" I asked.

John hadn't; I could tell he needed prodding.

"The melody is beautiful," I coaxed. Periodically throughout the day I reminded him of how I was looking forward to the completed song.

A day or two later when John woke up, he told me he had had a dream, which he described for me.

"There were two women. They were echoing my name. It was very strange. I felt like I was in a whirlwind." He began to write on his pad. In the dream he had heard the words *ah, bowakawa pousse,* and he wrote them down.

Two days later John finished his dream song. "I'm ready," he announced. As he had promised, all of the material had been completed in time for tomorrow's first rehearsal.

On the first day of rehearsal John walked into the studio to greet Jim Keltner, Jesse Ed Davis, Kenny Ascher, Nicky Hopkins, and Klaus Voormann. Guitarist Eddie Mottau and percussionist Arthur Jenkins were also there to work on the album. After a round of hellos, John said, "Okay, we're goin' to go in and work. Then we party after." There was not going to be any drinking or dope smoking on that one. John handed out lyric sheets with the chord changes written on them. Then he picked up his guitar and began playing his new songs. The musicians listened intently. It was obvious that they liked what they heard. When John was finished, there were congratulations and praise.

I was especially interested in everyone's reactions to "Scared," but no one else seemed to have the same visceral response to the song that I had had. The players were interested in making music, not in reflecting upon the lyrical content of John's songs. They all knew John very well, but they knew the kind John, the professional John, the John who was out of control only when he drank. They had little awareness of the deeply troubled John that I knew. What they wanted to do was go right to work, and they did.

Under John's supervision the players began to work out arrangements for the songs. Almost instantly they were caught up in John's musical precision, and it was stunning. Once, for example, when Kenny Ascher was at the piano, John stopped him. "No, no, no," he said. "Don't change it." Kenny had added a single eighth note to one of John's rhythmical patterns, and John had heard the slight change.

"Boy, is your ear sharp," Kenny observed.

When it came time for Kenny to do the string arrangements, John simply sang the string line to him, Kenny would take down the line, then he would make suggestions.

"Whatever you think. But it's got to sound like what's in me ear," John said.

At the end of the two-day rehearsal period the entire album had been arranged. The sessions began the next day.

At night when we went back to the hotel after those sessions, John would look at me and say, "Fung Yee, this is goin' to be the fastest, easiest album I've ever made. Fuckin' amazin'."

Indeed, things were moving so quickly that John did produce a rough track of "Goodnight Vienna" for Ringo during one of his own sessions. As soon as it was finished I mailed the tape to Ringo in Los Angeles.

At the end of June the musicians went home thrilled, and we moved out of the Pierre and back to my apartment. "I want Julian to be able to stay with us when he comes over. So we have to find something with a room for him. I know you like this place, Fung Yee. So do I, but the time has come to find a bigger apartment right now," John said after we unpacked.

From the time Julian had gone home after the New Year, I had gotten John to call him once or twice a week. John had not only accepted the fact that he had a son but also enjoyed talking to him, learning in the process that Julian was really quite an intelligent little man.

The difficulty of staying in my apartment was compounded by the fact that it was summer, and because of the warm weather, there were lots of people hanging out on the street during the day and at night. Fans began to recognize John's station wagon, which we'd been driving since my return to New York in the beginning of June, and would congregate around it. When we came out, those fans would try to engage

John in conversation. John would exchange a word or two with them before we drove off, and I'm sure none of them ever suspected how unnerved he was by those experiences. Even in New York it appeared that it was impossible for John to have his privacy.

One night at the studio we announced that we were looking for an apartment and asked for any leads people might have. A few days later Eddie Germano, who managed the Record Plant at that time, told us that there was a vacancy in his building, a small apartment house facing the East River.

"That's a good idea. We'll have to check it out. At least we'll have some friends in the building." John also liked the idea that Eddie had a son who was Julian's age.

The next day, during one of Yoko's calls, she announced that she wanted to come over to visit. Yoko and I hardly spoke anymore, and I couldn't imagine that she would ever come to visit me in my own apartment.

"What does she want?" I asked John.

John shrugged his shoulders and said nothing.

An hour later, a stretch limousine pulled up and Yoko got out. I buzzed her into the building and she climbed the three flights to my apartment. I opened the door and said, "Hello, Yoko. Please come in." Yoko looked very sullen as she stepped inside.

"Hello, Yoko," said John.

Yoko did not reply. She looked around and frowned. It was the kind of expression you expect to find on someone's face when he goes into a dirty public bathroom. She lit a Kool and paced back and forth, lost in thought. Finally she sat down and stared at John, not saying anything. John and I stared back at her.

"John," she said softly, "how can you live in a dump like this?" Then she turned to me. "May, do you plan to sit in this dump forever?"

"I think it's a lovely apartment," I replied.

Yoko looked very sad. "You're going to live in this place forever. Don't you understand that there are nicer places to live?"

"I'm sure there are," replied John.

"I want you two to move out of here. It hurts me to see you living this way." Yoko looked very hurt.

"We may do that, Yoko," John said.

"It's important for you to be comfortable. I think you'd want to be more comfortable."

"We do want to be comfortable," I told her.

"It hurts me when you're not comfortable."

John said nothing. I said nothing.

"You know how much better off all of us would be if you moved."

We remained silent.

"I can't understand how you could do something like this and be happy about it."

We said nothing.

"It's so easy to better yourself once you make up your mind to do it. Do you know what?" she asked. "There's an empty apartment at the Dakota. Would you like to take it?"

"Is there?" asked John.

I tried to maintain a neutral expression, but I was horrified. The idea of John and me living in the same building as Yoko appalled me.

"Let me find out. I'll call you." Yoko had planted the seed; I did not know how John would respond.

Yoko pounded away at the two of us for the next hour. When she was finally convinced that she had persuaded us of how much she was suffering because of the way we had chosen to live and how we could alleviate that suffering by moving, she said, "I have to go now," and she got up to leave. When she got to the door she turned. "You know what?" she asked.

"What?" asked John.

"John, I think you'd be very happy in a bigger apartment."

"I don't want to live in the Dakota," I said sharply as soon as John closed the door.

"I got a funny feeling she thinks I'm goin' to make *her* move out of the Dakota so that we can move in," John replied. "She couldn't stand that. It's important for her to live at the Dakota. She likes the address because it's *One* West Seventy-second Street. She likes it because famous people live there."

He paused and I didn't say anything.

"There is an apartment there. Wouldn't it be funny if we took it? People would never know what to think."

"We can move into Eddie Germano's building."

John thought for a moment or two. "The Dakota's nice, but I really always wanted to live by the river."

Germano's building was a small twelve-storied apartment house right off the East River, on East Fifty-second Street. Eddie had told us that the apartment was called the Tower. The vacancy turned out to be a small penthouse and it was charming. There was a living room with a wood-burning fireplace, a narrow kitchen, and a small but adequate bedroom. Glass doors in the living room opened onto a tiny terrace facing the river. The kitchen window opened onto the roof. If we moved in, we would have the entire roof to ourselves.

John breezed through the apartment. "Fung Yee, the kitchen is too small," he observed.

That morning John had brought up the vacant apartment at the Dakota. If the Tower was at all reasonable, I was determined to take it.

"We hardly ever eat in," I told him. "This kitchen will do. I think it's a lovely apartment."

"Do you really like it?" he asked again.

"I like it a lot."

John turned to Eddie. "What's the rent?"

It was $800, which doesn't sound like much today, but in 1974 it was a great deal for people who were trying to live on a budget. John frowned.

"Let me talk to the landlord," Germano said. "We're on very good terms. I think I can get the rent down." Eddie really wanted us to live in his building.

That night at the studio he told us the rent had been reduced to $750. "Let's take it," John said, beaming because of the fifty-dollar-a-month bargain.

When Eddie Germano told him that Greta Garbo lived on the block, he was even more intrigued. "I'd love to see her," John said. "Let's keep an eye out."

After we got up the next morning, we began to plan our

move. John and I looked over my possessions, thinking about which of them we were going to take with us. It was not until then that it dawned on me that John really was intent on me giving up my apartment to live with him in this new one.

"John, let's talk," I said quietly.

"What's the matter?"

"I'm very nervous about giving up this apartment. It's the first one I've ever had. It's an apartment I'll always be able to afford."

"Listen, Fung Yee, we've been together for a while and living at everybody else's place. And now it's time for us to live in our own place. So don't worry. It'll be okay."

"You know I love you and you know I want to live with you in our own apartment. But I'm still nervous."

"It'll be all right. Haven't things been all right up to now?"

Things were not only all right, they were wonderful. We had gone a month without any incident at all, and John, who used to make so few decisions on his own, was making all of them and seemed determined to continue to do so. He wasn't drinking, it did not appear that Yoko was pulling him by a string, and he had never been more loving. I didn't know what was going to happen but I did want to take the chance. I took a deep breath, looked at John, and decided to submerge my fears and take the plunge. "I'm ready if you are," I said—and like newlyweds we plunged into making a list of things that we'd need.

"What about a bed?" asked John.

I picked up *The Village Voice* and thumbed through it, stopping at an ad for Loftcraft, an inexpensive store that sold beds. "Let's go," said John. We took a cab downtown to the store. We were both fast shoppers, and by the time the clerks had gotten over their amazement about John's turning up to buy a bed, we had chosen one and had paid for it with John's American Express card. That afternoon I and Jon Hendricks, Yoko's personal assistant, went to Macy's, where I bought a mattress.

The next day John and I went off to Carlyle Custom Convertibles to buy a sofa bed for Julian to sleep on. As we were walking around the showroom John noticed a brown velvet couch and pointed to it. It was pretty. We sat down on it, and it was comfortable. We opened it, and it was easy enough for a child to open.

"That's it," said John, and we bought it.

John thought our new living room was too small and wanted to create the illusion of space. "Mirrors will do it," he said. "Let's hang mirrors over the fireplace." Jon Hendricks found a man who went to the apartment to take measurements for some large smoked-glass mirrors that would be installed later.

We knew Roy Cicala could get stereo equipment at a discount through the Record Plant. He and John planned a sound system for the apartment that featured huge three-feet-high, three-feet-wide Altec speakers. We also got a television set through Roy.

"Listen, we had those rugs from Tittenhurst Park shipped over. They were never used. They're just sitting around." John was referring to a number of beautiful rugs, some white and some black, that had been specially woven in China for his Ascot home. He called Jon Hendricks to ask him to find the rugs and then to deliver them. When he told Yoko, she said that it was a wonderful idea.

A little while later Yoko called and asked to speak to John. "Really . . . fine," snapped John. He slammed down the phone. "Yoko is afraid she is bein' left out," he told me. "Now she wants the rugs."

John and Yoko began to trade calls back and forth to discuss the rug issue. Finally John said, "We'll use one white one. Whatever's left over she can have. That's gotta be enough." On the next call, John was firm with Yoko, and the matter was closed.

After looking over our new apartment again, John said, "Listen, we need a separate room for Julian. We'll use the living room as our bedroom, and he can sleep in the other room."

We laid the white carpet in the front room and placed our bed there, to one side. John had his piano sent over from the Dakota, and we also placed it in the front room. Then Roy sent over a man and we had the sound system installed in that room.

When the television set arrived, we placed it in front of the bed. Then we bought two director's chairs and put them there as well. After we had the mirrors mounted over the fireplace, we moved the new sofa bed into the other room for Julian, and the apartment was furnished, except for the roof.

As time went on, John had a large tree hoisted onto the roof. It looked rather lonely and strange up there. "It's a beginning," said John. "Who knows what else we'll put on this roof before we're through."

Early one evening while John was in the studio, I went to see my mother to tell her about the move. She had known for months that John and I were together and she had refrained from asking about it. While I told her she remained silent, but I could see that she was nervous. "I don't want you to be upset," I told her.

"May, you've been making your own decisions since you moved out of my house. What is there to say?" she replied.

"I'm as nervous as you are," I explained, "but I'm in love with this man."

She looked at me, and I could see that she was puzzled. In her world you did not *love* a man, you worked for him. "I'd like you to meet John," I said. "When you meet him, I'm sure you'll feel better about all of this." The idea of meeting John seemed to excite her. It was inconceivable to her that, even though her daughter was living with the man, she would ever meet someone as famous as John Lennon. Still, she smiled. "I'd like to meet him," she said shyly.

"How did it go?" John asked when I got back to the studio.

"She was a little nervous, but it went fine."

"Good."

"John, it would be much easier for me if you met her. You'll really like her. She's a very sweet lady."

My mother's nervousness about meeting John was nothing compared to John's fear of meeting her.

"I can't do it. I can't do it. I don't want to meet anybody's mother."

"All you have to do is say hello once."

"I can't. I just can't." Then he said by way of explanation, "Yoko hates her parents."

"John, there's a big difference between my mother, a little Chinese woman who's worked hard every single day of her life, and Yoko's mother, who just happens to be a Japanese bank president's wife."

John would not listen and the matter was closed, much to my regret.

I tried to be as tactful as possible when I explained to my mother that John couldn't bear being around families because of his own difficult childhood. I knew that she would never understand that a grown *man* was afraid of meeting her. "I understand," she said gently, after my explanation. "I don't want to impose." I could see that she was a little hurt. "Still, I would love to bring you some food from time to time, if I may."

I thought I understood John's reasons for not meeting my mother, and I had explained them to my mother as well as I could. Nevertheless at the bottom of my heart, in the place that I avoided looking at, I was hurt and angry. The fact that John couldn't be kind to my mother and to me and usually reserved his great gestures only for strangers really upset me. But as long as I loved John and was with him, I knew it would do me no good to dwell on his refusal.

From the time we moved in, twice a week after work, my mother would arrive at our apartment, carrying shopping bags filled with delicious home-cooked Chinese food. I would buzz her in and meet her at the door. We'd stand in the hallway outside the apartment and talk while John hovered inside, waiting until she was gone. When our conversation was over, she would hand me the shopping bags. Because she had so little money, I always offered to pay for the food, but she refused to take a penny. I would thank her and kiss her good-bye. She would go home to Spanish Harlem to my father, and I would go inside to John, who couldn't wait to dig into the food.

Then, when our apartment was nearly decorated and we were almost ready to move in, we heard from Tony King, who told us that he was coming back to the United States. He was planning to sail in mid-July on the S.S. *France* with Elton John.

John was very excited. "I can't wait to see Tony and Elton!" he exclaimed. A little later he had a brainstorm. "It'll be a good idea when Julian comes over for him to go with them. They can look after him on the boat."

I called Tony back, and he loved the idea of escorting Julian to the United States. Then I called Cynthia and told her of John's plan.

"It's a wonderful idea," she told me. She asked to speak to John, and I gave the phone to him.

When John spoke to Cynthia, he was extremely curt. "Okay . . . fine . . . good," he said, wanting to get off the phone as quickly as possible.

The next time John spoke to Julian, Julian told him that Cynthia was planning to go with him. John was furious. He was counting on Julian to travel alone. It took all of my powers of persuasion to convince him to allow Cynthia to accompany her son.

After a few phone calls, it was arranged that when Cynthia and Julian arrived in New York, Julian would stay with us, and Cynthia would stay with friends.

John did not want to stay in our new apartment until the phones were installed, and so we moved back to the Pierre for a day or two.

I had to laugh. In so many ways our lives resembled a soap opera, and it seemed as if we were always packing our bags and moving somewhere.

While we lived at the Pierre we continued to go to the studio, where John worked on vocal overdubs. One night John's dream song, "#9 Dream," was to be overdubbed, but the backup singers did not turn up. John specifically wanted two male and two female voices. He also wanted a female voice representing one of the two female spirits in the dream to call "John . . . John . . ." periodically during the track. He wanted me to play that part, but he did not want me to be one of the background vocalists.

"I can sing background," I told him.

"I don't want you to."

"I know it's not hard, and you know I can sing. Let me try it."

"No."

John rounded up a boy and Roy Cicala's wife, Lori Burton. He needed another female voice. He decided to sing the other male harmony line, and when he could not find a second female, he finally said in desperation, "Fung Yee, give it a try."

I had no problem doing the background voice. But when it came time for me to call "John . . . John . . ." I had to have the lights in the booth dimmed, because it embarrassed me to say those sexy, erotic-sounding *John*'s with him looking at me. Nonetheless John was delighted when I was finished.

"I told you to trust me," I said.

"You were right." He still seemed nervous.

"You don't have to worry about me, John," I told him. "I don't want a solo recording career. And I don't want a gig at Kenny's Castaways."

He laughed. "You always read my mind."

Three days after we moved into the Pierre and were getting ready to leave it, Cynthia, Julian, Elton, and Tony arrived. When John saw Cynthia, he said quietly, "Hi, Cyn." When he saw Julian, he gave him a big hug. Then he embraced Elton and Tony.

They had all had a marvelous crossing. "Julian was a dream," Elton told John. "He waited for us outside our staterooms, escorted us to the dining room, always made sure we had good seats at all the events on board."

"Well, folks, we have a new apartment and we have a new album." He put his arm around my shoulder. "We've been a very busy little couple since last you saw us." He turned to Julian. "And you've got your own room."

"When are you moving?" asked Cynthia.

"Tomorrow."

She laughed. Cynthia knew what life with John was like. Things always happened at a moment's notice.

We had been in our new apartment only an hour when our phone rang. Our first call was from Paul McCartney. In Los Angeles we had told Paul and Linda that they could always call the Dakota to get our number. When Paul discovered that we had just moved in he wanted to come over and say hello. The McCartneys had an uncanny knack for showing up whenever a new event occurred in our lives.

That evening they were at our door. Julian had not seen Paul in years, and Paul's appearance added to his surprise at suddenly finding himself living in an apartment with John. At ten Julian had a storehouse of memories of his childhood as the son of a Beatle, and he told Paul he could clearly remember Paul and his father playing together.

John and Paul chatted back and forth. Again the conversation was exceedingly casual. They liked each other, yet they seemed to feel fragile and uncertain and they dealt with the feelings by pretending nothing at all had ever been wrong. It was as if no one dared say anything substantial, in that way making sure that there would be no arguments to interrupt the rebuilding of the kind of friendship that would allow them to work together again.

Whenever there was a musical instrument in the room, Paul's eyes would automatically dart back and forth to it. As Paul spoke to John, his eyes, as usual, kept resting on John's piano. Paul couldn't stand it anymore. He got up, went to the piano, and began to play and sing. Linda burst into a huge smile. In a few minutes I could see John becoming annoyed, but he said nothing and maintained a neutral smile during Paul's concert.

Throughout the evening, every time I looked up, I found Linda staring at me. I felt as if she were trying to determine who I really was and how I had gotten there.

After two hours, Paul and Linda got up to go. "Let's see each other again," said Paul.

"Let's," John replied.

When they were gone, we poured a glass of wine, toasted each other, then went out to sit on the terrace and look at the stars. We were growing sleepy, so we went inside, got undressed, and went to bed. We had never been happier.

The next evening we had another visitor, Mick Jagger, who began to make a habit of calling and asking if he could drop over. We were always delighted to see him. Nattily dressed and always looking roguish, he'd turn up with a wicked grin on his face. Mick usually brought something to drink, and John and he would spend their evenings together, drinking wine and sitting back and relaxing. Mick loved takeout

Chinese food. During those visits I'd call out and order our favorite dishes. Then, after we ate, John and Mick sometimes played their guitars and sang a bit, or we all watched television.

Mick's visits were low-key, yet I still sensed an air of mischief about him. At a moment's notice he was capable of surprise, and he and everyone else knew it. John and I affectionately nicknamed him "The Phantom." We never knew when he'd materialize, how long he would stay, when he'd call again, or what was really going on behind those devilish eyes and big pouting lips. Eventually he and I became friends, and I grew to like him a lot. He was his own man and he seemed to relish his success and his life. However, he always seemed a bit removed, like an actor who was enjoying his role but at the same time knew he was playacting and was always watching his own performance.

On our third night at the apartment Elton and Tony dropped in. Whenever Elton and John saw each other, they loved to have a good gossip about everyone they knew. For an hour they entertained us with their observations and witty one-liners.

When the laughter finally died down, John played Elton the tracks of *Walls and Bridges*. Elton was very impressed.

"I'd love you to do something on the album," said John.

"Anything you say," Elton replied.

"Which track would you like to play on?"

After a pause, Elton said, " 'Whatever Gets You Thru the Night.' "

"One of my least favorites!" John spat back.

"That song is a smash. It could be a number one," Tony told John.

John still looked skeptical.

"John, it gives me the most space to do something on," Elton explained.

A few nights later Elton and Tony went to the studio. If John was all business, Elton was equally quick. He listened to the song a second time, then sat down and expertly began to lay down the piano track. John stared at Elton's hands while Elton played.

"I'd like to play as fast as that," he said to me with genuine amazement. After a couple of takes, the piano track had been completed perfectly. John had not done the vocal yet, and it was decided that they would sing together. The harmony came very easily to them. Instantly a new singing team was formed as John and Elton ripped through the vocal a couple of times, getting looser each time they sang it. By the time they were done, their duet had a really infectious rollicking feel to it.

When they were finished, John said to me, "I'd like Elton to sing harmony on 'Surprise, Surprise.'" He knew how thrilled I'd be to have Elton perform on the song John had written for me.

"Let's do it," said Elton. John had already done his vocal, and Elton understood that his harmony line had to match John's phrasing exactly. After a series of takes, Elton began to grow frustrated. "You do have a special way of phrasing," he told John. Determined to match John's phrasing perfectly, he did a number of new takes; none worked, which only stimulated his determination. At two in the morning, after trying for over two hours, he became exhausted.

"Okay, Elton, it's fine," said John.

"Great!" Elton turned and left abruptly.

Even though it was impossible to get a perfect match, John was overwhelmed by Elton's efforts and he thoroughly understood his sudden exit.

During the days I had decided to devote my efforts to making our apartment a wonderful home for both John and Julian. I got a cookbook, and on the first Sunday after we moved in I started a ritual that John adored. I made an English Sunday breakfast for the three of us. The breakfast consisted of bacon and eggs, stewed tomatoes, beans on toast, and fried potatoes. John loved black pudding—I found a butcher who had that special kind of sausage—and I fried it for him. I also found a newsstand that got the English newspapers and had them delivered to the apartment. After our breakfast, we drank lots of coffee and read the newspapers.

John loved the water, and the Germanos had a boat

moored near Orchard Beach in The Bronx. The weekends were a wonderful treat. Early on Saturday mornings John, Julian, and I would set out. When we got to the boat, we'd cast off and just lie there quietly in the sun, letting the boat drift. After a picnic lunch, we'd rest some more, then we'd spend the rest of the afternoon swimming. Those weekend days were very quiet and they were also very special—special because the three of us enjoyed just being together, quietly lazing away the days in the summer sun.

At night when we were recording, we always took Julian to the studio. It was his summer holiday, so we didn't think it wrong to keep him up to eleven or twelve at night, as he could sleep late the next day. He could also nap at the studio. Julian followed John around the studio, watching in awe while his father worked on the album. John would casually explain things to Julian, allowing him to sit at the control board so that he could work the equipment side by side with John.

One night Julian was practicing on the snare drum and John told the engineers to turn on the equipment. Then he went into the studio and sang and played "Ya, Ya"—another old standard he had done in the early days of the Beatles—while Julian accompanied him. Later, after *Walls and Bridges* was pressed, John gave Julian a huge surprise. He told Julian that the performance had been included on the album.

Julian was astonished. "Why did you do that?" he gasped. "If I'd known it was going on the album, I would have played better."

John was taken aback. He turned to me and said, "I thought he'd get a kick out of it."

"You see," I replied, "he's as fussy a musician as you are."

John continued to refuse to speak to Cynthia, so I kept in touch with her. As it turned out she was alone, her friends having been called away. I could sense that she was lonely, yet she was always very cheerful with me and made no demands. She was delighted by John's sudden interest in Julian, and she was determined not to do anything to provoke his temper.

Whenever Yoko called, John was cordial but distant. From their brief conversations Yoko learned that everything was going splendidly: The album was being completed in record time, and everyone who heard it loved it; John loved the new apartment; he was delighted with Julian; Cynthia had done nothing to upset him; and John and I had never been happier with each other. Then Yoko suddenly decided that she wanted to go on a solo tour of Japan. John was not enthusiastic. "Do you know how much it will cost to fly you and your band to Japan, put you up in hotels, and travel you around? We're never going to sell enough of your records to pay for this tour."

Yoko was adamant. "I'm very big in Japan," she kept telling John, suggesting that by refusing to pay for the tour he was not allowing her the opportunity to maintain her own career, even though he was actively pursuing his.

"She's goin' to get awful reviews," John told me. "She's goin' to be hurt. I don't want her to go."

The calls came fast and furious. Finally, wearily, John capitulated. From that moment on Yoko had a reason to call even more frequently as she reported every detail of her tour to him. Her biggest problem seemed to be that David Spinozza had refused to go to Japan with her, begging off by telling everyone that he had other commitments. He had promised, however, to rehearse the band before they left. John told her to hire any guitarist of her choice.

I sensed danger. It seemed to me that no matter how much Yoko tried to control things, her life was full of surprises. I was sure she had been surprised when John had run off with me; then I was sure that she was also surprised when Spinozza refused to go to Japan with her. Surprises only made her more desperate, and I knew her desperation could only spell trouble.

During the following week there were a lot of calls back and forth concerning the tour, and I learned from friends who were close to Spinozza and the other members of Yoko's band that the guitarist was tired of Yoko's contemptuous attitude toward John. Reportedly Spinozza and Yoko argued constantly about how John and Yoko could present themselves to the world as the "peace-and-love couple" when Yoko had such contempt for John and kept remarking that John was like a child who would do anything she asked. Finally, carefully, Spinozza bowed out of the tour.

While Yoko was in Japan, Ringo called to invite John to go to Los Angeles to help him record "Goodnight Vienna." Then Tony King called and told us that Elton was planning to record his new album at the Caribou Ranch in Colorado. Tony told John that Elton was going to do a version of "Lucy in the Sky with Diamonds" and hinted that Elton would love to have John sing on the record with him. The two invitations excited John.

"I'd love to help Ringo and I'd love to help Elton and see Caribou," he told me. John was very curious about that legendary recording facility, which was designed to have musicians living in a beautiful, isolated setting so that they could concentrate fully on their music.

I shook my head. "I'm never going back to L.A."

"Why?"

"You know how I feel about the place."

"But we've got to do it for Ringo. It will only be for a few days."

In reality I hated the idea of what John might once again become as soon as he hit the fast, empty L.A. night life. John had to work really hard to persuade me to go. Repeatedly he promised that we would stay for only three days and that he would not drink or run around. I told him that if we were there for a fourth day, I was leaving, with or without him.

We worked it out so that we could go to Los Angeles for three days, then fly to Caribou for another two or three, then come back to New York. I was pleased when John agreed that Cynthia and Julian would accompany us to L.A.

The recording of "Goodnight Vienna," the song John wrote for Ringo, went quickly and smoothly. John advised Ringo's producer, Richard Perry, on exactly how he thought it should be done, and Perry, responding to John's lead, produced the session expertly. Ringo was very happy.

The next day at the studio Ringo said, "We're still one song short." John thought for a second. "This is one I wanted to do, but I'll give it to you." John went into the vocal booth and played and sang the old Platters hit "Only You," accompanied by Ringo and Jim Keltner on drums. His intention was to retard the tempo of the song, giving it an even more tender, personal feel than the version done by the Platters.

Ringo and Richard Perry went to work immediately. That day Ringo recorded "Only You," which became a top-ten single. During those sessions Perry and John worked very well together. It was obvious that Perry had bent over backward to please John. "He's been on his best behavior," John told me. "I think he wants to produce me."

When we heard the final mix, I was convinced that John's voice was bleeding through Ringo's and that his version of "Only You" had not been destroyed. John agreed with me, and it stayed on his mind for a long time. He even told Mick Jagger, "One day I'm goin' to go up to Richard Perry and ask him, 'Where's my version of that tape?' " John was right. His version of "Only You" is also still in existence.

After three days, true to John's word, we got ready to leave for the Caribou Ranch in Colorado to work with Elton. When John told Julian that we were leaving, Julian refused to go with us. It appeared that Julian did not like the idea of leaving Cynthia behind. John and I both tried to persuade him to go, but he wouldn't budge. I felt that Julian really needed a breather—all the flying around and all those superstars seemed a bit too much for him—and he wanted the familiarity of his mother for a while.

At any rate the two of us set out for Caribou without him. We flew to Denver, where we were picked up for the two-hour drive into the mountains to the ranch. The three-thousand-acre site was amazing. The recording studio was lodged in a large log cabin, and the performers lived in log cabins as well, which were decorated with antique furniture and beautiful brass four-poster beds. Surrounding those cabins were mountain streams and lakes, and there was a ghost town at one end of the ranch. Caribou was serene and beautiful, and we loved it. Because the elevation was so high, the air was very thin, and John had trouble breathing the first day we were there.

That night after we unpacked, we joined Elton in the studio. As soon as they saw each other, John and Elton fell into each other's arms. As they did every time they met, they began to trade one-liners. They were both in rare form, and everyone stood around laughing. Then the session began under the direction of Elton's producer, Gus Dudgeon, who was outfitted in western garb. During the session John suggested that a reggae break be included in Elton's version of "Lucy," and it was quickly worked up. The session was a long, painstaking one. Everyone worked efficiently, the changes made sense, and each of the musicians was given precise directions. Both perfectionists, Elton and John set the pace, and everyone buckled down to make a perfect record.

At the end of the session, when we left the studio to go back to our cabin, we stepped out into a beautiful summer night. The air was clear, and stars sparkled in the sky. "I can't stand it," John said in jest.

Three days later we were back in New York.

The following morning we made a number of calls to tell people that we had returned from our one-week whirlwind tour of recording studios in Los Angeles and Colorado. During the day I also spoke to the Apple offices in London and learned two strange things about Yoko. I was told that after her Japanese tour, she had gone to London. When she went to the Apple offices, she asked that her yen be converted to pounds. That was cash she had received from selling interviews to the Japanese press. Since John refused to restrain her excessive spending, I wondered why she felt the need to make a little money on the side. Then I learned that she had gone to visit John's aunt, Mimi Smith, the woman who had raised him and upon whom he doted, and had told her that John was about to be deported from the United States, that his life was going to be ruined, that he was living with another woman to whom he wasn't married, and that she, Yoko, was the only person who could save him. Mrs. Smith had called Apple in a panic.

I could see that Yoko was desperate, and when Yoko was desperate, I got nervous. I didn't say a word to John. In matters such as those, I knew that no matter what I did, I would end up in the wrong.

The rest of the summer passed in a whirlwind. During one of her calls Yoko suggested that John call Allen Klein, with whom she had just spoken. John called Allen immediately—it was rather disquieting to see how fast he responded to Yoko's suggestions—and to my astonishment I found out that we were going to be Allen Klein's Hampton houseguests.

"We'll have fun," John said. "I really do like Allen."

Klein turned out to be a very charming host and a terrific conversationalist. He left the next day, and as soon as he was gone, John said, "Let's do some acid later." He had been carrying some "windowpane" around in his wallet for months.

I must have looked panic-stricken.

"Trust me. You'll love it. It's beautiful. You'll be normal by Johnny Carson time," he said.

Early in the afternoon John said, "Let's swallow it now. I want us to be really high as the sun goes down." We stretched out on the bed in Klein's house, and I must say that I was very scared as I took the drug. "I'll take care of you," John said. As the acid took effect I suddenly burst into tears. John cried, too.

We alternately talked and cried for what seemed like hours, then we began to hallucinate. I told John that when I looked at him, I could see him changing forms. When we looked up, we saw two triangles: a May triangle and a John triangle. We wanted those triangles to fuse. When we kissed, the triangles got closer and we felt very happy. We kissed some more, and the triangles got even closer, making us feel better still.

We pulled off our clothes and began to make love. Only then did the fusion become complete, and we felt wonderful. It seemed as if John and I made love for hours and hours. I couldn't believe anything could ever make me so passionate. Every sensation was incredibly intense, and both of us kept screaming out in delight. Finally we lay there gasping. Later, as we were coming down, we got dressed and went out for a walk on the beach.

The sand glittered and began to change colors. I looked at the moon and somehow I believed I could hear it singing to me. It was all so unbelievably beautiful.

When we went back into the house, John turned on the television and we heard a voice say, "Here's Johnny!" We burst out laughing, and throughout the Carson show we kept looking at each other and giggling.

"Can I take some more?" I asked John.

"You like it that much?"

"Yes. Yes."

He cocked his head. I think even he had doubted that I would have such a wonderful trip. He didn't have any more, so we just fell onto the bed and held each other until we fell asleep.

When Julian and Cynthia returned from Los Angeles, Cynthia went back to the hotel, and Julian rejoined us. We had a week with Julian, and once again we resumed our city routine with him. Then it was time for Julian and Cynthia to return to England.

"Julian, you're goin' to see me again this Christmas," John told his son before the child left, "and this time you're really old enough to come by yourself."

I had just stepped out of the shower one Friday night toward the end of August when I heard John shout, "Fung Yee, come here."

"In a minute," I called back.

"Now, Fung Yee. Now!" he screamed.

He sounded panic-stricken, so I ran into the living room. I could see him standing naked on the terrace, and I ran out and stood beside him.

"What's the matter?" I asked.

"Look up there!" He pointed to the sky. "Tell me what you see." I looked up and couldn't believe my eyes. There was a saucer-shaped object surrounded by blinking white lights gliding through the sky. I was convinced it was a UFO.

"I can't believe it!" I exclaimed.

"You're seein' exactly what I see."

"I can't believe it!" I repeated.

I was astonished. Then I began to laugh.

"What are you laughin' at?" asked John.

"Suppose it's looking at *us*. Maybe they think that everyone who lives on the East Side wanders around naked on their terraces on Friday evenings. We look like Adam and Eve."

We watched the object gliding through the sky. Then we went inside, got our telescope, and studied it some more. "I almost didn't call you," John said. "I was afraid you wouldn't believe me. I thought you'd say, 'What is John on?' I didn't think anyone would believe me."

We went to the phone and called Harold Seider and Elliot Mintz to tell them about the UFO. Seider was skeptical. Elliot, of course, was not. John spoke to Bob Gruen, a photographer who did a lot of work for him, and asked Gruen to come over and to get on the phone to find out if anyone else had sighted the object. Gruen made a few calls and learned that there had been reports made to both the local police station as well as to the newspapers. That sighting eventually was recorded in the official UFO journals. On the liner notes of *Walls and Bridges* John wrote, "On the 23rd of August 1974 at 9 o'clock I saw a U.F.O.—J.L."

We couldn't stop talking about the UFO. "I never believed this stuff before," I said. "Now I've seen it and I *do* believe it."

"It was real enough," said John.

When Yoko called, John told her about the spaceship.

"What did she say?" I asked when he got off the phone.

"She was upset because she hadn't seen it."

Yoko called back two or three times to complain about being left out.

In bed that night we continued to talk about it.

Just before he fell asleep, John said softly, "I wish it had taken us both away."

If only it had been true, we would both have been much better off.

18

The summer was over, and a very busy fall loomed ahead. John and I discussed all the things we had to do. *Walls and Bridges* and a single from the album, "Whatever Gets You Thru the Night," were both going to be issued at the end of September, and Al Coury, the Capitol Records promotion man, wanted John to attend a number of promotional meetings and also wanted him to participate in a round of promotional activities for the album. Then Harold Seider informed John that the negotiations to dissolve Apple were getting much closer to a settlement. He wanted John to attend a series of meetings with all of the lawyers to go over the last-minute arrangements.

Harold also reminded John of another problem: a copyright matter with music publisher Morris Levy. The settlement of Levy's infringement charge over the song "Come Together" included a commitment by John to include three songs published by Levy on John's next album. At the time the agreement was made, it was anticipated that the Spector album would be John's next project—a perfect one for Levy's golden-oldies–type songs. But those sessions had come to a halt, and John's "next" album had turned out to be *Walls and Bridges*. The Levy matter was something John took very seriously. He was a professional and he viewed the fact that he had not kept his end of the bargain with Levy as *un*professional. He was determined personally to rectify it.

John assumed it could be rectified only by finishing the Spector album and including three of Levy's songs on it.

The Spector tapes had been lying in the Record Plant vault since the end of June. Usually John could not bear leaving an album unfinished, but that album brought back such bad memories that he could not bear to face the tapes.

I told him that we had to listen to them.

"I don't want to listen to them," he replied.

A week or two later he relented. "Let's do it," he said.

That night we went to the studio and listened to the nine of the eleven tracks that had been recorded by Spector in Los Angeles ten months earlier. (Spector had kept two of the tracks for his own use as part of his settlement.) John listened to the best and next-best Spector mix of each song. As we listened John said over and over again, "These are awful. I must have felt terrible when I did these."

It appeared that Spector had kept all twenty-four tracks on during the recording, and none of the instrumental lines had enough clarity. Guitar tracks bled over keyboard tracks; electric guitar lines bled into acoustical guitar lines.

"Can't we take down some of his wall?" I asked John, referring to Spector's recording techniques.

He frowned and began to listen to the tapes again.

By the time we finished listening we were lost in gloom. First, the music was terrible; second, it brought us back to the nightmare of Los Angeles. "Well," John said finally, "what's past is past. At least I know what I've got to do now."

This disappointment was compounded by the release of *Pussycats,* which was preceded by a single, "Many Rivers to Cross." The single failed to sell, and this made it almost inevitable that the album would also fare poorly. John had many rationales for the album's commercial failure, but he was so disappointed that he preferred to push it all out of his mind.

Then, a few days later, Harold called and told John that the meeting with Levy was all set. Although he was nervous about finally meeting Levy face-to-face, John was also determined to resolve the matter. As soon as we sat down at that meeting, John launched into a sincere explanation of why *Rock* 'n' *Roll* had been delayed. Now that *Walls and Bridges* was finished, John concluded, he had every intention of completing the Spector album.

To John's relief the meeting went smoothly and quickly, and when we got home he told me that he had found Levy fascinating.

"Why?" I asked.

"He's such a character."

"He seems like a businessman to me."

"He is a businessman and he *is* a character."

A few days later Levy called and arranged another meeting. We met with him a few more times during September. These were social meetings and no lawyers were present, although a lot of the time at these meetings was taken up by extended discussions about the material John would record in order to finish the Spector album. John was so friendly that it must have appeared to Levy that he had acquired a new best friend, the legendary John Lennon. Morris told John that he owned a dairy farm in Upstate New York and he invited John to bring his musicians to his farm in October and rehearse them there before John went into the studio to finish the album. John eagerly accepted Levy's invitation.

When he told Harold Seider, Seider said, "I don't think you should go." The lawyer reminded John that basically John and Levy were adversaries and should not become friends until all their business matters were completely resolved and Levy had nothing to hold over John's head.

John ignored Harold. Occasionally he became so fascinated by a person that that person had real power over John and John would not listen to reason. As unpredictable as ever, John had become fascinated by Morris Levy.

There was nothing I could do about it, so I got on the phone and organized the rehearsal weekend. We arranged to fly Klaus Voormann, Jim Keltner, and Jesse Ed Davis to New York, where they would join Kenny Ascher and guitarist Eddie Mottau. In New York the band would be limousined to Morris Levy's dairy farm.

The musicians were as bemused as I was. They had never

expected that the next time they would be playing with John would be on a dairy farm owned by Morris Levy.

It was no surprise that John found the days to be exhausting, and we mainly spent our evenings relaxing with friends. Paul and Linda continued to show up, as did Mick. Mick, however, always called first. They'd turn up with a bottle of wine and we'd all sit around, discussing music and gossiping about our friends. One night he brought Glyn Johns with him. Glyn had engineered for both the Beatles and the Rolling Stones. During the evening Mick pulled me aside.

"Glyn is very angry at John," Mick said with a glint in his eye.

"Why?" I asked.

"It's something John said."

Mick and I began to whisper together, and after a minute or two, he had me laughing in anticipation. He was such a tease. Then I noticed John staring at us. He became instantly jealous when any man spoke to me. Mick noticed too and he said suddenly, "Glyn, why don't you tell John what's on your mind?"

"What's the matter?" John asked.

"He's angry at you."

"What's the matter, Glyn?" John could not bear anyone being angry with him.

"I'm trying to be mad at you, but you're so nice, it isn't easy," Glyn replied. Then he explained that he had been upset by John's comments about him in the "Lennon Remembers" interviews. John had said that *Let It Be,* which had been remixed by Glyn, had wound up sounding awful, and Glyn, a true professional, had been very offended by John's comments.

John did not remember saying it at all and he was very embarrassed. He explained, "I had just done primal therapy. I was just lettin' off steam. That interview was just a lot of anger."

Glyn stared at John. John's words had hurt him, and he had never expected that John would not remember what he had said, nor had he perceived that the comments would be dismissed as "just lettin' off steam." Like everyone else, he believed *everything* the public John said and took him very seriously.

John repeatedly apologized to Glyn, and eventually the matter was dropped. Neither Mick nor Glyn said anything, but I could see that they were genuinely puzzled by the fact that John's most influential interviews, interviews which people took as gospel truth, were for John occasions to blow off steam and then to forget what he said. Even they had to reckon with the difference between John the public myth—a man of devastating truth and honesty—and John the man behind the myth—a human being who could behave as capriciously as the rest of us.

We also renewed our friendships with Tony King and with David Bowie, who was eager to get John's reactions to his many new projects.

Mick and Bianca had been spending the summer and early fall at the shore, living in Andy Warhol's house in Montauk, and they proved the source of our one extended fall break at the ocean.

They had driven into town at the end of September to attend the fall opening of the Metropolitan Museum of Art. Before the opening Mick called and asked if he could drop in to visit us. He came to the door dressed in a subdued dark fall suit, looking wonderful as usual. After an hour he got up to leave. Suddenly he said, "Why don't you two come to the museum with us? Then we'll all go back to Montauk together."

John liked the idea of going to the beach, but he didn't much care about the museum opening. Mick began to twist his arm. "Come on. Come on. Let's go." John looked reluctant, but Mick would not take no for an answer. "All right, we'll go," John finally said.

"What should I wear?" I asked.

Mick flicked the lapel of his suit. "Oh, come as you are," he said.

John was dressed in jeans and a T-shirt. I was wearing a jump suit.

John looked at me. I knew that if I told John to get

dressed in something more conventional, he would just lose the impetus to go. So I looked at him very coolly and said, "I'm ready if you are. Just let me throw some things into an overnight bag." We slipped our matching black velvet jackets over the clothes we were wearing, and after I packed, we all went down to Mick's limousine and went to the hotel to pick up Bianca. When Mick left the car to get his wife, John, who had already met Bianca, said, "Now you're finally goin' to meet the mythical wife." I laughed. "Then when we get to the house, we'll meet the mythical child," he added. Neither of us had ever seen Mick's daughter, Jade.

Ten minutes later Mick returned with Bianca. "This is B.," he said. Bianca was elegantly dressed for the museum opening in a beautiful black double-breasted suit. She smiled at us and said hello. Then she settled back in the limousine and said nothing.

"I wanted to fly to Montauk," said Mick, "and I called the airport. But there was too much fog and I couldn't charter a plane. So I decided to keep the limousine and send it back to New York after it drops us off."

The museum opening was black-tie, and at the museum entrance the guard collecting the invitations stopped us and said to John, "I'm sorry, sir, but you can't come in. You're not dressed for the occasion."

"This is John Lennon," said Mick.

"I'm sorry, sir."

John was ready to turn away, but Mick wouldn't have it. He stood there arguing with the guard. "How could you turn away John Lennon? I can't believe you wouldn't allow John Lennon in." Then Bianca stepped forward. She was very charming, then she was very firm, and then she was charming again. Her determination was awesome. Finally the guard gave in and let us all in.

The museum was filled with rich, elegantly dressed women accompanied by formally dressed men. A bar had been set up on the second floor of the museum, and we gravitated toward it. Mick and John began to gossip about the guests, commenting on what they were wearing and what they looked like. Bianca, meanwhile, floated through the museum, looking extremely cool and collected. The opening was hosted by Diana Vreeland, who greeted Bianca warmly.

Among the guests was Jacqueline Onassis. When she spotted John, she smiled and said, "Hello. How are you?" and extended her hand. Then John introduced me to Mrs. Onassis, whom I was delighted to meet officially.

That world was an extraordinary one that I had never experienced before. I must admit I liked it, and not until that moment had I thought about how inelegant the world of rock 'n' roll was. This touch of sophistication pleased me very much.

After an hour or so, we were ready to leave. During the ride to the shore we all sat in the backseat of the limousine, and I sat between John and Mick. The car had a bar, and Mick, who loved to play host, kept pouring wine for us. First Mick turned to John, and they chatted casually about music. When that topic came to a logical conclusion, Mick turned to Bianca and gossiped about the jet set. When Bianca drifted off, Mick turned back to John. It appeared that Mick existed comfortably in two contradictory worlds and he seemed to have the best of both of them.

It was very late when we got to Montauk. "We'll call you at the end of the weekend so that you can come and pick up Mr. Lennon," Mick told the driver before the car was sent back to New York. Then we followed Mick and Bianca into Andy Warhol's house. John and I were very tired and we said good night and went straight to bed.

When we got up, we looked around Warhol's house. An old mansion at the water's edge, the house was very large and did not have a folksy feel to it, and John and I didn't really like it. The Jaggers had their own housekeeper, as well as a nanny for Jade, and the housekeeper had prepared breakfast for Bianca on the patio. We joined her, and she introduced us to Jade, who was an adorable little girl.

Mick, like John, thought that the children of celebrities should never be photographed. He too thought it unfair to the children and that it gave them the illusion that they were special only because their parents were famous. They both felt that public exposure also made the children ideal candidates for kidnapping. That's why there were so few published pictures of Jade.

When Mick walked outside, the little girl ran to her father and threw her arms around him. She obviously adored him and loved teasing him and playing with his hair. John whispered to me, "She's a regular little daddy's girl." She was.

After breakfast, Mick said, "What should we do?"

"What do you suggest?" asked John.

"Let's go fishing!"

"I'd love to go fishing," Bianca agreed. "But first I have to change." She got up and went into the house. We all went down to the car and waited. While we were waiting Mick grew more and more impatient. Finally he bellowed, "What's taking her so long?" It took Bianca forty-five minutes to assemble and put on her fishing costume. Looking like a natty female admiral, she finally emerged dressed in yellow trousers, a blue blazer, and high platform sneakers; a captain's hat was perched on her head.

Mick was driving a rental car. We all hopped into it, and Mick drove us to the Montauk pier. I had to notice that Mick really enjoyed being in charge.

There were clam sellers all along the pier. "I love clams!" Bianca announced as soon as she got out of the car, and she bought herself a plate. Meanwhile Mick rented a fishing boat for the day. It was rather beat up and came with a crew of four. As soon as we boarded the boat I began to talk to Jade. I looked up and saw Bianca staring at us. She looked annoyed. "Jade! Jade!" she called out as she ran across the deck to her daughter. Suddenly she slipped, fell, and screamed out in pain. We all ran to her, and Mick helped her up. "Are you all right?" he asked.

"It's nothing."

"It doesn't look like nothing," said Mick.

"I'll be all right." Bianca's face was twisted in pain.

"Are you sure you're all right?" Mick asked again. "Do you want to go to the hospital?"

"I think I've torn a ligament in my knee. I've done it before. There's nothing you can do for it." Looking brave, she leaned against the railing as the boat set sail. We were all concerned about Bianca, but whenever we approached her, she pooh-poohed us. Finally she said, "What I need is a scarf or a handkerchief to tie around my knee. Do you have a scarf?" None of us had one, and she hobbled away to speak to the crew. One of the men pulled a handkerchief from around his neck. It had been used to catch the sweat that dripped down to his face. Bianca tied it around her knee.

"Only my wife could find a color-coordinated handkerchief," Mick observed.

As the boat sailed into the bay, John spotted a house in the distance, perched on a cliff overlooking the water. "I love that house!" he exclaimed. "Look, it's made of stone. I'd love to live in a house like that."

He turned to the captain, who told him, "I think it's been vacant, and I happen to know it's for sale."

"I'd like to see it," John replied.

The boat was coming closer to the house. A small stone cottage, it looked like a storybook house. As soon as I saw it I fell in love with it also.

We spent the afternoon fishing. Most of the fish were caught by Bianca, who would grimace in pain and then expertly cast her line. Every time she cast, a porgy bit, and she would reel in the fish with great glee. Occasionally when Mick and John were talking, she would turn and interrupt the conversation. Mick would say, "Yes, B." "You're right, B.," Mick would respond. It had the effect of pacifying her without allowing her to get Mick's attention away from John.

At the end of the afternoon, when the boat docked at the pier, Mick dropped Bianca at their house—she said she was in so much pain she had to go back home—then he drove us to the stone house John had spotted from the boat. A next-door neighbor had the key and let us in. We stepped into the living room, which had a wood-burning fireplace. The sun was just setting, and the room was flooded with one last burst of sunlight. There were also two small but cozy bedrooms and a tiny kitchen. The kitchen equipment was old, and the floorboards were rotted. Nonetheless the house had a wonderful feel to it.

The neighbor told us that there was also an erosion problem: The sea had been eating away at the ground beneath the edifice.

"I wonder what they're asking," John said. The house was for sale for $250,000. He was given the realtor's number, then we drove back to Warhol's house. Dinner was ready, and the housekeeper had set the table for four. Then Bianca told us she wasn't going to join us. "I'm in too much pain to eat. I'm going straight to bed."

"Are you sure you don't have to go to the hospital?" Mick asked.

"No." Bianca twisted up her face in pain and stared at Mick. "I'll be fine. Good night." Then she hobbled from the table to her bedroom.

After dinner John, Mick, and I sat around while Mick strummed his guitar and John and he had a few drinks. We felt very relaxed. John could see that Mick was drinking a lot. On this night John wasn't. We had spent a tiring day, and Mick began to nod off. "I'm goin' to look in on B.," John said. "I want to make sure everything is all right before we go to bed." He thought that if Bianca was really in great pain and Mick got very drunk, he might not be able to help her.

After John left the room, Mick suddenly opened his eyes and leered at me. "What lovely legs you have," he cooed. "I didn't realize they were so long." Charming, flirtatious, and mischievous, Mick made me giggle. He giggled, too. He was being *Mick Jagger,* and we both knew it.

When John came back, he told us that Bianca was fine. It was not late, but we were both sleepy, so we went to bed.

I decided to go straight to sleep. John was reading a history of the Crusades and decided to stay up and read himself to sleep. As I lay next to him, beginning to drift off, he remarked, "You know, I love the house. We should really ask Harold to check into it." Then he asked, "Are you sure you can work with the kitchen?"

"I love the house. I just love it," I replied.

A little later he looked down at me. "Bianca is just like Yoko," he said. "She wants all the attention and she always finds a way to get it."

A few minutes later we heard a car pull up to the house. Flashing lights flooded our bedroom.

"Maybe it's Keith," said John.

"Why would Keith be turning up so late at night?"

Just then there was a knock at the bedroom door. "John," said Mick, "I don't have any cash. Can I borrow some money? It's the police."

John opened the door. Mick was very nervous and upset. John gave him all the cash we had—one hundred dollars. Mick took the money and left, then we heard some noises in the house.

I got up and looked out of the window. All I could see in the dark were three cars parked in the driveway. There were flashing lights on top of each. Then I saw Mick and Bianca leave the house, accompanied by police. John had become very panicky.

To him, police meant a raid, and he hated the idea of the two of us lying there in bed, vulnerable and defenseless, just as the police charged into the room. It reminded him of 1968 and the time he and Yoko had been raided. That raid, which led to a conviction for the possession of marijuana, was the cause of his ongoing immigration problem in the United States.

A little while later the phone rang. "Answer it," said John. I got up and went to the phone. It was Mick. "Everything's all right," he told me. He sounded very drunk. "While we were all sitting in the living room Bianca called the hospital. They sent the fuckin' police, an ambulance, and a fuckin' fire truck. We're in the hospital now. She's having her knee fixed."

I got off the phone and told John. "Why didn't she tell him she was callin'?" he asked. "I hate surprises like this." Before I went back to sleep he said, "You see, she *is* just like Yoko."

I could see the comparison. During the day, however, I had observed that when Bianca began to annoy Mick, he pacified her but remained unaffected by her games. He was always his own man. *John* had been the one who had responded deeply enough to Bianca's cues to go to her bedroom to see if she was all right.

The next morning, when Bianca appeared for breakfast, she was walking with a crutch. After breakfast she replaced the crutch with a cane, and she spent the morning alternating between the two.

Later John Phillips and Genevieve Waite came to visit. "It's gettin' a little too crowded," John told me.

We called for the limousine to take us back to New York.

The next morning John called Harold Seider and asked him to call the Montauk realtor and open a discussion about buying the house.

"Next summer's goin' to be even nicer than last summer," he told me after he got off the phone. "Next summer we're goin' to have our *own* fuckin' house."

A few days after we got back from Montauk, Mick and Charlie Watts invited us to join them at a party at Bud Praeger's apartment. Praeger managed rock 'n' roll bands. A little while after we got there, I saw John follow a girl into the bathroom. I didn't wait until things got out of control—I went and banged on the bathroom door. John opened it, and there was a sheepish look on his face. Later he explained that the girl had offered him cocaine.

The next night he decided to visit Yoko. An hour after he left, the phone rang. "Listen, May," said Yoko, "John's sick. It's his nerves. You know how nervous he gets. He's too sick to go home. I'll keep him overnight and send him home in the morning." I didn't like it, but there was nothing I could do about it. When John turned up the next day, I asked him, "How do you feel?"

"Better," he replied. "Better." That's all he had to say about his night with Yoko at his old apartment.

Early one morning a few days later, after a phone call from Tony King, John bounded out of the apartment. When he came back, he looked ashen. "Fung Yee, I have to talk to you," he said. We sat down beside each other. "The night after I met that girl at the party, I went out with her."

"I thought you were at Yoko's."

"I called Yoko and had her lie to you."

I was upset by John's behavior and puzzled by Yoko's.

Why would she cover up for John? I assumed she had to be up to something.

"I took the girl to The Bottom Line, and our fuckin' picture was taken. It's in the trade papers this mornin'. I've been out all over town, tryin' to buy up every copy so you wouldn't see it, but it's just no use. So I had to tell you."

I glared at John. He had lied to me, Yoko had lied to me, and yet again, John didn't care enough about me to avoid embarrassing me in public. However, as upset as I was, I was not *that* upset. There had not been a shadow of an argument for four months, and that incident—as unpleasant as it was—was certainly not in the category of his incredible drunken rages in California and the night he had nearly killed me in a Jacuzzi in Palm Springs.

"I didn't *fuck* the girl," said John. "Not really."

"The point is not what you did to her or what you allowed her to do to you, John. The point is, you lied to me."

"I love you. It fuckin' scares me. It scares me so fuckin' much, I had to do something. Whenever things go well, I've got to do something. Now I've done it. It's over."

Once again I was reminded that the better things were, the more chance there was of trouble. I remembered how, when we were in California, John had asked me to leave because we were getting too close. The fact that John really was so afraid of closeness made me feel awful.

He put his arms around me and begged me to forgive him.

"I don't want to be hurt again," I said quietly.

"I'll try. I'll try."

Then the girl called. John refused to speak to her, and she kept calling and calling. I took the phone over to John. "Your date is on the phone," I said. John shouted into the receiver, "I don't want to talk to her. I don't want to see her," then he slammed down the phone.

Later Yoko called. "John told me that he asked you to lie for him and you did—" I began.

"Listen, May," she interrupted, "I did it for your own good."

"What do you mean by that?"

Yoko's words stunned me.

"Did you know John gave the girl your home number? Why did he give her your number? He had to have a reason for giving out the number. If he didn't care about her, he never would have given out the number."

"I don't know why John gave her our number."

"He gave her the number because he was planning to get rid of you and replace you with her, that's why." I was stunned. "Do you know what I had to do? I had to talk him into keeping you. It was very hard, but I did it. So if I had to tell a little lie, it was for your own good. May, you know you should trust me. You really should."

I stared at the phone and then I stared at John. At that moment I didn't know whom to trust. Suddenly all the old bad feelings hit me at once, and I felt trapped. No matter how well John and I were doing, there were always surprises—ugly surprises. Once more I felt as if I were in water over my head, and I didn't know how and when John and Yoko would pull the plug. John smiled at me. The only thing I could feel at that moment was the chill of dread.

19

We had been together for fourteen months and our birthdays were soon approaching. John was going to be thirty-four on October 9 and I was going to be twenty-four on October 24. John loved the sitar sound, and Jimmy Iovine and I prowled around the guitar pawn shops until we found an old sitar-guitar, a model that was not being made anymore. I had a plaque made that read "With all my love" and had it mounted on the back of the instrument. John loved chocolate, and I also bought him a rich chocolate cake from his favorite baker, William Greenberg, Jr.

A day after his birthday, when Yoko called, she said, "John was very uptight by what you said on the back of the present. He thinks you want to marry him. That upset him very much. You made him very nervous. You know you shouldn't do things like that."

About a week after John's birthday, Elton's present arrived in a box from Van Cleef & Arpels. John unwrapped the box. Inside it he found a large black onyx pendant attached to a gold chain. The pendant was rimmed in gold, and there was an inscription from Elton on the rim. One side of the pendant was made of equal parts of gold and platinum, standing for gold and platinum records. The gold was shaped in the form of a wall, the platinum in the shape of a bridge—Elton's salute to John's album *Walls and Bridges*. On the other side the name

Winston O'Boogie—one of John's favorite pseudonyms—had been inscribed in flashing stones.

John stared at the inscription. "They're rhinestones," he said. His innate cheapness made him doubt anyone's generosity.

"I don't think so. Elton wouldn't go to Van Cleef & Arpels to buy rhinestones."

John studied the pendant for a minute or two, then dropped it on the floor near our bed.

Later when I was talking to Tony King, I asked him, "Tell me the truth. Are they rhinestones?"

"You must be kidding," Tony replied. "They're diamonds, my dear!"

When I told John, he dashed over to the bed, scooped up the pendant, held it above his head, and studied the inscription. The stones were diamonds. He carefully put the pendant on a shelf over our bed.

That weekend John rehearsed the musicians he was going to use to finish the Spector album, and Monday we took them into the studio and quickly performed and produced the basic tracks that would complete the album, which John later named *Rock 'n' Roll*.

In October and November John also worked very hard to promote *Walls and Bridges*. His efforts paid off, for John had both the top single and the top album in the country at that time. This stunning achievement both amazed and delighted him. Finally he had his number ones.

"It's what I always wanted, Fung Yee," he told me excitedly. "I didn't think I could do it, but I have."

When Yoko called on the morning that we got the news of John's triumph, I gave her the news. John was still asleep.

"May, everybody knows it's all a hype; that's all it is." I didn't say a word. She sounded so bitter and jealous that I couldn't even talk. However, when John called her back, she congratulated him profusely on his triumph.

A day or two later Elton also called to congratulate John. Then Elton reminded John that he had promised to perform "Whatever Gets You Thru the Night" with Elton in New York at his Madison Square Garden concert if the song made it to the number one position.

Looking at John, I could see that he was panicky. "I did make the promise," he told Elton.

"You don't have to do it if you don't want to," Elton said generously. "We were just kidding around."

"No, no. A promise is a promise. . . . But we'll talk more about it."

Old friends had also prevailed upon John to promote a stage show of Beatles music, *Sgt. Pepper's Lonely Hearts Club Band on the Road,* which was scheduled to open on November 14 at the Beacon Theatre. As the fourteenth approached, John invited Yoko to the show, but she did not want to go.

I just knew she would show up unexpectedly, though. It seemed inconceivable that she would miss the opportunity to embarrass John in public by forcing him to acknowledge her presence when he was with me, and I told him so.

"She told me she wasn't goin'," John said firmly.

That night, after we arrived at the opening and were in our seats, Harold Seider walked over to us. "Yoko's here," he said. "She doesn't want to sit in the back."

John froze. Then he gave me one of his helpless looks. I was right. Yoko, who had gone with Arlene Reckson and Arlene's date, had decided to give John a public test. If I stayed put, I knew John wouldn't ask me to move. Inevitably, though, he would wind up wallowing in guilt about the way he had treated Yoko, and I would have to deal with his upset. It was something I did not look forward to. "Will it make it easier if I switch seats with her?" I asked.

John thought for a moment, then he snapped, "Tell her she'll have to sit in the back."

I was amazed. John knew that I would willingly switch seats with Yoko so that she could save face. That was the first time that John had been willing to show the public that he was with me, not with her. Arlene told me that Yoko made no comment about John's decision. During the show she did announce, "You know, a lot of those songs are pretty good." It was the first time she had ever bothered to listen to all of those classic Lennon-McCartney songs, even though she had known John for seven years. The Beatles' music simply had no meaning to her.

At the end of the performance we got up and dashed down the aisle, hoping to avoid being caught in the crowd. We moved so quickly, we did not realize that Yoko had gotten up and had followed after us, calling out, "John . . . John." She even stood on the street, watching our limousine pull away while she continued to call for John to stop. Then she became moody, especially since the mob surrounding the theater had seen John ignore her.

In the limousine John said, "Who would have known Yoko was coming tonight," and then he froze. He smiled warily at me, and we let the subject drop.

There was a party after the show at a discotheque called Hippopotamus. As soon as we arrived John marched straight over to the bar. After a drink or two, he began to flirt with any woman who passed by. Soon women were hugging and kissing him and sitting on his lap. I watched for a few minutes, then I said, "If you don't cut it out, I'm leaving."

He had become drunk very quickly; his expression was glazed and he could hardly hear me. This time I was determined not to be around if he used liquor as an excuse to run riot.

"I'm leaving," I said again, then I got up and walked out. After a few hours, it was apparent that he was not coming home. Suspecting that he might employ Yoko in some scheme to deceive me, I called her. "John's not home," I said. "Is he with you?"

"No, May."

"Have you heard from him?"

"No, May."

"Do you know where he is?"

"No, May."

"If you do hear from him, I'd like to know," I said.

"Was he on liquor?" asked Yoko.

"Yes."

"Was he on cocaine?"

"Yes."

There was a pause. Then Yoko said, "You know, May, I'm thinking of taking him back."

"What did you say?"

"I'm thinking of taking him back."

Even though she said it evenly and with no trace of emotion, I knew she meant it. Yoko always meant everything she said. Just as she had wanted to get John and me together and had gotten what she wanted, I knew she wanted John back and would get that also. John had defied and embarrassed her in public—to reassert her power over him, and, knowing Yoko, that would be reason enough to avenge herself for the slight. I knew I would have to pay a thousandfold for that moment of pleasure I felt a few hours earlier when John told Yoko to sit in the back of the theater. I was heartbroken. I sat up that night until dawn, by myself, my back pressed against a chair. Yoko's voice played over and over again in my head: *"I'm thinking of taking him back."* Tears ran down my cheeks. I knew that it was the beginning of the end.

When John returned the next day, he told me he had left Hippopotamus with a group of people and had wound up in the apartment of a well-known black model. Then he had left that apartment and wound up in the apartment of the black wife of someone who worked in the music business.

"I didn't fuck her," he said. "Not really."

I said nothing.

"Fung Yee, you look like a jealous housewife."

"You're wrong," I replied. "Jealous housewives stay and defend their property. I left because I knew you were going to go crazy. What bothers me is, you drank and you used your drinking as an excuse to raise hell.

"And what really bothers me is that when I spoke to Yoko, she told me she was thinking of taking you back. What that really means is that she wants you back and she's got a plan to get you back, and I know she knows how to get you back."

John froze. "That's just Yoko," he finally said.

"You're right. That is Yoko, and that's why I'm upset. I don't want any surprises. If you're thinking of leaving, I want to know about it."

"I'm not goin' back."

John glared at me and I did not challenge him, even though I did not believe him. From that moment on John was very cool to Yoko on the phone. I could see him making a real effort to resist her. Looking back, I only wish I could have helped him more.

20

A few days later, arrangements were made for us to travel with Elton to see his performance at the Boston Garden before John appeared with him at Madison Square Garden. Elton's forty-four-city tour had been arranged so that during the eastern part of the tour he could live at the Sherry Netherland Hotel in New York City, fly to his engagement on a chartered jet, the *Starship Two*, and then fly back to New York and sleep at the hotel.

Elton really liked John, and once again I was reminded of the efficiency of Elton's machine. From the moment we left our apartment until we returned from Boston late that night, Elton made sure that we were comfortable and happy. He was as generous as he was efficient, and it really pleased him to see John happy.

John and I loved the concert from the moment Elton made his entrance, prancing on stage wearing a four-foot-high ostrich plume headdress, until the finale almost three hours later.

After Elton did his first three numbers, John turned to me and said, "This makes me want to be back on the road. I'd love to tour. I'd love to tour." By the time the show was over his mood had changed. "You know, it's too much responsibility for me. At least with the Beatles there were four of us to share the load. This time it would only be me. I don't think I can do it all meself."

After the show, John and Elton threw their arms around each other. The performance had been a great triumph. All we could talk about on the flight back to New York was how John's appearance at Madison Square Garden would make Elton's show even more exciting.

During the days John continued to mix *Rock 'n' Roll*. When John had a completed rough mix of the album, he said, "I'm goin' to give Morris [Levy] a copy of the rough tracks. It will show him that I've acted in good faith." Once again Harold Seider warned him. "You're crazy," he said. "What does he need a tape for? You can send him the album when it's finished."

"Morris has been a real gentleman to me," John replied. "And besides, these mixes are so rough, no one would put them out anyway."

During the two weeks before the Thanksgiving night Madison Square Garden concert, we spent a lot of time hanging out with Elton. One night in Elton's suite at the Sherry Netherland, there was a knock at the door, and Elton opened it. A group of policemen stood outside.

Elton was told that an anonymous call had been made to the police. The caller had stated that he was in the hotel with a gun and that he was looking for Elton. The policemen warned Elton to be careful, just in case.

After the policemen left, everyone became very upset. John was especially nervous, since he was about to appear live on stage for the first time in three years.

A Sunday afternoon rehearsal was scheduled at the Record Plant for the weekend before Elton's New York opening night. When we got there, Elton had already thoroughly rehearsed the band. He was a perfectionist and he felt honored by John's desire to appear with him. Determined that when he and John performed they would sound exactly as they had sounded on record, he had gone to the extent of making sure that the horn section would play their parts note for note like the horns on the record. The precision was astonishing.

The rehearsal went quickly and smoothly. After they ran through "Whatever Gets You Thru the Night" and "Lucy," they began to discuss an encore. Someone suggested "Imagine," which John instantly vetoed. "We've done a song of Elton's and a song of mine. Let's pick a neutral number." He thought a second. "Let's go all the way back."

"How about 'I Saw Her Standing There'?" asked Elton.

John loved the idea. "It's one of the few Beatles songs I *didn't* sing lead on."

The number was worked up quickly and then the rehearsal was over. When John got home, he was a wreck.

During the week Elton kept in close touch with him and kept trying to reassure him. He really wanted John to make the date.

When Yoko called, John told her about the preparations for the show. She told John she wanted to go. "She doesn't want to be left out of the excitement," John observed.

I wondered if she thought that if she turned up unannounced, John, once again, would tell her to sit in the back.

I called Tony King. "Would you mind arranging tickets for Yoko," I said, "and getting her there? This time she *wants* to go."

Even though in the future John would tell the press that he did not know who was going to be there that night, he not only knew, but Yoko had also complained a number of times about her seating location.

On the night before the show we visited Elton at the hotel. People came and went all night long. It was a relaxed and pleasant evening.

As soon as we got home John ran to the bathroom and threw up. He looked green. I had seen him drink a few glasses of champagne as the night went on. "Is it the liquor?" I asked.

"It's the cocaine."

I had not seen anyone offer John any drugs. "When did you get some?"

"When you went to the bathroom."

"Who gave it to you?"

"I don't know who the person was."

"Who was it?" I asked again.

"I won't tell. You'll yell at him."

"How much did you have?"

"A lot."

If there was such a thing as cocaine-and-champagne poisoning, John had it. He was sick in the bathroom for a while, and so I got into bed. When he came out of the bathroom, he came over to me, climbed on top of me, and began to kiss me. He was very affectionate and he wanted me to hold him tightly and to hug him very hard. Then he started to cry.

"What's wrong?" I asked.

"Please forgive me."

"Why?"

"Please forgive me. I don't want to hurt you. I know I hurt you in the past. I don't want to do it again."

"It's all right, John. It's all right."

I rocked him in my arms and stroked his hair.

"I'm serious," he sobbed. "I mean it. I don't want to hurt you."

I continued to speak soothingly to him, telling him again and again that everything was all right, and finally I calmed him down. John looked gratefully at me. Then, happily, we made love through the following morning.

When John got up the next day, he still felt sick. Throughout the afternoon he suffered from attacks of vomiting and diarrhea. Phone calls were traded back and forth between our apartment and the Sherry Netherland, and Elton told us that he felt sick, too.

"It's just his nerves," I kept telling everyone who called. "He'll make it." I wanted John to make the performance. Just as he had finally been able to prove himself as a solo recording artist, I thought it important that he prove to himself that he could also perform in front of a live audience.

I sat with him, holding his hand, reassuring him. "I'm not nervous anymore," he told me. "I'm too sick to be nervous."

As the evening approached he grimly got up and dressed in his black suit. Then he put on Elton's pendant, and numbly we went to the limousine. John was numb during the ride to the Sherry Netherland, where we picked up Elton and went to Madison Square Garden. All of us were very quiet in the limousine. It was as if we were going to a wake.

There was an almost eerie calm backstage at the Garden.

Yoko had sent a single large flower each to John and Elton, and John took his and stuck it in his lapel. We were led to John's dressing room and we sat alone together.

"I can't wait until it's over," he said.

"Don't worry, you'll be fine."

"I'm very sick."

"You're going to be terrific."

He got up and looked in the mirror. "How do I look?"

"Wonderful."

"Are you sure?"

"I'm sure."

For two hours I kept gently reassuring him.

"Fung Yee," he finally said, "just be around when I go on, so I can see you."

"Anything you say, John."

When John was called, we both stood in the wings. Then Elton announced John, and John walked to center stage to an incredible ovation, and I walked on stage and stood near the speakers near Elton's piano, so that John could see me. The difference between the private and public John was startling. John was nervous when he first began to sing and play, but he quickly picked up steam. Occasionally he turned and looked at me. I sang and danced and gave him reassuring smiles, and with each note he grew stronger and stronger. It was an amazing performance, and the audience went wild. I thought the building would collapse during "I Saw Her Standing There."

I was convinced that a whole world of touring had opened for John. He had experienced the love of his audience first-hand, and he had been able to communicate his love to them. Though he didn't say too much, I could tell that he was also deeply moved.

After the show, we went to a party at the Pierre. John was in a jubilant mood, but he also did not want to spoil the evening by drinking and he did not want to stay too late. So we decided to do a quick round of table-hopping, and Yoko joined us for a short while. "May, it was a nice concert, wasn't it?" she told me when she sat down. John and she made small talk for about twenty minutes, but John was very distracted. Uri Geller, a psychic, was at another table and was using his powers of concentration to bend keys, and John preferred seeing Geller's tricks. Finally he took my arm and we got up and left Yoko and went over to Geller's table, where Geller was busy bending the house keys of a young couple. We learned later that he had bent their keys so badly, they found themselves locked out of their apartment.

A little while later John said, "Let's go," and we did. He hadn't even said good night to Yoko. He was still working hard to resist her and he did not spend too much time with her on the phone during the following week either.

As early December arrived John told me to make arrangements to bring Julian over for Christmas. On the day that I made them Morris Levy called to chat with John, and John told him about Julian's forthcoming visit. Morris had a son, Adam, who was approximately Julian's age. He suggested that after Julian arrived, we join them at Levy's condominium in West Palm Beach, Florida. John eagerly accepted Morris's offer to have a Florida vacation.

When John told Harold Seider, Harold said, "I don't think you should go. Your business with Morris isn't finished yet."

John was adamant, in part because he would be able to show Julian Disney World.

Then John's past began to catch up with him. The Apple negotiations were drawing to a close, and George Harrison had arrived in the United States and launched a solo tour. One night John's lawyers visited us at our apartment. Many years had been devoted to negotiating an agreement to dissolve Apple. The lawyers had had innumerable meetings with John; they had answered every one of his questions clearly and had sent him copies of each piece of correspondence concerning the negotiations. The whole experience had been exhausting and extremely difficult.

John wanted takeout Chinese food that night, and we sat in bed eating from cartons while Harold, Michael Graham, and David Dolgenos sat on the edge of the bed for hours, once again going over the settlement point by point. As always, John cocked his head to one side, listened carefully, and asked pertinent questions. At the same time the lawyers could see that he remained distant. He wanted to get it over with.

When they were finished, Harold turned to the subject of Lee Eastman, Linda McCartney's father, who was then managing Paul's career. "Lee Eastman is determined to get Paul out of this agreement. He wants Paul to get his solo royalties directly and he's willing to pay anything to accomplish this. Because of that fact, this is a really good deal for you, John. In fact, you've come out better than we all thought you would. I think you should sign."

"I'm just glad it's over," John replied. "Let's just get the fuckin' thing over." After the lawyers left, all John wanted to do was watch television. I knew he didn't want to reflect on any aspect of the official end of the Beatles and I knew better than to ask him any questions.

John seemed to be in a very strange state of mind about the dissolution. From the hints he had dropped since we had been together, I had learned that John's departure from the Beatles had essentially been Yoko's idea. Without Yoko to drive him forward, he felt strangely ambivalent about officially ending the Beatles at that moment. By nature, also, he felt inclined to take a position opposite from that of Paul McCartney. Paul desperately wanted that agreement signed. Whether or not it was the best thing for him to do, John, on principle, was inclined not to want to sign it.

After the meeting John turned his attention to George's tour and he learned that George was not getting good reviews and that business was off. George was so upset, he was considering not playing New York.

"Tell him I'll do anything—anything I can—to help," John told Neil Aspinall, who had been managing director of Apple and had come to New York to attend the final Apple meetings.

A few days later, as soon as George arrived at the Plaza Hotel after his gig in Washington, D.C., John called him and told him we'd like to see him, and we dashed to the hotel. We were to meet George in the hospitality suite, a suite where the people on George's tour could spend their free time. In a few minutes George entered the room. He was accompanied by his friend Olivia Arias, an attractive young Mexican-American who had been George's secretary and had run his Dark Horse Records label in the United States, and whom George subsequently would marry.

George looked very tired and upset. The difficulties he was having with his tour were written all over his face, and he seemed reticent to me as John and he greeted each other and sat down. George remembered me from the time we met when I was working at ABKCO, and he told John, "I'm glad you're with May. She's really a lovely girl." George's disapproval of Yoko went back at least as far as the original *Imagine* sessions in 1971.

John smiled appreciatively. "I know she is. I'm glad you like her, too."

John was determined to be open and friendly. George, however, seemed edgy, and all of his replies were curt and had a hostile edge to them. A long hour went by, filled with off-and-on talk about the tour. Then John finally hinted that he would be willing to play with George when he appeared at Madison Square Garden. "Well, maybe I can come and help ya," he said.

"That'd be nice." George glowered at John. Then George's anger really burst forth. "Where were you when I needed you!" he snapped. It was the first of a series of explosions, each of them followed by moments of tense silence. "I did everything you said. But you weren't there," he repeated.

"You always knew how to reach me," John would reply evenly to each of these outbursts.

There was no doubt in my mind, watching those two, that George's anger with John had been accumulating for years. It was exactly the kind of situation that John usually ran from. But I could see in that moment that he loved George enough to remain calm and still as George drilled away at him.

George said that repeatedly in the past he had sung what John wanted him to sing, said what John wanted him to say. Because John wanted it, George had gone along with the decision to go with Allen Klein. In the nearly four years since, John had virtually ignored him, a fact that pained George deeply. George's voice grew even more harsh as he blasted John for his sudden appearance, as if out of nowhere, to offer an evening's worth of help.

Yet again George said furiously, "I did *everything* you said, but you weren't there."

Suddenly he leveled his gaze at John. "You know, John," he snarled, "I want to see your eyes. I can't see your eyes."

John was wearing sunglasses. He reached up and quickly took them off and put on his regular glasses. He was willing to do anything to pacify George. But the gesture was not enough. It looked as though George was going to slap John.

"I *still* can't see your eyes." Suddenly he reached over, yanked John's glasses from his face, and dashed them to the floor. His face was a mask of fury and contempt; I had never seen an angrier man. George's anger even paralyzed John.

I knew how panicky John became when he could not see. I expected him to jump up and hit George. I was terrified that George might be satisfied only by a fistfight.

Yet, miraculously, John stayed calm. There was a long silence. Then George returned to the basic theme of his anger, but I could see that the worst moment had passed.

Finally, well after midnight, it all wound down. John and I were bone weary, and we took a suite right there at the Plaza. When we were alone John told me, "I saw George goin' through pain and I know what pain is about. So I let him do it.

"I'll go out and help him or whatever it is he wants me to do. If he wants me to go out on stage, I will."

John looked at me. I was crying.

"You two are like brothers," I said. "I can't stand it when people like you who love each other so much can't get along."

Then *I* was the hysterical one. The tension in George's suite had been so great, I couldn't hold my feelings in, and that night, after his scene with George, John had to spend another hour calming me down.

The next day we saw George, and everything was fine. As soon as George saw John, he hugged and kissed him. "Please forgive me," he said. "I wasn't feeling well last night. I didn't mean to get upset." It was as if the previous night had not occurred. Yet again I realized how unpredictable they *all* were!

That night we went with George to Nassau Coliseum to

see his show. John was delighted when he discovered that George's opening act, Ravi Shankar, was sick and could not go on. "Thank God," he said. "At least we don't have to go through that."

We watched from the wings, and some kids sitting in the first few rows spotted us and began to scream for John, so we stepped back. John didn't want to take the spotlight from George, and George had not asked him to go on.

At the end of the show John, who could see how ragged the show was, said, "I can help him." He felt that a surprise appearance by him would give the concert the punch it lacked.

On the way back to New York John again told George that he was willing to appear on stage with him.

"Thank you," said George quietly; no commitments were made.

By the time George was scheduled to play the Garden, Paul had arrived in New York. Julian was also scheduled to arrive on the day of that concert. During the day John was notified that the Apple negotiations were rapidly drawing to a close and that the final documents were about to be photocopied. John was told to be prepared to sign the final documents at midnight, after George's concert. At that time three of the four Beatles would gather together for the purpose of signing the papers that would officially dissolve their partnership. (Ringo had stayed in London to avoid being served with an Allen Klein subpoena and would sign the papers there.)

After John got the news, he said nothing. We were sitting in the bedroom, and I got up to go to the kitchen when John suddenly slammed the door and locked it behind me.

"John, what's the matter?" I called out.

"I'm not goin' to sign the agreement," he said through the closed door.

"What?"

"It's not fair. I've got to pay more taxes than the others. I'm being taxed twice as much."

I went to the door and tried to reason with him.

"Harold has told you again and again that this is the best deal you can have. He's told you that you've come out better than he ever thought you would. It's taken years to reach this point. I think you should sign."

John said nothing.

"Open the door."

There was more silence.

"What's going on?"

He refused to reply. I stood outside the door, wondering what to do. I knew that the settlement included a provision that John pay $1,000,000 in United States taxes, based on his income while he resided in the United States. Still, Harold Seider repeatedly had explained that there was no way around it. At that moment John was at his most unpredictable. Suddenly his fears that his money was going to be taken away from him, that he was going to be cheated, that he had to have as much money as possible, had all come into play. This was also John's way of resisting the reality that the Beatles were officially about to come to an end and that Paul was about to prevail.

I continued to try to coax him to unlock the door, but he would do nothing. It was one of those horrible moments when I knew that the only thing I could do was call Yoko, ask for help, and hope that *she* would behave in a rational manner.

I picked up the phone, called her, and told her, "John has decided he doesn't want to sign the agreement. He's very upset and he's locked me out of the bedroom. Yoko, you know it's taken a long time to reach this agreement. You know it's in both of your best interests to sign it. I don't often ask you for help, but I need your help this time. I want you to tell him to sign it."

"I knew it. I knew there would be trouble," she replied.

"That's not the point. The point is, we've got to avoid trouble."

"Don't tell him you spoke to me. I'll have to think of something. I'll call you back."

Half an hour later John unlocked the door. He was very shaky. He called Harold and told him of his decision not to sign the agreement. Harold told him not to worry, that he would take care of it. A little while later Julian arrived. Even though John was distracted, he had a warm reunion with his son. We took Julian out for a walk and something to eat before we sent him off with Hilary Gerrard to the first of George's two concerts at the Garden. When we returned, a messenger had left a letter to John from Yoko. It was lying in front of the door. John picked it up and opened it.

His reaction was astonishment. "Yoko's astrologer told her to tell me I shouldn't sign the agreement. She's written a letter to warn me. Isn't that amazing?"

"It is amazing," I replied. Amazing for all the wrong reasons.

George called just before his concert. "Do you want to speak to John?" I asked.

"No." George had heard about John's decision and he was livid. "Just tell him I started this tour on my own and I'll end it on my own," he snarled. Then he slammed down the phone.

Later that night Paul called, too. Unlike George, he was exceptionally even-tempered. John explained to Paul his feelings about the unfairness of the tax provision, and they both agreed that they would try to find a solution.

The next day John abruptly decided he had to see Lee Eastman, choosing after three years of legal maneuvering suddenly to become his own lawyer. I was astonished by John's decision, and so were all of our lawyers, but there was nothing anyone could do about it. John had decided he had to see Eastman, period. A meeting was arranged for that evening.

When Paul and Linda called, I told Linda, "We're going to see your father tonight." Even she appeared to know nothing about the surprise meeting.

"Well, I'm always in favor of that!" she replied chirpily.

George was scheduled to give a second concert at the Garden that night, and just before we left, John dispatched Julian, with Hilary, to George's show and told him to tell George that he had gone to visit Lee Eastman in an attempt to solve the problem.

The Eastmans lived in a vast, elegant Park Avenue apartment, which housed an impressive collection of Picassos, Cornells, and de Koonings. Eastman shook hands with John and led us into the study. He beckoned us to a couch, and we sat facing him while Neil Aspinall, who had accompanied us, found a chair at the side of the room.

Eastman did not seem pleased by the visit from John. They spoke for an hour, and it was easy to sense Eastman's resentment. To him, John was a troublemaker: He was the one who had insisted that Allen Klein be hired to manage the Beatles; he was the one who was refusing to sign the agreement. At the end of a rather unpleasant hour, Eastman said contemptuously, "John, you don't know the trouble you've caused. It really is all your fault. That's why George hates you. He'll never forgive you. He never wants to speak to you. He'll never speak to you again."

"We'll see about that, Lee. I'm just tryin' to work it out," John replied.

"There's nothing to work out." Then Eastman tried again to convince John to sign the agreement, repeatedly returning to the point that George hated John and that the only shot John had at ever being George's friend again was by signing the document.

The tug-of-war continued for over half an hour. Then the phone rang, and Eastman answered it.

It was Julian calling John, and John asked me to speak to him. I took the call in another room. "I just saw George," Julian told me excitedly. "He has a message for Dad. He wants to tell him that all is forgiven and he still loves him and he wants him to come to his party tonight."

When I stepped back into the study, I announced, "Julian has a message from George to John."

"Yes?" asked John.

"George says all is forgiven and he still loves you. He wants you to come to his party tonight."

John beamed. So did I. Eastman, however, was dismayed. Five minutes later the meeting was over, and Neil took us to George's party at the Hippopotamus discotheque, and we all had a wonderful time. John finally signed the agreement in early January.

During the next few days, we took Julian to Montauk to see the stone house John was thinking of buying. "This will be our house by next summer," John told him. "Next summer you'll be staying here with us." Then we left for Florida, where we celebrated Christmas early. When we returned to New York, we decided to give Julian a second Christmas and we shopped for gifts and a tree. John told me that he would put up the tree and wrap the presents, because he could see that I was exhausted. Gratefully I went to take a nap. When I woke up, John was asleep beside me. I got up, and Julian and I put up the tree, decorated it, and wrapped all the presents. At two in the morning John finally got up, only to discover that the job was done.

Then Yoko began to call John to tell him how much she had missed Julian and how much she wanted to see him, despite the fact that she had once made it clear to me that she found being with Julian very upsetting, because John had Julian, while she did not have Kyoko. Yoko kept insisting upon seeing Julian, and a time was set for her visit. As soon as Yoko entered the apartment, she threw her arms around Julian's neck and kissed him. "I've missed you so much," she said. Then she launched into a lengthy, loving conversation with him, asking him about his life and school. Butter couldn't have melted in her mouth.

She was also very cordial to me. John and I showed her our apartment. She was especially fascinated by the mirror over the fireplace. After she had looked around, she turned to me and said, "Not bad." Later she would mirror the ceiling above her bed. After an hour, she kissed Julian good-bye.

Then she started to call, urging John to bring Julian to the Dakota for a visit. John took him there after New Year's and before the boy returned to England. The short visit to the Dakota was the only time John had seen Yoko without my being there during the previous two months.

Julian left soon after the New Year, and John returned to the job of mastering *Rock 'n' Roll* and also started to write new songs.

I had a hunch he was eager to make a new album.

A few nights later we went out with Paul and Linda. During the evening Paul had a brainstorm. "Let's call David." We called David Bowie, and he invited us over to his suite at the

Pierre. John and I had seen him a couple of times before our Christmas holiday, and he had always insisted upon playing us the tracks of his new album, which he would title *Young Americans*. That night he played the album for Paul and Linda, even though John and I had heard it many times before. When it was over, he played it again. I could see Paul getting restless. "Can we hear a different album?" he asked. David ignored him, and when he began to play it a third time, John said, "It's great. Do you have any other albums that might be of interest?"

For a moment Bowie seemed startled by John's request, then he smiled and told me to pick another record. I selected an Aretha Franklin album and put it on the turntable. Then David said, "Excuse me for a second." He marched out of the room.

"I think you hurt Bowie's feelings," I told John.

"Paul's been askin' him all night to change the record," John replied.

"His feelings are hurt, John."

Linda suddenly piped up. "Oh, no. That's just the way he is."

As soon as we got home that night David called John. They talked quietly for a while, and when John got off the phone, he told me, "David really did feel hurt when I asked him to change the record. He was very upset. I kept tellin' him I didn't mean it that way." John was very distressed by David's reaction.

"When David looks at you, his eyes are always filled with admiration," I told him. "You've got to be especially careful when you're around people like that, because every little word and gesture means something special to them. Whether you like it or not, you've just got to be a little more thoughtful."

We continued to talk about how hard it was to be John Lennon, even in the company of other rock stars like David Bowie. I said to John, "Are you going to tell Paul?"

He grimaced. "Are you kiddin'?" he snapped. "It's not worth it. He wouldn't understand anyway."

Soon afterward David called to invite us to an overdubbing session of *Young Americans*. During the session John and guitarist Carlos Alomar began to jam on a riff that had a really funky feel to it. It took David half an hour to set a lyric to the riff. The song was "Fame." Coauthored by John, "Fame" became David's first number one hit.

Disaster hit when John discovered that Morris Levy was planning to take the tape of *Rock 'n' Roll* that John had given him and market it as a TV mail-order record called *Roots.* "He can't do it. The tape sounds terrible. I don't want anyone to hear it. It's got stuff on it no one's supposed to hear."

But it was too late. Ads had already begun to appear on TV. John was furious. I thought his bad mood might drive him to drink, but it didn't. He decided to throw all his energies behind putting the finishing touches on *Rock 'n' Roll* and then promoting it as vigorously as he could. He wanted to fight Levy and he was determined to win. Eventually the two would wind up in court.

A day or two later the phone rang, and I answered it. "John, it's Yoko," I said as I brought him the phone. When John took it, his expression changed to anger. Before she had said a word he shouted, "Yoko, I don't have time to speak to you," and he slammed down the phone.

John turned to me. "That's it, I'm through."

The phone rang again. Yoko was enraged. "May, I never want you to do that again to me. He hung up on me. I don't understand what's going on. I don't understand what you're trying to do to me."

"I put you on the phone with John the way I always do."

"But he was angry. How could you put him on the phone if he was angry?"

"To tell you the truth, he didn't get angry until he picked up the phone."

Yoko paused. "Is he angry now?"

"No."

There was another pause. "May, don't do this again. This must never happen again."

"Yoko," I replied, ready to go further than ever with her, "there's nothing I can do about how he acts when he starts to speak to you. That's a problem between the two of you."

There was no answer. She had hung up on me.

When she called later, John refused to speak to her. Yoko tried that night, then several times the next day. Whenever she asked to speak to John, he signaled me, and I had to tell her that he would not come to the phone. She tried repeatedly for another day or two, then she stopped calling, and we did not hear from her for a week. When she finally called again, John decided to say hello.

He listened while Yoko talked to him. As he listened I could see his expression changing as he grew more interested in what she was telling him. "Did it really work? . . . How long did it take? . . . How do you feel?" he asked excitedly.

"She's stopped smokin'!" John exclaimed when he got off the phone. "She hasn't smoked in a week. She's going to try to set it up so that I can stop, too."

"How did she stop?"

"Yoko says she found a new way to stop smokin'. But she won't tell me what it is. She hasn't wanted a cigarette from the moment she stopped. Isn't that amazin', especially the way she chain-smokes."

"It sounds like Yoko."

"I'd love to try it." John really did want to stop smoking. He hated the fact that smoking two packs of Gauloises a day had shortened his breath and given him chronic cigarette cough. An hour later Yoko called, and a time was set for the meeting between John and the man who had gotten Yoko to stop smoking. I remember it was on a Monday. John was madly enthusiastic.

I sensed danger. "Everything is going so well. Please don't start these games again," I told him.

"Oh, Fung Yee, it's over, and Yoko knows it. All she's tryin' to do is help me."

"I want to come with you when you take the cure," I replied.

"No, no. Yoko doesn't want to see you, and I don't want to upset her. This is just between us." John threw me a look. He did not want to hear any more.

For the next few days Yoko called John repeatedly to tell him how effective the smoking cure had been. She kept telling him she hadn't smoked a cigarette but she wouldn't describe the "cure" to him. Each time she called John grew even more excited and curious.

"She's playing with you," I said.

"You're bein' silly," John replied.

To be logical with John about that matter was to deprive him of his fun. I did not want to admit it, but I knew I had been trapped again. Nonetheless on Monday morning, the day that John was supposed to go to the Dakota, Yoko called.

"The stars aren't right," she told him. "I've canceled the meeting." She said that she would call back with a better time. That same day Yoko called with an appointment for Wednesday at seven in the evening. John was very pleased.

"John," I said, "can't you see you're being teased?"

He did not respond. What he did not want to see he ignored.

That evening we got a call from Paul. He and Linda were going to New Orleans to begin a new album, which turned out to be *Venus and Mars.* "We'd like you to meet us there," Paul told John.

"I'd really like to go," John said to me after the call. "I've never been to New Orleans, and it's Mardi Gras season, and I'd love to see it. And it will be fun to watch Paul record."

I was pretty sure that if I could get John to New Orleans, Paul would do the rest and get him into the studio to record with him. It was a very exciting prospect, but I said nothing about it, because I did not want to put John off. But he kept bringing up the trip, and each time he mentioned it he grew more enthusiastic. He seemed unaware of the possibility of recording with Paul again, but I think, deep down, that he also realized that he and Paul finally were ready to work together again.

A meeting was scheduled that night for Al Coury, Harold Seider, and us to discuss the promotion and marketing of *Rock 'n' Roll.*

"Fung Yee, listen to the tape with me," John said.

After John played the tapes, he looked at me and shrugged his shoulders.

"John, you wanted a classic Spector album. I don't have

the best ear in the world, but I do know the classic Spector hits had extreme lows and highs. These tracks are all middle.''

In the silence that followed, I realized he was listening seriously.

''You've got to pick the best of these tracks and be done with it. This album is a dream gone wrong. Years from now when people listen to it they'll know how upset you were before you got it together and made *Walls and Bridges.*''

John wasn't depressed by what I said. ''Let me think,'' he said.

That night at the meeting John stated that he was taking ''Angel Baby'' and ''Be My Baby'' off the album. He had come to the same conclusion about *Rock 'n' Roll* that I had—that less of it was more.

''What do you think of me decision?'' he asked me when we got home.

''If you believe they're the weakest tracks, then you should take them off the album.''

John abruptly changed the subject, not wanting to think about the album anymore. ''Do you know what I'd like to do this weekend? I'd like to drive out to Montauk and look at the house. Just the two of us. This time we'll be alone together. It will be winter. It will be beautiful, and I just really want to see it one more time.''

It was a wonderful idea.

''Then we'll go to New Orleans next week, and then I'll come back and finish masterin' *Rock 'n' Roll,* and then we'll start the new one. What do you think?''

''I'm with you every step of the way.''

''I'm up. I want to continue on . . . so after we go away, we'll come back and think about a new album.''

I felt very happy. The John I loved most was the productive John, a man deeply committed to making good music.

We got undressed, watched television for a while, and then made love. We drifted off to sleep together.

In the morning, as soon as John woke up, he wrote on his pad. He spent a lot of the day writing the album he planned to make when we returned from New Orleans. Every so often he stopped to play me what he had written to get my reactions. John was working on a sad song that he called "Tennessee." It had been inspired by his rereading of Tennessee Williams's *A Streetcar Named Desire*. I loved it and I told him so.

John seemed determined to write as much of the new album as he could, and by the end of the day he had another song, "Popcorn," a very funny, catchy tune. Yoko called two or three times that day to remind him of his appointment that evening to stop smoking, finally telling him that the method that had been used on her was "a new form of hypnosis." John was so busy writing, he got off the phone as quickly as he could.

Just as John was about to leave, Yoko called. The stars weren't right again, and the session was canceled. Yoko called back three or four times during the evening to schedule, then reschedule, the meeting. The session was then supposed to occur Thursday at four. On Thursday there were two reminder calls, followed by a cancellation an hour later. By then Yoko had spent two full weeks enticing John with the promise that he would stop smoking.

Each of those calls increased my anxiety. I tried to control myself, but I wanted the calls to stop and I couldn't hold it in any longer. "John, don't you realize what's going on? You could go to Smokenders; you could go to the meetings we see advertised in the newspapers; you could hire your own hypnotist. You don't have to go to Yoko's hypnotist."

"Yoko's really good at findin' people who can do these things."

"But everything is going so well."

"Fung Yee, nothing can happen now, because everything is goin' so well."

He was determined to go to Yoko's hypnotist. I became so upset, I began to cry.

Later Yoko set the new appointment for Friday at six.

At five fifteen on Friday John and I stared at the phone. I hoped that it would ring and that Yoko would cancel the meeting, but it didn't. "The fuckin' stars are finally right," John said. "It shouldn't take more than a few hours, and when I come home, who knows? I may not be a smokin' man anymore. Let's go out and have a late dinner. Then we'll try to get up early and go to Montauk."

As John walked toward the door I suddenly called out, "John, John, please don't go. I've never asked you for anything, but I'm asking you for this. Don't go."

"Fung Yee, you're makin' too much of this."

That was John. He never listened to what he didn't want to hear. At the door I threw my arms around him and held him tightly.

"I'll see you later," he said.

I tried to put on a bold front, but when John left, I was shaking. I knew he was again going to get locked into the game he played with Yoko and I knew the game was too powerful for me.

I made a cup of tea and turned on the television. Five hours later John had not returned. I picked up the phone and called the Dakota.

"I can't talk to you right now," Yoko said abruptly as soon as she heard my voice. "I'll call you later."

"Is John there?"

"Yes."

She hung up.

I waited another hour. Then I called again. "I still can't talk," she said, slamming down the phone. I knew there was no way to get her to put John on the phone. I was miserable. I watched television until the last late movie, then I fell asleep.

When I got up in the morning, John had still not returned. I called the Dakota.

"I'd like to speak to John," I told Yoko.

"You can't. He's exhausted. The cure was very difficult."

"Are you sure he's all right?"

"He's fine. Fine. I'll have him call you later."

I sat by the phone all day, but John did not call. I also sat up for most of Saturday night, alone, once again staring at the television, doing my best not to think about what was going on at the Dakota. My stomach ached and I did not want to make myself sicker, so I just sat still, trying not to think at all. Whether I liked it or not I knew I would find out the truth soon enough. On Sunday morning I got up and waited for the phone to ring. Again it didn't. I had never felt worse. I wanted some news—any news—and I knew I wouldn't get it. I could not imagine why John was treating me so cruelly, but he was. At two that afternoon I called Yoko.

"Yoko," I said as soon as she answered the phone, "I *must* talk to John."

"He's still sleeping."

"He's got to wake up sometime."

"When he does, I'll have him call you."

"Wake him up now. I want to talk to him."

"May, I'll have him call you."

I knew she was never going to put me through. There was nothing to do but wait.

Of all the silly, incongruous things, we had both made appointments with the dentist for the next day, Monday. I was going to keep mine and hoped that he would keep his. Unless he came back that night. Unless he called.

Everything had been going so well, yet I had not been able to stop John from going to the Dakota. I felt powerless and I felt awful. At that moment I hated both of them—hated them because they were so unpredictable. And I hated myself because I had allowed myself to be the victim of that unpredictability, because I loved John so much, because I knew our relationship was ending and I did not want it to end.

On Monday I got up, got dressed, and spent the morning waiting until it was time to go to the dentist. When I looked in the mirror, I hated the way I looked. I had hardly slept or eaten since Friday night and I looked even more haggard than on the night John had been tied up by Phil Spector, or on the night John had accused me of flirting with David Cassidy, or on the day that John had suddenly asked me to leave the house in Bel-Air, or on the night when he had attacked me in Palm Springs. I looked so exhausted and burned out, I decided to wear sunglasses.

John was not at the dentist's office when I arrived, but at the end of my appointment I found him sitting in the waiting room. He looked even worse than I did. His eyes were red-rimmed and there were bags under them. He looked at me vaguely and seemed dazed. It was the look that followed an evening of drinking when he awoke and could remember nothing.

"Hi," I said.

"Hi."

There was a pause. John got up and went into the dentist's office, while I sat there, waiting. When he came out, I got up and began to walk to the door. John followed after me, saying nothing, and I walked out to the street.

"Where are you goin'?" John asked when we reached the street.

"Home. . . . Aren't you coming?"

John blinked. "Uh . . . right . . . okay."

He seemed extremely disoriented. I stared at him, trying to figure out whom he resembled just then. Suddenly it came to me. It was corny, but he seemed like one of those characters in *Invasion of the Body Snatchers*. He looked and sounded like a zombie.

We walked in silence the three blocks to the apartment. When we got upstairs, I opened our door, and John followed me in.

"I guess I should say this to you now," he said after he stepped inside. "Yoko has allowed me to come home."

I had suspected it. I knew it. But I was still stunned when I heard it.

"What?"

"Yoko has allowed me to come home."

I stared at him.

"I'm goin' to pack a few things and then I'm goin'."

I slumped into a chair. There was nothing I could say to John. He seemed automated, and I knew I couldn't break through. He got a suitcase and began to pack. "It wasn't anybody's fault. It just happened," he said as he threw his socks and underwear into the suitcase.

He looked up and blinked at me. "It wasn't intended to be," he said softly, and he continued to pack his clothes.

Tears streamed down my cheeks, but I was too stunned to say anything. I was too numb.

From the moment eighteen months before when Yoko had suggested that I go out with John, I had known that she had the upper hand. But as our relationship had progressed, I had allowed myself to think that John had changed. He had stopped drinking. He had had the time of his life with Julian. He had stopped being a recluse and had learned to have friends once again. *He was writing.* And yet, although I hated to admit it, deep down I believed that Yoko would always know how to get John to do what she wanted.

I should have realized that John would walk out on me at the moment of our greatest happiness. The truth of it was, the closer John and I got, the greater was my chance of losing him. It was Yoko's moment of triumph, and I felt humiliated and cheated. I don't know why I did it—to this day I don't know—but I got up, went to the telephone, and dialed her number.

"Congratulations, Yoko," I said icily when she answered the phone. "You've got John back, and I'm sure you'll be very happy."

Her response was a surprise. "Happy? I don't know if I'll ever be happy," she said bitterly. I had never heard her sound so miserable. Her response stunned me and her mood was so dark, it momentarily shocked me out of my numbness.

"Yoko, isn't this what you wanted?"

"May, this is not the time to talk. I'll call you." She hung up and never called back.

I walked back into the living room and watched John finish packing. When he was through, he looked up and smiled at me.

"Tell me about the cure," I asked.

"It was horrible."

"Why was the cure horrible?"

"I don't know. It was just like primal therapy."

"Primal therapy?" I gasped.

"I was throwin' up all the time. I kept throwin' me guts out. I kept fallin' asleep, and when I woke up, they would do it to me again."

I couldn't believe what I was hearing and I felt sick to my stomach. Things raced through my head. For a moment I too was in a science fiction movie and I thought I might even call my own hypnotist or primal therapist. Then I realized how silly that was. I knew that whatever the "hypnotist" had said or done had touched something very deep in John, something that was *always* there. John's childish fears once again had risen to the surface. I was furious with the infantile part of him. That was the hardest thing for me to face: that John wanted to be a child again—a child taken care of by a very strict mama.

"When did she tell you you could come home?"

"It just happened."

He looked nervously at me, confusion flickering across his face. "I don't know . . . it just happened. Nobody wanted it . . . it just came up."

He looked even more confused. Then he looked helplessly at me. "It just came up," he said again.

Even though I was enraged, I cared so much about John that his confusion made me even more upset. I hated the fact that John was leaving me, but I would have felt better if he at least had a clear reason for what he had chosen to do.

"What about us, John?"

"What do you mean?"

"What about the love we felt for each other? What about the closeness? When did that stop?"

"I still love you. I love you very much."

"John . . ." I began to sob out loud and couldn't say any more.

"Yoko knows I still love you. She's allowed me to continue to see you. She said she can be the wife, and you can continue to be the mistress."

There were so many thoughts I had when I was with John that I didn't have the courage to face. At that moment the thought I didn't want to deal with was that the three of us were probably crazy.

John suddenly jumped up and went to get his coat. "I almost forgot this. Yoko sent you a present." He took two little vials from his pocket and placed one in my hand. "One is for you, and one is for me." I stared at my bottle. John opened it. "I'm supposed to put some on you." He poured some of the liquid in it onto his fingers and then dabbed it on my neck. The smell was horrible.

"Smell mine," he said. He opened his vial. It had a sweet smell. I closed mine. I knew it was something horrible and I pushed the vial to the other side of the table.

John sat down beside me, took my hand, and caressed it. "It's goin' to be all right," he said. "You'll see."

John reached over and kissed me. "I've missed you, I've missed you so much. I love you so very much."

I was heartbroken and scared and I felt desperate. I clung to John tightly, never wanting to let go. John began to undress me.

We made love, and it seemed to me that nothing had changed. He had been telling me the truth. He still wanted me very much.

When we were finished, John lit a cigarette, and we just lay there quietly, caressing each other. Then John said, "I have to go home now." He got up, and I watched him as he dressed. "Don't worry," he said. "Don't worry about a thing. Everything is all right between us. You'll see. I'll call you tomorrow."

He left me lying there. I was stunned. Finally I got up and spent the rest of the day sitting by myself. I was too numb to move.

Occasionally the phone would ring. Calmly I told everyone who called that John had gone back to Yoko and gave the callers John's number at the Dakota. Everyone was very gentle with me. When my girl friends got the news, they were extremely sympathetic and they volunteered to stay with me if I needed them. No one wanted me to be alone, but I felt so crushed that I didn't want to face anyone—even my friends.

Mick called, and we chatted for a few minutes. Then I said, "Mick, I have something to tell you. John has gone back to Yoko."

There was a long pause. "I guess I've lost a friend," he replied.

That night I stayed by myself. It was almost as if I had entered a period of mourning. I watched television for a while and then I turned off the set and tried to sleep. As I lay there my panic began to grow. John had left me without a job, without a place to live, and with no money at all. Of course, John hadn't brought those subjects up. It was not like him to think about them, and I had been too shocked by his decision to bring them up either. I did not want to think about them then. I was too overwhelmed by my aloneness—I had not been alone for more than eighteen months—as well as the lunacy of what had happened and my fears about what the future would bring.

Hope dies hard, and in a certain part of me I did think John might come back. I thought Yoko might even send him back. But I also knew that each day he spent at the Dakota would make it easier for him to stay there even if he did still love me.

I was so upset, I couldn't stay in our bed. Even though it was freezing, I went outside on the terrace. I looked up at the sky and stared at the place where John and I had seen the UFO months before. I had never felt lonelier. I looked down at the street. I knew I wasn't the kind of person who would ever kill myself. I was too furious. I loved John. But how could I love someone who could treat me so badly? Had I merely been dazzled because the man was John Lennon? Had I confused the sexual passion we had for each other with love? I couldn't pretend that the end came out of the blue. I had always known John was capable of anything, but once it happened, I felt more awful than I ever could have imagined. Still, at the moment of my bleakest stress, I was not surprised. Deep inside, I had always believed that my relationship with John had essentially been initiated, controlled, and now terminated by Yoko. To love John was to accept the fact that anything could happen—anything.

Even though I felt sick I got back into our bed and tried to sleep. Lying there, one thought kept coming back to me: Despite the pain and horror of what I was going through then, given the chance, I would do the whole thing over again.

Part
Three

21

When I got up on Tuesday, nothing had changed. I was alone, and I felt awful. There were two things I wanted to deal with that morning, and I was afraid of them both.

I pulled myself out of bed, had a cup of tea, and got dressed. Then I went looking for books about hypnosis, even though I knew I would never really be sure whether or not John had been hypnotized. Back home, as I pored over them, I learned that when a subject is in a hypnotic state, he can easily be made to experience his entire past. Until then I did not understand why John's hypnosis had reminded him of primal therapy, which also leads a person back through his past. I learned that both hypnosis and primal therapy can lead a person back in time to the core of his being. I also learned that while in a hypnotic state a subject becomes increasingly susceptible to suggestion, but he cannot be made to do anything he does not want to do. The experience John had had could have taken him back in time to the source of his misery, then some specific solution to that misery could have been suggested, such as going back to Yoko. But even if that had happened, the point I still had to face was that part of John had received and accepted the suggestion. I had to see that the most palpable part of John wanted to regress, and that part of him was far more powerful than the part that wanted to grow up.

I used to feel guilty that I could not satisfy all of John's needs, but most people learn to live without all their needs fulfilled. They choose the most important ones and learn to satisfy them. They also learn to enjoy satisfying the most important needs of the person they choose to love.

I hated to admit it, but John was like a baby. He really did not want to deal with the fact that *some* of his needs would never be satisfied, and so he went back to an environment in which his needs were controlled for him. I suspected that as time went on his life would be made simpler and simpler. It was horrible, but John felt most secure when his life was the most childlike.

John had seemed to enjoy everything about the last few months. It was hard to accept that he was willing to throw away all the hard-earned progress in order to feel safe.

I closed the books, once again realizing I was no match for John's impulsiveness and that I was no match for Yoko as a strategist.

There was one other thing I wanted to attend to. At lunchtime I met a Spanish-speaking friend and accompanied her to a *botanica*—an apothecary's shop—to find out the meaning of Yoko's "gift." My friend showed the bottle to the woman behind the counter. She opened it, smelled it, winced, and shut it quickly. She spoke to my friend in Spanish.

"You must throw this away *now*," my friend told me. "It's not good for you."

"What is it?" I asked.

I learned that my scent was a mixture of sulphur, arrowroot, and chili powder. The sulphur had made it especially foul-smelling.

The woman behind the counter spoke again in Spanish.

My friend listened, then said, "She says whoever gave it to you must really hate you."

"Ask her what kind of liquid has a rose smell," I said.

I learned that the combination of rose, jasmine, gardenia, and lemon oil makes a potion that the woman called Come to Me. The liquid would be used to force someone to feel a strong sexual response.

"It's incredibly powerful," my friend translated.

*   *   *

As soon as I got home I flushed my gift from Yoko down the toilet. A few minutes later John called.

"How are you?" he asked.

"I'm as well as can be expected, John."

"Are you really okay?"

"No, I'm not really okay."

"I'll call you later."

John called four more times that day. During our last brief conversation he asked me to go to the Record Plant to help him make sure the work on *Rock 'n' Roll* was finished properly.

I was so confused. John was eager for me to continue working, and despite everything I knew, I still wanted to be with John and work with him. I guess one of the things I was learning about myself during that experience was that no matter how much you learn, you may not learn anything at all.

When I went to the Record Plant the next day, John smiled. He ran over and began to kiss me, then he froze. It was as if he were hearing a voice in his head that was telling him to stop. He stood there deep in thought for a moment or two, wrestling with himself, then he snapped out of it and kissed me again.

Suddenly there were two Johns in my life. The first John was incredibly affectionate. He spoke gently to me, seemed very caring, and was eager to make love to me at any opportunity. Two or three times a week for the following two months we continued to work side by side, and when our work was over, we would go back to my apartment to make love. As soon as were were through, the other John would become extremely nervous. He would jump up, quickly shower and dress, then reapply the rose-smelling perfume and say "I'll see you" as he headed out the door.

I realized that whatever Yoko might have told him, John did not want her to know that he was still seeing me.

The other John was horrible. A few days after our official breakup, when we were lying in bed, he turned to me and said, "I think you should know that Yoko wants to announce to the press that we're back together. We discussed a number of statements to make. We've decided to say that the separation failed."

He looked at me with the same quizzical expression he used when he wanted my reaction to a mix or to a piece of ad copy or to a mockup of a record jacket cover. I couldn't believe that he wanted my approval of his press statement and said nothing. John lay there, staring at me, waiting nervously for my reaction.

"I think it's fine," I said finally.

"Good." He smiled, delighted by my positive reaction. His insensitivity amazed me. Always one to be hurt, he refused to deal with how much I could be hurt by being involved in that discussion. The quote appeared in *Newsweek* a few days later.

At the beginning of the next week I needed his opinion about the release dates of ad copy for *Rock 'n' Roll* before I authorized them, and I called him at the Dakota.

I got the other John on the phone. "Don't you ever call me here!" he screamed. "What's wrong with you?" Then he slammed down the phone.

Toward the middle of the week the other John called and said that he was bringing Yoko's assistant, Jon Hendricks, over to help him move back. John had taken most of his clothes, and I did not know what else he wanted. When he arrived, I asked, "John, what else are you going to take?"

John was very nervous. "I'm not goin' to take the furniture," he said, "until you find a new place of your own." He added quickly, "You can stay as long as you like." I could see that he wanted me out. He did not offer to help me find an apartment, nor did he seem capable of figuring out that since I was penniless, I couldn't afford to move at all.

He seemed to have also forgotten that I had given up my old apartment—an apartment that I could afford—at his request. John pointed out to Hendricks that as soon as I moved he would send moving men over to take his piano, jukebox, and desk back to the Dakota.

John went to the closet. He took out the leather pants he had bought me. "These fit me. I'll take them." He handed them to Hendricks. He then went through the closet, looking for other clothes of mine that fit him and that he might like to have. He couldn't find any. He then went to a bureau drawer and began to go through the T-shirts. We decided to divide them equally between us. He handed the ones that he wanted to Hendricks. When he was finished, he sent Hendricks back to the Dakota.

"I'll get you some money," he said after Hendricks left. He looked at me imploringly, wondering if I would ask him for any. I knew him well enough to know that he knew how nervous and upset I would become about discussing money with him. He knew me very well, in that my behavior was governed by a sense of being honorable. It was impossible for me to ask him for money.

"You know I can't ask you for money. I just can't," I told him.

I thought John might say, "We've meant a lot to each other. I know how difficult this is for you. I'd like to make your life easier, since you've given me eighteen months of your life and I'm returning to the Dakota and you have to start from scratch. It's only fair for me to help you. We'll always be friends, so why shouldn't I make your life a little easier. . . ." But John seemed too dazed to be able to do that. He wanted to do nothing for me. He behaved as if it were important for him to do as little as possible. John wanted to do nothing for me in order to prove to himself that I had lived with him not because he was John Lennon but because I really loved him. That was all that mattered to him. I must admit that the man I went to bed with that afternoon was a man that I knew was behaving terribly toward me in a great many ways. This John wanted to sleep with me, yet it seemed as if he didn't care if I starved on the street.

"You may have been John's girl friend, but you also continued to work for him," Harold Seider told me a few days later. "You refused to let him hire anyone and you worked harder than an army of assistants. You saved him plenty of money. You deserve your back salary and you certainly should be paid for the work you're doing now."

"I can't ask him for anything," I replied. "That's just not me."

"Let me do it, then." Harold spoke to John and Yoko, and they came to an agreement: I would be allowed to keep my job at a salary of $15,000, but I would be paid nothing for any of the work I had done over the past eighteen months.

At least it was enough money to start looking for a new apartment. I was eager to get on with it.

A month elapsed, and one afternoon toward the end of February, the first month of our official breakup, after we had made love, the other John reared his head once again. "I have to ask you a favor. Yoko wants us to make our first public appearance together at the Grammy Awards. Are you plannin' to go?"

"Yes."

"If we were together, we wouldn't have gone. You know that, don't you?" he shouted.

"Yes."

"But now we're not together, so I don't think you should go."

"I'm not with you, John. When I was single, I always went to events like these."

"Why do you want to go? Do you think it will further your career?" John screamed. "Do you think that you'll make new contacts?"

I sat up and stared at him. "That's not the way you or I think, is it? Do you really believe that about me, or are you just repeating what's been drilled into your head? Tell me the truth," I shouted. "Do you believe I want to go to the Grammy Awards to further my career?"

John stared at me. He looked confused. I hated it when that blank expression crept across his face.

"Tell me the truth," I shouted again, loudly enough to break through his confusion. Suddenly he started to cry.

"You can't shout at me anymore, John."

"Just please don't go," he said quietly.

I didn't.

Rock 'n' Roll was finally released in February 1975, a year and half after work on it had originally begun. It found itself competing against *Roots,* the tape released by Morris Levy.

The critical reaction to the album was disappointing, as were the sales. Around 340,000 copies of *Rock 'n' Roll* were sold, compared to the 425,000 sold by *Walls and Bridges*. John's last album for Capitol was to be a collection of greatest hits, *Shaved Fish,* and even though he was busy writing a new album when he was with me, in fact he would not record again for another five years.

It was the beginning of March, and I was ready to look for a new apartment. I saw a number of them and finally found one I liked and could afford, a lovely one-bedroom apartment on the Upper East Side.

John was very pleased when I told him about the apartment. "You can keep the bed and the couch," he said. "That will get you started."

I had to laugh.

"What's so funny?" he asked.

"Julian slept on the couch. I slept on the bed. No wonder they won't fit into the decor at the Dakota."

"I'm doin' the best I can, Fung Yee," he said softly. "That's all I can do."

"I know you are," I replied.

"After you move, I'll have the movin' men take the rest of the furniture. I'll take the television set then."

"Do you really want the television? You've got seven sets of your own."

"I like this television."

"John, I really can't afford to buy a new television."

"You can use it until you move." John glared at me. I sensed that it was important for him to show that he could take it back, and eventually he did.

I continued to see John throughout the month of March. In April I was sent to London to work in the Apple offices. There was no real reason for me to go. I sensed John had been told to get me out of town. In London I had a pleasant visit with John's aunt, Mimi Smith.

When I returned to New York, I did not see him, but I did hear from him by phone occasionally. His voice always seemed low, his conversation slurred. It seemed as if those were stolen moments, and I could sense his tension as he asked me how I was and what was going on.

Then one day after I had been back about three weeks, John walked into my office in the Capitol building. "Let's go out," he said to me.

"What?"

"I've come to see you. Let's have a cup of coffee."

We went to the nearest coffee shop. After we had ordered, John said, "I don't think you can work there any longer."

"John, I've been expecting it. When do you want me to stop coming into the office?"

"Now. It's impossible for you to come and work here anymore. I'm very sorry about it."

"I'd rather get a new job anyway. . . ."

He looked at me blankly. "This is the best I can do, Fung Yee. I really want to help you, but you know I can't."

"John, I know you well enough to know that this is all you really can do."

We were both quiet for a few minutes. Then John said, "Yoko's havin' a child." He paused. "We haven't discussed it with too many other people."

I found myself with nothing to say.

"It's goin' to be a boy," he added.

"Another son! What are you going to name him?"

"I don't know. The only name that's come to me is Paris."

"Paris?"

"Yes." Then John suddenly asked, "Don't you wish it was your baby?"

I was shocked. "What do you mean by that?"

"You could have become pregnant to keep me."

"Do you really think that, or have you been told that?" John looked confused. "Yes, you're right," I replied. "But I was always careful not to. I never wanted to trick you or trap you. Do you really believe I wanted to trap you?"

"No . . . no, of course not, Fung Yee."

"Did someone tell you that I wanted to trap you?"

"No . . ."

"You shouldn't believe everything you hear."

John became very uncomfortable. Changing the subject, he asked, "What's new with you?"

"I've got a new boyfriend."

"Oh." He smiled. It was the smile that masked his real feelings. I knew that he did not like the fact that I had a boyfriend.

"Tell me about him."

"He's a bass player. I met him at Home. He's Irish."

"Irish?" John looked displeased.

"John, I don't want to be alone, and this man is nice to me."

"Richard Ross wants to go out with you."

"I don't want to go out with Richard."

"He's handsome and he's got a bit of money."

"John, don't try to fix me up. You're not as good at it as Yoko."

"What about Mick? He wants to go out with you also."

I wondered if John knew Mick had called.

"Mick really likes you."

"As far as I'm concerned, one superstar in a lifetime is more than enough for me."

After we had our coffee, we began to walk down Park Avenue.

"I heard about Pete Ham," John said. I had briefly dated Pete Ham in 1971, when he was a member of Badfinger, and we had remained friends over the years. Pete had fallen on hard times and he had become very depressed. A few weeks earlier he had been found hanged in his garage in London. "I really wanted to call you, but I didn't know what to say. I wanted to say I was sorry about what had happened. I wanted to say I was sorry about how I acted about him. God, I couldn't believe it."

John was always sorry when it was too late.

"People lost interest in Pete and they stopped caring about whether he lived or died," I told John. "I saw Pete when I was in England, and I saw how the indifference of others had worn him down and he had lost the will to survive. When people treat you that badly, there are just no excuses."

"There are no excuses."

"I think it's better to do the right thing than feel guilty because you didn't, or ignore the right thing because you don't have the courage to do what must be done."

"All I can do is tell you the truth. I still care about you. I miss you very much."

"I know you do."

We walked in silence a few more blocks. "Come on," he said.

"Where are we going?"

"Let's go someplace where we can be by ourselves."

We couldn't go to my new apartment, because my roommate was there. John said, "Let's go to our old apartment and see what it looks like."

He still had the keys. Even though I had just told him off, I wanted to go to the old apartment with him. Even though I was very angry with John, I could not deny it to myself: I still loved him and wanted to be with him.

The apartment was entirely empty except for the mirrors, which were still mounted above the fireplace. I had been out of the apartment for almost a month. Yet, it seemed as if I had lived there a century ago.

"I wanted to take these mirrors," John said, "but I couldn't get them off. I think I'm goin' to give 'em away."

"Who are you going to give them to?"

"I don't know."

"Didn't it ever dawn on you that I might want them? John, I'm amazed at how difficult it is for you to ever think of me."

"You know why it's difficult, don't you?"

"Yes, John. Thinking about me makes you feel guilty. So why think at all?"

He looked embarrassed.

"John, I've got a new apartment and I've got a new boyfriend. You're home and you're going to have a child. Life is going on for both of us, and I hope we'll always be friends, no matter how difficult all of this has been."

He put his arm around me and kissed me gently. We spent the rest of the afternoon making love. Before we left I looked at the apartment and said good-bye to it for the last time. I never wanted to go back. I believed that part of my life was over. I had no idea then that for the next three years, although circumstances would make it more and more difficult, John and I would continue to see each other whenever we had the chance.

Although I wasn't in any immediate financial danger, I realized it was time for me to go back into the real world. During the previous eighteen months I had received official credits on *Mind Games, Pussycats, Walls and Bridges,* and *Rock 'n' Roll,* and I had learned a lot. I was going to apply at all of the major record companies for a job.

After two weeks of turndowns, a friend who was a record company executive said, "Let's have lunch."

"Listen," my friend said, "there's a rumor floating around the industry about you, and I think you should know about it. With the completion of *Rock 'n' Roll* and one more LP, John's deal is up with Capitol. All of the labels are going to want to sign him. Everybody's afraid that John won't sign with any label that you're working for. I don't know how the rumor got started, and I don't know who's fueling it, but I'm sorry, May. I think you're being blacklisted."

Then John gave a long interview to *Rolling Stone.* I didn't want to be mentioned and I was glad I wasn't. In it John said that Yoko and he had met backstage at the Elton John concert and that the meeting had been a surprise. He said that they had looked silently at each other while the photographers went wild and that in that moment of silence it was obvious to everyone around them that they were very much in love.

I knew that none of it had ever happened—so did John. I couldn't stand the fact that he wasn't playing straight with me, the public, himself. I couldn't stand the truth either: that what he really wanted to do was tell those lies.

A few days later he called and said, "I've been talkin' to the press, you know. I've had to say a few things. I'm sure you'll understand."

"I understand," I replied icily, "I do really understand."

During that period John continued to call me once or twice a week. His calls were tense and hurried, and I was too upset to want to stay on the phone with him. I spent a large portion of each day searching for a job in the music business. Usually during interviews I could see the nervousness of the executives who were interviewing me. I did not want to take a job in another field, but as time went by I knew I might have to, and that made me even more furious with John and Yoko.

One afternoon I called Jimmy Iovine, and he asked me to meet him that night at Ashley's, a popular music business hangout on lower Fifth Avenue.

I set out for Ashley's with two of my friends. As I was about to walk into the restaurant a man came out and walked past me. I thought it was John. "John . . . John," I called out.

It was John. He dashed over and grabbed me by the shoulders. "Where are you goin'?" he asked.

"I'm meeting Jimmy Iovine."

"I'm with Albert Brooks. We're goin' to some girl's house." He looked guilty.

"You don't have to explain. I'm not your wife and I'm not your girl friend anymore. As far as I'm concerned, you can go wherever you want to go."

"I'm comin' back for you. Don't leave. Promise you won't leave until I get back."

I looked at him skeptically. "See you later, John."

John went to his limousine. Before he got in it he turned and called out, "Now, don't forget. Wait for me."

"Sure, sure, John. I'll be inside, waiting," I replied, and I went inside.

I had a lot of trouble sleeping those days. Every time I got into bed I began to worry about my future. Rather than go home after our long, pleasant evening, I asked Jimmy to drop my friends and me off at the Brasserie. There I spotted Richard Ross, the owner of Home. Richard was obsessed with John, and John was the first thing he always talked about.

"My bartender told me John was looking for me at Home, but I missed him," Richard told me.

"I saw him at Ashley's," I replied.

"Really?"

"Really."

"What are you doing?"

"I just don't want to go home."

"Let's go for a ride."

We drove to Westchester in his elegant new sports car and had breakfast. I didn't get home until eight in the morning.

I had just begun to get undressed when the phone rang.

"Hello."

"Fung Yee, where are you?" John screamed. "I need to hold you. I went back for you. You weren't there. I got so sick. I thought I lost you."

I told him matter-of-factly how I'd spent the night.

"I must see you. I want to see you now. I feel terrible. I'm sick."

"Where are you?"

"I'm at the Drake Hotel. In Albert Brooks's suite. Do you think you could come over for a while? I miss you so much."

Knowing that a psychiatrist could have a field day with our story—that *I* could have field day if I heard it from somebody else—I knew also that I loved him and I wanted to be with him, so I rushed to the Drake.

As soon as John saw me he picked me up, carried me to the couch in the living room of the suite, and buried his head in my lap. Brooks, I realized, was asleep in the bedroom.

"I'm sick because I miss you," he told me. "I miss you all day and all night. Missin' you has made me sick. Fung Yee, I can't forget you. I just can't. I need to hold you."

For a long time we simply sat there, holding each other, not saying a word. Then we made love on the couch. When we were through, I said, "I have to go. I have things to do."

"Do you have to go? I don't want you to go."

Suddenly I realized I had my own life to lead, even though I still loved John. I walked to the door and said, "I have to go now, John."

I couldn't believe my own voice. Without looking back I left the suite.

After the meeting at the Drake Hotel, John started to call again two or three times a week. Those calls were even more tense and hurried.

Then one day Cynthia Ross called. She had bad news. Richard had contracted Hodgkin's disease and had gone to the hospital to have his spleen removed and to have chemotherapy treatments. When John called, I told him about Richard.

"Shit," he said. "I never wanted anyone I know to go through anything like this again without me help. How can I tell Yoko that I know about Richard? Wait a minute, I can say someone called the office and I got it from there. I'll think of something."

"I think if you can, you should go to the hospital to see Richard."

"I will."

When I went to see Richard, I was shocked by his appearance. The chemotherapy had caused chunks of his hair to fall out and he was horribly emaciated. We spoke quietly for a few minutes, then Richard told me that John was on his way over. When John arrived, he too was taken aback by the way Richard looked.

John and I kept meeting at the hospital. At the end of those visits we walked together in the street. I realized that my anger at John had passed. As always, we felt very relaxed with each other and were happy being together. We both wished we had someplace to go. Our old apartment had been rented, my roommate was working out of my new apartment, and John was afraid to use his credit cards because Yoko looked at his bills and gave him only a little cash to spend. The idea of getting a secret credit card or bank account panicked him, and if he did, he was always afraid someone would talk. So he did nothing—and gave away control.

Toward the end of our next visit to Richard, despite his sickness, Richard said to us, "I think you two need your space. I'm tired of being in this bed. I'm going to go for a walk."

"Richard, are you going to be all right?"

Richard slowly got out of his bed. "I'll be fine."

He left the room and closed the door behind him.

When he was gone, John and I climbed onto Richard's bed and made love. As crazy as it was, that was the only place we could be alone together.

John and I continued to meet in the hospital for the next

three weeks. Occasionally during those visits Richard would leave the room to give us our "space."

To our great relief Richard's treatment was successful, and after he went home, it seemed natural that he continue in the role of our secret agent. The phone would ring, and I'd answer it.

"May, it's Richard."

"Hi."

"A friend called."

"Really."

"He's coming over. He'd like to see you."

John explained these absences to Yoko by telling her he was going to visit his convalescing friend Richard at home. Later Cynthia Ross discovered that John had worked out a plan with Richard. When Richard and John went away to New England together, Richard was visiting a girl friend of his own.

John and I began to meet at Richard's apartment two or three times a week. After a few minutes of conversation with Richard, he would leave so that we could be alone. During those afternoon meetings we were very close. We liked to talk to each other, and the passion between us was still at a fever pitch, fueled, perhaps, by the fact that we were not together anymore. Occasionally a blank expression crept across John's face and he became very quiet. Thankfully those zombielike moments happened infrequently. They made me very nervous.

Sometimes John discussed his impending fatherhood, an event he was really looking forward to. He was especially excited about the baby being a Scorpio. "You're a Scorpio," he kept reminding me. "Scorpio people are very special."

John told me that he planned to raise the baby differently from the way Julian had been raised.

"Yoko explained to me that if she has to go through these nine months of hell, it's my job to take care of the baby from the moment it arrives. She refuses to function as the mother just because it's the role society puts on women."

One day Cynthia Ross and I were talking. "John told me the baby is due in early November," she told me.

"I'll make a bet it will be born on John's birthday," I replied.

"But that would make it October 9, almost a month early."

"I'll still bet you the baby will be born on October 9."

I had assumed that John and I would stop seeing each other once the child was born. I was right on both counts: Sean was born on October 9, and John did stop calling.

As Christmas approached I realized I had not heard from John in more than two months. I took a short trip to Florida. When I got back, my doorman told me that John had been looking for me.

While I was away John and Yoko had gone to dinner with Tony King and Elliot Mintz. Suddenly John turned to Yoko and began screaming, "I want May! I want May! I want May! I don't want you!" He grew progressively more agitated. "Get me May. Get me May." It was impossible to calm him down. He pointed to Yoko and turned his head away. "Take her home. I don't want her! Take her home!"

Tony got Yoko out of the restaurant while Richard Ross and Elliot took John to search for me.

A week later I went to Ashley's with a couple of friends. Ashley's had two floors. The lower level consisted of a restaurant. Above it was a dance floor and a bar. We decided to go to the bar and headed for the staircase. When I reached the top of the staircase, I came face to face with John. John was smiling, and I could feel the corners of my lips tugging upward.

"Oh, hi," I said.

"Hi."

John turned and walked quickly back into the crowded room. We went to the bar, which was fairly empty at that time, and sat down. There was a mirror over the bar. In it I could see the reflections of John and Yoko, who were at a table in the corner of the room, along with Peter Boyle and his girl friend, Loraine Alterman. Yoko's eyes were fixed on me. We ordered drinks. A little while later John came over and sat beside me. I was amazed by his lack of diplomacy. By walking over, he had to know that he was going to upset both Yoko and my date. John's attention embarrassed me and I did not want my date upset, but it was John, and it was always impossible for me to turn John off. I sat there feeling very uncomfortable.

"I was lookin' for you," John whispered. "You know, I really wish you weren't with him. I don't think he's right for you. I don't get a good feeling from him."

John was right. My date was not giving me a good feeling either.

We made small talk for another few minutes. Every so often I looked into the mirror. Yoko's eyes hadn't left me. Then John said, "I gotta go back." As he turned I watched him in the mirror and I saw Yoko's eyes fixed on my back. Ten minutes later he came back. "I want to remind you that whatever you read in interviews that I give about our time together are things I have to say. You know how I really feel about you. You know why I have to say these things," he told me.

Once again I said nothing. Every time I read those interviews about John's "lost weekend" I hurt. But I knew that John cared more about pleasing Yoko than respecting my feelings. I knew saying something would change nothing.

I looked in the mirror. Yoko was whispering to her guests. Then Boyle got up and came to the bar and sat beside John.

If Peter had been sent to get John back to the table, he changed his mind quickly. He said, "I think you're having more fun here than I am at the table."

Peter was very witty, and we started laughing together. Suddenly Ashley Pandel, the owner of the restaurant, came over to speak to John, and John got up and followed after him. Then John came back. He was very excited. He ignored me and whispered to Peter. Peter got up and followed John.

A few minutes later Loraine got up from the table to search for the two men. It was obvious that she did not want to speak to me, even though she had been especially friendly when I had been with John.

Yoko was alone at the table and she continued to glare at me. Then Loraine walked out of the back room and whispered to her, and she followed after Loraine.

I did not want to be there when they returned to their table. All of a sudden, after John had defied Yoko by speaking to me, he had disappeared after the slightest prodding from Ashley, and all of the bad feelings started up again. I realized that people who quit their addictions by going cold turkey were better off than the people who said they were going to taper off! Every time I got a little John fix, I suddenly felt awful all over again. I turned to my date and said, "I've had enough excitement for one night. Let's go."

As we were leaving a Beatles song was playing on the jukebox. When we got into the cab, "Mind Games" was playing on the car radio. When we got into the elevator of my building, I said, "Thank God, Muzak doesn't play in this elevator the minute these doors close."

My date said, "I've met John Lennon. I don't like anything that's happened tonight. But I can't help it. He's hooked me, too."

Soon Richard began to call again, once more telling me about the "friend" who wanted to see me. I had to be honest with myself: There was only one thing I wanted more than to be free of John, and that was to be near him. There were many bitter pills to swallow—the interviews John had given; the fact that I was having a very rough time and that the most powerful man in the music business would not pick up the phone and make a single call to help me, even though he kept telling me how much he loved and missed me—and I swallowed them. The times I was with John made me so happy that I decided to let all my anger pass. I missed him and I wanted to be with him.

From February 1976 until the end of 1977 we met at Richard's at two-, then three-month intervals. There was also a meeting that occurred one night when Richard called and said, "Your friend is at Home. Would you please come over?" When I got to Home, Richard was waiting for me outside. He escorted me upstairs to the apartment he kept over the restaurant, where John was waiting for me.

The form of those meetings was essentially the same. John would reminisce about how much fun he had had when we were together. We told each other stories about the time we had spent together, starting from the day we had first met in December of 1970, six years before. We reminisced about the bad times as well as the good. John seemed eager to remind himself of what had gone on. It was as if he had been forbidden to remember me and was denying that prohibition by discussing the past with me. He also repeatedly told me how much he missed me.

John referred to Yoko either as "Mother" or "Madam" and did not tell me too much about his life with her or Sean, knowing that it might be painful for me to hear about his domestic situation, and in turn when he asked me how I was doing, I did not want to tell him about the hard time I was having getting a job. The music business was the only place I was sure I would get a job that would consist of more than filing, and I was determined to stick it out. I found myself surviving by getting occasional free-lance assignments when a friend hired me as a consultant on publicity campaigns or to devise marketing strategies. Finally, however, in 1977, after more than two years of looking, I got my first full-time job since John had left me. I was hired as assistant to the president of Island Records.

During my interview I was complimented on my credentials. The man who hired me knew all about my relationship with John and understood why I had so much difficulty getting a job.

"Who gives a crap," he said. "John Lennon is never going to sign with this record company, and I know you can do the job."

22

When John left me, he had been in a very creative phase. He was actively pursuing a solo recording career and was determined to become a first-class solo recording artist. By contrast, the John I encountered in the years since seemed totally lacking in ambition. He was in many ways unlike the man I had lived with. He seemed capable of concentrating for only short periods of time. Sometimes he would just sit there and look at me through glazed eyes. His spirit, his wit, his insight, seemed to have disappeared and he appeared to have no energy at all.

John told me that Yoko had told him repeatedly that he need not worry that he was not recording. She told him he did not have to prove himself anymore, because he was already there.

He wanted me to agree with her, but I couldn't. "I think your spirit dies unless you keep challenging yourself to learn and grow."

John looked hurt.

"The truth is, John, I think you're very depressed."

"No. No. Why do you say that?"

But I could get nowhere with him on that front.

In one area, though, John was certainly his old self. He was even more passionate than before, and he brought to those meetings the deep, exuberant sexual desire that he had had when we first began our relationship.

After we made love, he would hold me tightly for a long time. Finally, reluctantly, we would both let go. As soon as we were dressed he would sink back into his remoteness and passivity.

One time he said quietly, "I wish I could spend the whole night holdin' on to you. I want to wake up with you just like we used to. But you can only get out once."

I burst into tears and sat up. We got dressed quietly and kissed each other good-bye. Neither of us said anything.

One afternoon early in 1977, Mario Casciano, a young fan of John's, called me. He had just been taken to lunch by John. "Guess what John told me," Mario said. "He's closing down the office in the Capitol building and moving everything back to the Dakota. He said that Yoko and he are having a 'clean-up time.'"

"I beg your pardon," I said.

"That's exactly what I said. I asked him what 'clean-up time' was. He said it's a way of breaking the umbilical cord to the past. He said that Yoko and he have hung a Civil War dagger over the bed. It's to remind them every day that they've both cut all ties with the past. You won't believe what else they've done. Yoko got John to hang up his guitar also, because music is part of John's past. The guitar is to remind him that he's said good-bye to music as well."

"How awful. Was he serious?"

"You bet he was. After lunch, he said good-bye to me, because I'm part of his past, too. Everything that he ever liked has been gotten rid of."

I had been afraid that after John left me he would allow his world to be shrunk to minuscule size. Mario's phone call confirmed my worst apprehensions.

I saw Yoko alone once during the spring of 1977. I was invited to meet with Hilary Gerrard, Ringo's manager, and Neil Aspinall invited me to join them at the Plaza Hotel after they finished an Apple meeting. I was walking toward the elevator in the hotel when Yoko stepped out of it. She was flanked by two huge men.

"Hello, Yoko. You look well today," I said boldly, and I started to walk toward her.

"Hello, May." She backed away in a panic, and that time I followed after her. I couldn't believe it, but she was on the run.

"You look well," I repeated.

"You look well, too." She turned and hurried away.

I realized that there were times when even she could be scared off, and at that moment I could have chased her down the hall, into the elevator, through the lobby, and down Central Park South.

Why hadn't it ever occurred to me to do that years before? Why hadn't it occurred to anyone else? It amazed me yet again how everyone had allowed her to seize control. Only Harold Seider had ever had the courage to stand up to her.

Later, at the end of the fall of 1977, I ran into both John and Yoko in public. Robert Palmer, Spencer David, and I had all been invited to a party for Rod Stewart at Regine's, and we all went off to it together. A few minutes after we arrived, John and Yoko turned up. They had just come from Loraine Alterman's marriage to Peter Boyle, and the Boyles were with them.

When John and Yoko walked into the room, they came face to face with me. John stopped dead in his tracks and stared at me. Yoko smiled contemptuously. Suddenly a music business acquaintance—a minor concert promoter John and I both knew very casually—stepped forward, literally pushing me away so that the Lennons would not see me. It was amazing to see the lengths to which people would go to be in John and Yoko's favor. There was no reason for that man to do what he did, except for his entertaining the fantasy that someday he might be doing business with John and that Yoko, John's "manager," would remember the gesture. John and Yoko were seated at a table directly next to mine, and my chair was back-to-back with John's. I headed for my chair, but the man who had held me back sat in it and stared defiantly at me. Other people surrounded John. I stood there trying to get close to him—I just wanted to say hello—but it was impossible. I saw John staring at me through the crowd of people around him. A short time later he got up and left.

A week or two later, when we met in Richard's apartment, John said, "When I first walked into the room, I couldn't believe it. You were the first person I spotted. I was horrified. I didn't know what to do. I couldn't stand bein' so close to you and not bein' able to talk to you. It was makin' me crazy. I had to get out of there."

I also had wanted to talk to John that night, and again I was reminded of how often and in how many ways John had set up his life to make it impossible for us to do even that.

Richard Ross and I had been friends for a long time. I had introduced him to John, and I had encouraged John to become Richard's friend. John's attitude had always remained the same about Richard: Richard was "safe"—he would go to any limits to please John—and, therefore, could be trusted. Richard had always seemed grateful for it all.

From 1976 until the end of 1977 Richard's attitude began to change drastically toward me. During those two years, whenever we spoke alone, his main topic of conversation was John and how much closer he was to John than I was. "I know John better than anybody," he kept telling me. "I know how he thinks. I know what John wants. John doesn't do anything without telling me first."

Once Richard called me to say, "I couldn't find John. Was he with you?" he asked nervously.

"No."

Richard was puzzled. I was the only person Richard believed John would go to without telling him first, and he felt that it was an incursion on his power over John.

I had been a fan myself and I have always respected and liked fans. There is a kind of hero worship, however, that resembles madness. I had heard, for example, that Elliot Mintz was still in contact with John and Yoko. People would call and tell me that they had heard from Elliot, who bragged that he was the only person in the world who was allowed to be in daily contact with John. He seemed as obsessive as Richard. That kind of obsession terrified John, yet people like Richard and Elliot seemed to be the only people whom Yoko allowed John to be close to.

In John's mind the only way he could see me was by utilizing Richard. It was unthinkable to John to pick up the phone himself and call me to arrange a meeting. He always wanted everything done for him. He wanted those meetings arranged for him also. Yoko must have left him alone sometime; he could have called then. When he was with Richard, he would not use a pay phone to make a date with me, because he did not want to offend Richard by doing his job for him and he didn't want to feel guilty. He could have stood over Richard and made sure that Richard called me. But that was not John.

Finally, however, at the end of 1977, at one of our last meetings that year, he spoke out.

"Where have you been for months?" he asked.

"I've been at home or in the office."

"I keep askin' Richard to call you, and he tells me he can't find you."

"How often have you asked him?"

"I ask him ten times, he gets you once."

John thought for a second. Truth always came slowly to him; he preferred to ignore the harsh realities. By ignoring them he would not have to deal with them. After a pause, he said, "He's fuckin' jealous of you. He thinks that if we get together, I won't spend time with him. We've got to think of someone else."

"Who?"

"Who do you think?"

John was so isolated that it was virtually impossible to think of anybody. When I mentioned a name or two, John said, "I don't trust him. People talk. I don't trust them. How could anybody keep his mouth shut about this?"

We were stuck and we knew it. It was hard to believe, but even harder to accept, that seeing John depended on the whim of Richard Ross.

* * *

I did not hear from John again until the end of 1978. As time went on I concluded that John finally was a part of my past and tried to push him out of my mind.

So 1978 became a realistic year for me. I felt I had finally put John behind me and was using all of my energies to launch a career and to find someone with whom I really wanted to share my life. Then one morning early in December I was awakened by my phone at 7:00 A.M. I picked it up and said hello. All I could hear on the other end was a click. It happened again half an hour later. I was in the shower when the phone rang a third time. I picked it up.

"Hi," said John.

I was amazed. Not only had it been eleven months since I had heard from him, but I could not believe that he was calling himself, especially that early in the morning.

"Hi, John," I said softly.

"What's happenin'?"

"John, have you been trying to get me?"

"No."

There was a pause. We were both very nervous.

"What are you doin'?" he asked.

"I'm getting ready to go to work."

"Do you have time to see me?"

"When?"

"In a little while."

"Well . . . I mean . . . does it have to be today?"

"I would like to see you today."

"Okay, I'll call in sick."

"I'll come over."

I gave him instructions, as he had never been to my apartment, and I told him I'd meet him downstairs. I knew it was an enormous step for John to call me on his own, and I knew he would probably go through millions of changes in the short trip between the Dakota and my apartment. I did not want him to get to my lobby and then panic and run away because he thought he might be recognized. I really wanted to see him and I didn't want any last-ditch obstacles.

I waited in the lobby for an hour. While I waited it seemed

as if every one of my neighbors stopped to talk. Finally John appeared. It was a rainy day, and he looked pale and frantic. "I couldn't get a cab," he said. "God, it was awful. I was standin' on the street and I didn't know what to do."

I took him upstairs and sat him down. His hysteria always manifested itself in dreadful physical symptoms, and he was so nervous that he was wheezing. He put my hand to his heart, and I felt it pounding.

"Calm down," I said gently. "Calm down."

"Can you turn off the radio? It's too loud. It's makin' me nervous." It was playing softly, but I turned it off anyway. John sat there, blinking and trying to regain his balance.

After a few minutes, he reached over, pulled me to him, and we hugged for a while. Major and Minor, my cats, spotted him and began to climb all over him.

"I've got cats now," John said. "I had a baby cat, a Russian Blue. Something went wrong with him. I took him to the vet. The vet said he had to put him to sleep. I held him while the vet gave him an injection. He was so beautiful. I wept."

I took John's hand and squeezed it.

"Mother's gone to an Apple meeting in London. On the Concorde. The minute she left I called you," he explained. "I was so afraid."

"Why?"

"I didn't know whether you were with someone or you were married. That's why I made those two calls. To see if you were with anyone."

"John, if I had gotten married, I'm sure you would have heard about it."

"I probably would have." He smiled. "I didn't want you to be with anyone."

"John!" John wasn't making any bones about his selfishness, and I decided to change the subject. "How's Sean?" I asked.

"He's beautiful."

"Have you called Julian?"

"Yes."

"When was the last time you spoke to him?"

"I just spoke to him the other day."

I rested my hand on John's shoulder, and he stroked my hair. Out of the corner of his eye he suddenly spotted my framed copy of the story about us in *The Daily Palm Beacher*, written while we were vacationing at Morris Levy's condominium in West Palm Beach.

"I remember that!" he exclaimed, and he jumped up and looked at it. "A disgrace to Palm Beach. That's my favorite story ever. I must have a copy."

"I'll trade you," I said. "I'd like a tape of the songs you were writing before we broke up. I still love them."

"Do you really like them?"

"A lot. They were the best."

John smiled happily.

"John, do you want to record?"

"Of course I do. I never stopped wantin' to make music."

Suddenly it was as if the year during which we had not seen each other had not taken place. We both felt relaxed. The color in John's face was better. His hands were not as clammy. He was less confused than he had been when I had seen him at other times, yet he still seemed a little melancholic.

"John, are you happy?" I asked.

"Yeah. I like Yoko bein' my manager. It's great when wives manage their husbands. Look at Elizabeth Joel and Billy Joel. He's doin' all right."

"John, Billy Joel makes records and gives concerts. He works at making music. Elizabeth encourages Billy to create."

"This is a nice apartment, Fung Yee," he replied, quickly changing the subject.

I took John's hand and showed him around. "I love it!" he said. "It's so bright."

When I showed John the bedroom, he stared at the bed and said, "I remember that!" Then he looked at the smoked mirrors. "And I remember these!"

We went back inside and sat on the couch again. John had never been skinnier. He was so skinny, he looked frail.

"My, you've trimmed down."

"I never want to weigh more than one thirty or one thirty-five, tops."

"You're five feet eleven. You could handle a little more weight."

"I never want to weigh more than one thirty-five, tops!" Then he said, "Watch out for the sugar blues," and he gave me a short lecture on the evils of sugar and told me about the strict macrobiotic diet he was on.

I smiled gently; I sensed he did not want to be contradicted.

"What have you been listenin' to?" John asked.

We spent the rest of the morning playing records while we hugged and kissed, stopping every now and then to talk. During the morning I played him Frankie Miller's version of "Jealous Guy." He loved it.

"Who is he?" John asked.

"He's Scottish."

"He sounds like a white Otis Redding." John looked quizzically at me. "There's a song I heard on the radio. It reminds me of us, but I don't know who sings it."

"Hum a few bars." He did. "It's called 'Reminiscing.' It's a song I love."

"Who does it?"

"The Little River Band."

"Who are they?"

"They're Australian."

"It's about time the Australians got a good group."

"I've got a copy of the record, John."

"Play it for me. Play it for me."

I got the record and played it for him. "Play it again," John said.

This time we both hummed and sang along; we began to kiss. We got up and went into the bedroom. "I'm so happy to be in my old bed, Fung Yee. I can't tell you how happy this makes me."

"I'm glad, John," I said. "But I wanted you to come over for another reason—because it would make *me* happy, too."

For an instant he stared at me in the way that only John could, and then he kissed me.

We spent the whole afternoon in bed, getting up only to

play "Reminiscing" again and again. We must have listened to the song eight or nine times.

As we were getting dressed John said, "I wish it wasn't so difficult to see you."

"Was it so difficult for you to pick up the phone yourself?"

"Yes. I had to wait until Madam left for England. Before I left I closed the bedroom door, so no one would know if I was in or out."

John noticed my puzzled expression. I had not seen him in almost a year, and while I still loved him, I was so removed from his game with Yoko that his telling me about it just didn't make any sense. As always he needed enormous reassurance.

"You were very brave today," I said gently. "I hope it's given you the courage to call me again."

"Well, we can't use Richard. We both know what he's like. If I have to wait for him, I'll never get through to you. As soon as I get an opportunity I'll call you."

John was beginning to get nervous. I knew he *wanted* to call, yet I knew how difficult a thing it was for him to do. Seeing him sinking back into his predicament began to make me feel sad. It was a feeling I did not want to have. "I've had a wonderful day," I said. "John, I love you so very, very much."

"I love you, too."

I walked him to the door and watched as he waited for the elevator. Then I blew him a kiss good-bye. I did not know that it would be the last time I would ever see him alive.

It was the Sunday afternoon of the Memorial Day weekend in 1980, and I was spending the day with three girl friends, Margie, Jae, and Nersa. We had just taken a stroll and had gotten back to my apartment to have a snack when the phone rang. I picked it up. An operator with a heavy French accent said, "This is the operator. Have I reached . . . ?" She stated my phone number.

"You've got the right number," I told her, "but are you

sure it's the number you want?" I couldn't think of anyone in France who might be trying to call me.

A voice suddenly said, "I know I've got the right number, May." When I heard John's voice, I froze. We had not spoken to or seen each other in seventeen months.

"John, where are you calling from?" I finally asked.

"Is that my husband?" asked Nersa, whose husband's name was also John. I motioned her to be quiet and I began to take the phone and walk toward the bedroom.

"Guess," said John.

"John, you must be calling from France." Nersa suddenly caught on. She looked almost as surprised as I was.

"Further, I'm much further."

"I can't guess." I went into the bedroom, closed the door, and settled down on my bed.

"I'm in Cape Town!" John exclaimed.

"Cape Town, South Africa?"

"Yes."

"What are you doing there?"

There was a pause, then John replied hesitantly, "It was time for me to take another trip."

"Why Cape Town?"

"Because I've been here before and I like it."

"When are you coming home?"

"Probably the day after tomorrow," he replied vaguely.

There was a pause, then John said, "Fung Yee, do you have time to talk to me?"

"Of course I do, John."

"Let me get a cig."

"So you're back on cigarettes?"

"Gitanes." He left the phone for a second, then came back. "Okay?"

"Okay." There was another pause. I could tell that John was very nervous.

"Fung Yee," he said finally, "what are you up to these days?"

I told him about my new job at ABC Radio.

"You're not in the music business? I can't believe it. Do you like working in radio?"

I hesitated. "I'm a rock 'n' roller. I wish I was still in the business."

Perhaps, at last, John finally realized that because of him, I had been forced to look outside the music business to find work.

"I wish I could do something for you," John replied, "but I can't. There's nothing I can do. I still can't come out and say things."

"Maybe I'll say things," I said jokingly.

"What do you mean?"

"John, we've known each other almost ten years. Maybe it's time for me to do 'Pang Remembers.' "

John laughed. "You do have some story to tell. I wish I could have been better to you, Fung Yee."

John suddenly sounded very happy. I had been kidding him, but I realized he liked the idea of my speaking out. It was just like John. He would have liked to have me relieve him of the responsibility of telling the truth. I decided to change the subject.

"Do you like Cape Town?" I asked.

"It's very interestin'. . . ." John searched for something to say. "Fung Yee, what have you been listenin' to?"

"The Pretenders. You should listen to them."

"I will."

I could not believe that John was thousands of miles away, and I had not heard from him in seventeen months, and he wanted to make casual conversation. There had to be something more important on his mind. He was testing the waters, and I knew that when he felt safe enough, he would speak up, so I decided to be very calm and equally as casual.

We talked more about music, then John began to ask me about our old friends.

"How's Tony King?" he asked. "Tell me about Harold." He was pleased to hear that they were both doing well.

"Fung Yee, you know I kept your number in my secret address book, which I kept hidden. You know me. I hid it so well, I couldn't find it.

"Then I found my address book. I smuggled it out of the house with me. I knew I'd have no problem callin' you once I got to Cape Town. I wasn't goin' to tell you, but I sent you a postcard. I wanted to know if you're goin' to be able to recognize it. It's just so weird."

"I'll always recognize it."

"We'll see. How long haven't we seen each other?"

"The last time we saw each other was a year and a half ago."

"I didn't realize it had been so long." John paused. "I want to see you. I want to take you to the Long Island house with me. Can you get a car?"

"Do you want me to get the car?"

"I can't call up the Esquire Limousine Service and order one."

"I'll get the car, John. I want to see you, too." I was very excited by the prospect.

"I don't even know how to get there. All I know is you take the Jericho Turnpike."

"We'll work it out. We always have before."

"That we have." We both laughed. Then John abruptly changed the subject.

"Sean's wonderful," he said. "He's very smart and very healthy and he's doing very well."

"I bet he is terrific."

"Fung Yee, I'd love you to see him. I'd love you to get to know him. You'll like him very much."

"I'd love to meet Sean." Then I asked John, "Have you spoken to Julian?"

"Yes, I've called him. I really have."

"As long as you keep in touch with him."

"I keep in touch. Fung Yee, make sure you can get a car."

"I'll make sure."

John thought for a second. "I want to see you again, but I can't do it until I finish me business. I promise to call you as soon as I'm done. Find a car, and we'll make plans."

"When do you think you'll call?" I asked.

"I don't know exactly. You know how I am about time. It could be a week or six months, but I will call. Suppose I went into the studio again. I'm not going to call until I'm done."

"Are you getting ready for the studio?"

John hesitated. "I've changed the lyrics on those songs you love so much."

"Why? Those songs were wonderful."

"I know. But I had to change the lyrics anyway. I couldn't use lyrics that I wrote when I was with you. That's just the way it is. You understand, don't you?

"If I do go into the studio, I will call you as soon as I am done. Then we'll go away. Okay?"

"John, I'm glad you called."

"Fung Yee, you've put up with a lot. All you wanted was for me to be happy. That's all you've ever really wanted. You know I know that, don't you?"

"I know it, John."

"I'll call. I promise you I'll call."

The conversation, our last, had taken an hour and a half.

Four days later I received a postcard: John had taken a message from a fan, scratched out his own name, and then re-addressed the message to me.

Two months after that, at the end of August, a friend who worked at The Hit Factory called to tell me that John and Yoko had suddenly begun to record an album together. I was delighted that John was recording again and I knew that he would probably record for two or three months. I did not expect to hear from him until the album was finished. One day I got a call from another friend at The Hit Factory. "What's with them?" he asked. "I expected them to be hugging and kissing all the time. They're really rather aloof with each other."

At the end of November I heard *Double Fantasy* for the first time. "Tennessee," which John had written when he was with me, had become "Watching the Wheels," and he had also composed the melody for "Beautiful Boy" during our time together.

Then, a few days after I heard the album, someone gave me an advance copy of John and Yoko's *Playboy* interview. It had been years since John had given a major interview. Once again even I, who knew him so well, was amazed on the one hand by the public John, whose remarks were honest, direct, and commonsensical. That was the John people modeled themselves after and the John even he himself sadly knew could never exist in private. On the other hand, there were many things about the interview that distressed me and forced me to come face to face once again with his worst aspects. As he had warned me in so many long-ago telephone conversations, John felt compelled to use this interview as an opportunity once again to give the party-line version of his separation from Yoko, five long years after it had happened. There it was, spelled out in print in *Playboy* all over again: John had been kicked out by Yoko; suddenly John was alone and unbefriended by anyone; John had a lost weekend that had lasted eighteen months; John wanted to go home, but Yoko would not take him back until she was ready.

Even though I had heard and read those falsehoods many times before, and it was totally predictable that, as sure as the sun would rise, under Yoko's influence John would cough them up all over again, I still felt upset and angry when I read them.

I knew the pattern only too well. The interview was scheduled to appear on the newsstands early in November, and John knew that it was inevitable that I would read it. I knew it was only a matter of days after the magazine circulated in public before John would get on the phone to apologize for all the lies he had told.

On December 8, the night that John was killed, I was having dinner at a girl friend's house. The radio was on, and I heard a bulletin stating that "a man believed to be John Lennon has been shot." I panicked and ran to the phone and began making calls. "Did you hear anything about John on the radio?" I kept asking. The people that I reached didn't know anything but promised to call back the minute they heard. I sat by the radio, nervously waiting for news. Then a newscaster announced: "The person who was shot on the Upper West Side was John Lennon. *John Lennon is dead.*"

I stood up and stared at my friend. I couldn't believe my ears. Suddenly I began to scream at the top of my voice. No matter how my friend tried to comfort me, I couldn't stop. She threw her arms around me and held me tightly. Still, it was impossible for me to gain control. People had begun to call back, but I could hardly speak, I was so much in shock.

My friend wanted me to stay over, but I was filled with frenzy and panic and couldn't sit still. I wanted to go home, and she went with me. The phone was ringing as I opened my apartment door. I picked up the phone. It was Ringo's secretary, Joan, wanting to know the name and the number of the hospital John had been taken to.

"It's too late," I sobbed. "He's dead."

"What's wrong with your goddamn country?" Joan screamed. "I've got to get off the phone. I've got to tell Ringo."

I kept getting call after call. Everyone was astonished and horrified. "I can't believe it," everyone said. Neither could I. I had recently seen David Bowie, who was starring on Broadway in *The Elephant Man,* and we had spent the evening talking lovingly about John and our delight that John had started to record again. I pulled myself together and picked up the phone. I felt the need to share my grief with someone who had been with us when we had been together and still cared enough about me to keep consistently in touch. Finally I reached David's secretary, Coco.

"Are you alone? Get here immediately!" Coco said as soon as she heard my voice.

My friend got me into a taxi. Coco was waiting for me when I got to David's loft. A little while later David arrived. When he saw me, he threw his arms around me, and we both burst into tears. I sat up the whole night, sobbing and shaking, while David and Coco looked after me. Once or twice we turned on the television and watched news flashes of the army of people converging in front of the Dakota. We both stared at the tube in disbelief.

For weeks afterward I remained numb. Like everyone else, I grieved for the public John, the man whose music and personality had such an extraordinary impact on the world. Having known the private John, I grieved also for the man who was too afraid to grow up and yet had accomplished so much despite the fact that his life was so incomplete. I had seen for myself that John had really made an effort to grow up, and yet, he couldn't. But he was so special. Who knows what he might have accomplished if he had had more time? How awful, I thought, that this time had been taken from him in such a bizarre, horrible way.

John was a creative genius in an extremely fragile vessel. His ability caused a legend to grow up around him, a legend he felt powerless, as a human being, to fulfill. I know that by remembering the bad parts as well as the good I am contradicting that legend. But to me, the man, not the myth, was the important thing. From John I learned how fragile we all are no matter who we are.

To this day I wonder if I could have done anything differently. Another human being might have. Given the human being I was at the time that I met him and the things I knew, I could only do what I had the capacity to do.

As for myself, John brought a touch of greatness and adventure to my life, and I miss him. I will always miss him. I miss him very much.

Acknowledgments

We are grateful to very many people whose cooperation was crucial in the writing of this book. We would especially like to thank the following, who willingly shared with us their recollections of the days when May and John were together. They are: Kenny Ascher, Pete Bennett, Mario Casciano, Al Coury, Fran De Angelis, Cynthia DeFigueiredo, Dennis Ferrante, Bob Fries, Wayne Gabriel, Steve Gebhardt, Joel Glazier, Michael Hewitson, Nicky and Dolly Hopkins, Doug Ibold, Peter Jameson, Arthur Jenkins, Jim and Cynthia Keltner, Norma Kemper, Steve Khan, Mark Levinson, Peter McCabe, Paul Mozian, Richard Perry, Jozy Pollock, Dan Richter, Brad Rosenberger, Al Steckler, and Linda Stein.

Special mention should be made of Tony King and Cynthia Lennon Twist, who were with us every step of the way and whose emotional support was unflagging.

We would also like to thank those people who spoke to us but would prefer to go unnamed. They know who they are and they will always have our thanks.

Thanks also to the management and staff of Warner Books, especially Ross Claiborne and our outstanding editor, Reid Boates.

The driving force behind this project was our good friend and very fine literary representative, Ron Bernstein, who worked unstintingly on our behalf. We thank him for his good counsel.

Nersa Miller and Caroline Shookhoff worked many hours, under great duress, to prepare this manuscript for publication. They also made many astute suggestions along the way, and we thank them now. Our researchers, Maxine Mark and Cynthia Savage, were also of great help, and we thank you. Special mention must be made of Cynthia Merman, whose reading of the first draft was of so much help.

Three friends must be singled out for their generosity of spirit during the writing period: Jerry Edelstein, Myrna Zimmerman, and our very special friend, Doug Hall.

Thanks to Renee Sacks, to whom we owe so much for painstakingly reviewing the manuscript word by word. Ms. Sacks was the person with the capability to take these experiences and lead us to the fullest understanding of them. Her contribution is immeasurable. Finally, our thanks to Dr. Eugene E. Landy, whose compassion for the frailties of human nature and dedication to growth and behavioral change served as our inspiration during the many difficult and painful days in which this book was written.

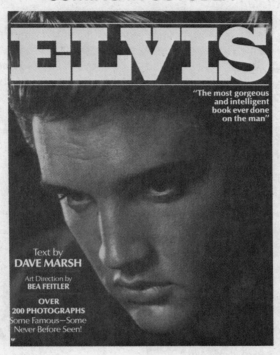

CATCH THESE HOT TITLES!

SHOUT: THE BEATLES IN THEIR GENERATION
by Philip Norman   (I30-337, $3.95)

At last! The complete story never before told! Behind the myths…behind the masks…behind the secluded walls…For the first time here's the definitive biography of the incredible rise of four boys in scuffed boots to beings more pampered and adored—and in many ways deprived—than any in the history of popular entertainment.

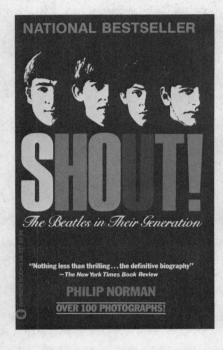

THE CATALOG OF COOL   (R37-515, $6.95)
Edited by Gene Sculatti   (In Canada R37-530, $8.50)

Let this loose talk summon you to enter the first and only compendium of cool ever assembled between two covers. In-depth, out of sight, it brings you the personalities, books, discs, flicks, threads, and wheels that define the essence of enduring style. Here is the swingin' world of sunglasses, James Bond, paper dresses, and Plastic Man. Be flip, get hip, and wig out.

Jim Morrison comes alive—
In these titles from Warner Books....

1 MILLION COPIES IN PRINT!

The bestselling biography of JIM MORRISON

JERRY HOPKINS and DANNY SUGERMAN

NO ONE HERE GETS OUT ALIVE
by Jerry Hopkins and Danny Sugerman   *(I30-576, $3.95)*

Here is Jim Morrison in all his complexity: singer, philosopher, poet, delin-
quent—the brilliant, charismatic and obsessed disciple of darkness who
rejected authority in any form, the explorer who probed "the bounds of
reality to see what would happen..." Seven years in the writing, this
definitive biography is the work of two men whose empathy and experience with Jim Morrison uniquely prepared them to recount this modern
tragedy.

BURN DOWN THE NIGHT   *A large-format, quality paperback*
by Craig Kee Strete   *(A37-071, $6.95 U.S.A.)*
                                          (A37-343, $7.95, Canada)

This is the fictionalized story of Strete's manic journey with Morrison, an
autobiographical novel that brings back the Day-Glo sixties, illuminating
the era and its generation with the neon, the mind-splitting acid rock, the
mind-expanding drugs, the casual and furious sex. With Morrison and
Strete we consort with rock's jokers and madmen; we mix it up with the
bands and the billy clubs; we descend into orgies with predatory California
ladies and child-woman groupies; we witness the death games.

THIRTY YEARS OF ROCK 'N ROLL TRIVIA
by Fred L. Worth   *(V91-494, $2.50)*

This book is packed with all the facts that the casual fan or serious aficionado could ever want to know about the music called rock 'n roll. More than another encyclopedia, it's a fascinating pastiche, a rock around the time clock, spanning three decades worth of colorful pop memorabilia.